Discover China

STUDENT'S BOOK FOUR 学生用书4

Introduction

Discover China is a four-level Mandarin Chinese course, specially designed for beginner to intermediate level students studying Chinese in English-speaking countries. It employs a communicative and integrated approach to language learning. Emphasis is placed on communication in real contexts through pair work, group work and a variety of independent and integrated activities to help students become confident Chinese language speakers.

Key features

Discover China's unique communicative course design includes a number of distinctive features:

- **Topic-driven content in real-life contexts** gets students engaged and motivated. The topics in each book are organized around the lives and travel experiences of five young students in China.
- **A truly communicative approach** lets students learn the language by using it in real-life situations, providing them with the tools they need to communicate in Chinese naturally.
- **Structured and effective learning design** based on the sequence "presentation, practice and production", with activities moving from controlled practice to personalized tasks, facilitates effective learning of the language.
- **Systematic vocabulary and grammar development** comes through topic-based practice and extension exercises. The lexical syllabus is based on levels 1-4 of the *Hanyu Shuiping Kaoshi* (HSK test) and the grammatical syllabus takes students up to the Vantage level (level B2) of the Common European Framework.
- **Student-centred grammar learning supplemented with detailed grammar reference** allows students to discover the rules for themselves through identifying patterns in the language samples. The grammar reference provides comprehensive and detailed explanations.
- **Meaningful and integrated character writing practice** through grouping characters with common radicals. These high-frequency characters are presented within the context of the unit theme.
- **Insights into Chinese culture**, through "Cultural corner" sections linked to the unit topics, promoting a deeper cultural understanding. Fascinating full-colour photos, showing the real China, provide visual appeal and draw students into this diverse culture.
- **Simplified Chinese characters** are used to facilitate learning of the written language used by the majority of Chinese speakers.
- **Pinyin matched to the word level** instead of individual characters helps students understand how to write and space pinyin meaningfully. *Discover China* follows the official pinyin orthography of the mainland of China. All pinyin shows the character's original tone, except in those parts of the pronunciation and speaking section where special rules about tonal change are introduced.
- **Extra pair work activities** for each unit provide additional communicative speaking practice.
- **Supported by free online resources** including teacher's books, assessment tasks, unit quizzes, extra character writing sheets and more.

Workbook

The Workbook provides extensive consolidation of the language skills and knowledge taught in the Student's Book.

Each Workbook unit features clear language objectives which correspond with the Student's Book unit structure and activities. A wide variety of vocabulary and grammar exercises, as well as extra reading and listening activities, provide practice of the core language presented in the Student's Book. Writing practice sections give students the option to extend their Chinese character writing skills beyond the Student's Book requisites. A self-assessment at the end of each unit using "I can..." descriptors enables students to reflect on their individual progress.

Characteristics of each level

Books 1 and 2 cover basic language relating to everyday topics. The focus is on listening and speaking, although there is a writing activity at the end of each lesson 2. Character writing practice is available in both the Student's Book and Workbook to help students learn how to write Chinese characters with the correct stroke order.

Book 1 is for beginners who have not studied any Chinese. To avoid overwhelming students with character reading at the very beginning, pinyin is placed above all Chinese words and characters to provide the necessary language support. However, to help students develop character recognition skills, pinyin does not appear for conversations and passages in the Workbook. Activities in the online unit quizzes, which simulate test questions from the HSK test, have no pinyin.

Book 2 follows on naturally from Book 1. Pinyin is used only in activities with new words and phrases, and the activities in the pronunciation and speaking section of each unit. Most other activities in the book do not carry pinyin. However, versions of all the main conversations and reading passages with pinyin are available for downloading from *Discover China's* free resources website.

Books 3 and 4 cover language from school life and the work environment. The focus is on the development of language skills, which is conducted through various approaches including guided writing. The lessons contain activities to further enhance students' language skills in all areas across different contexts and functions. A new guided writing section teaches students how to compose natural texts following authentic-like texts. The conversations and reading passages are longer, and pinyin only appears in each unit's vocabulary boxes.

Storylines

- **Book 1** presents the fundamentals of the Chinese language, following the characters' day-to-day lives in Beijing. From simple introductions to going shopping, eating out or playing sports, students encounter a broad range of situations and learn the basic language skills they require.

- **Book 2** includes "survival Chinese" for travelling and living in China, as the characters hit the road on their winter holidays. They see the Terracotta Warriors in Xi'an and try authentic Sichuan food in Chengdu, make new friends and broaden their knowledge of Chinese to handle typical subjects such as food and drink, hotels, sightseeing and going to the doctor.

- **Book 3** takes a deeper look at China's diverse culture. Steve lands his dream job and is sent on assignment as a photojournalist to exciting places all over China. Amanda pursues her love of Chinese history and takes the Chinese history class. This provides students with rich exposure to the use of Chinese language across various cultural and social contexts.

- **Book 4** prepares students to use Chinese for work-related purposes. Mark takes up an internship at a Chinese company in Shenzhen, and Yeong-min volunteers at a summer camp for international students studying in China. Both gain valuable experience working with different people and dealing with different situations. Encouraged by Wang Yu, Steve showcases his talent in a photo competition themed around Yunnan. Wang Yu herself goes to study in the US, and finds that living abroad gives her a new perspective on the experiences of her overseas friends in China.

Unit structure

Student's Book 4 | Unit 12 No pain, no gain. 有付出，才有收获。

Pre-listening
Pre-listening activities are designed to pre-teach the key words/expressions, or activate students' background knowledge about the unit topic in preparation for the conversation.

New words list
Target words are set out in the order they appear in the conversation.

Pronunciation
Difficult pronunciation points for English speakers are presented and practised in context to prepare students for communicative activities in the unit.

Post-listening
Comprehension questions are used to check understanding.

Controlled activities allow students to practise the target words/expressions, and role-play the conversation.

Presentation dialogue
Meaningful and authentic conversation between the resident characters sets the context for vocabulary and language presentation.

Further listening practice
A further listening passage based on the unit theme provides extra practice to develop students' listening skills.

Chinese to go
Simple and useful colloquial expressions or language "chunks" of immediate use are provided to students.

Pre-reading
Pre-reading activities are designed to pre-teach the key words, or activate students' background knowledge about the unit topic in preparation for the reading passage.

Post-reading
Controlled, guided and freer activities allow students to practise the target language in a sequence that is most effective for learning.

Reading
Reading texts cover a wide range of text types relevant to students' everyday lives, such as diaries, articles, blogs and online posts.

Guided writing
The reading passage acts as a model for the students to write their own short passage in a similar style.

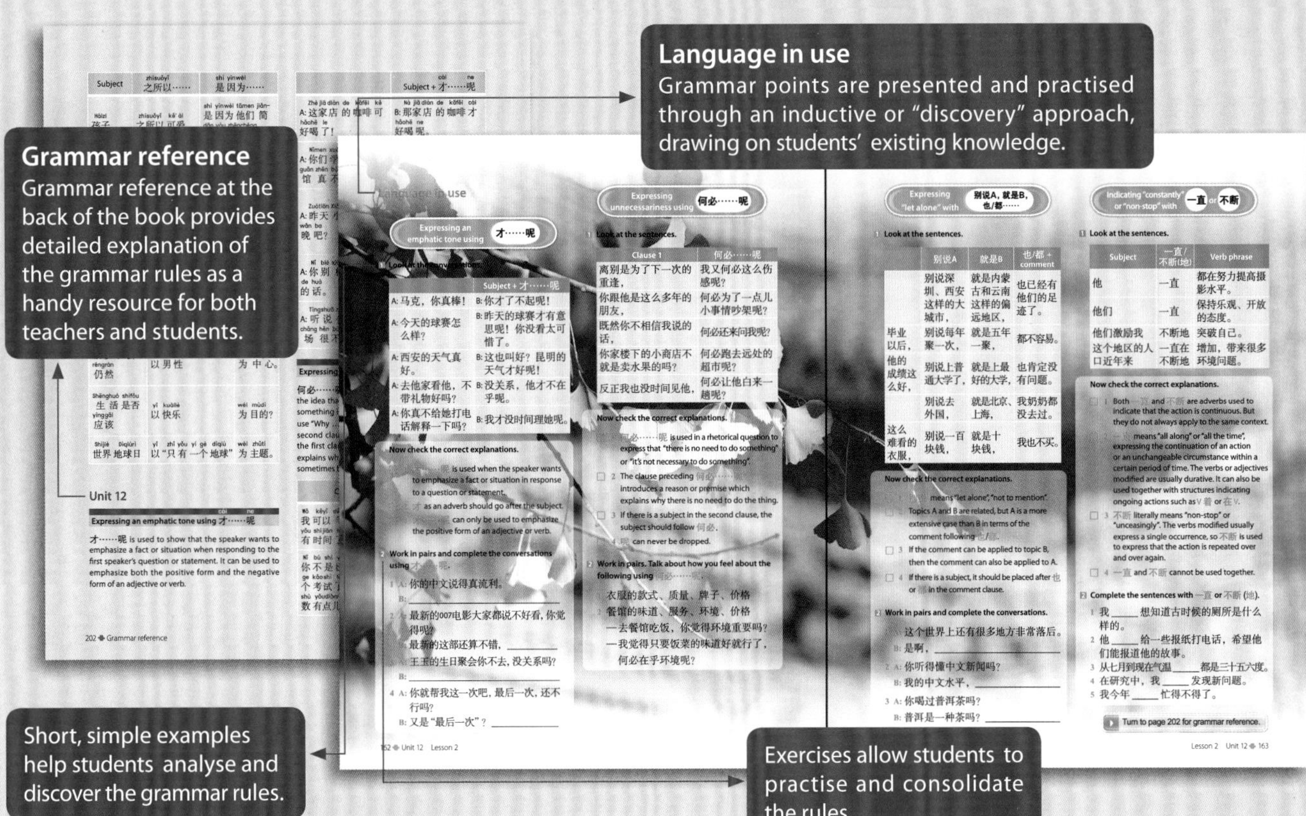

Grammar reference
Grammar reference at the back of the book provides detailed explanation of the grammar rules as a handy resource for both teachers and students.

Language in use
Grammar points are presented and practised through an inductive or "discovery" approach, drawing on students' existing knowledge.

Short, simple examples help students analyse and discover the grammar rules.

Exercises allow students to practise and consolidate the rules.

Cultural Corner
Cultural points linked to the unit topic enable a greater understanding and appreciation of Chinese life and culture.

Communication activity
Meaningful and realistic communication in relevant contexts is facilitated through role-plays and speaking tasks.

Review and practice
Builds on language acquisition by recycling previously learnt target language, through which students can also assess their progress.

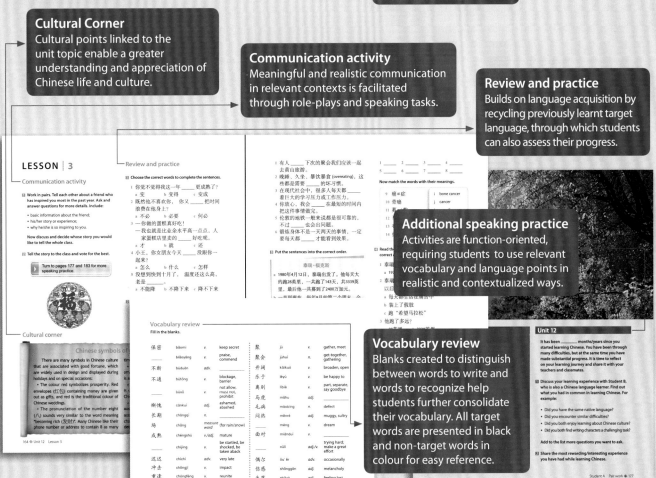

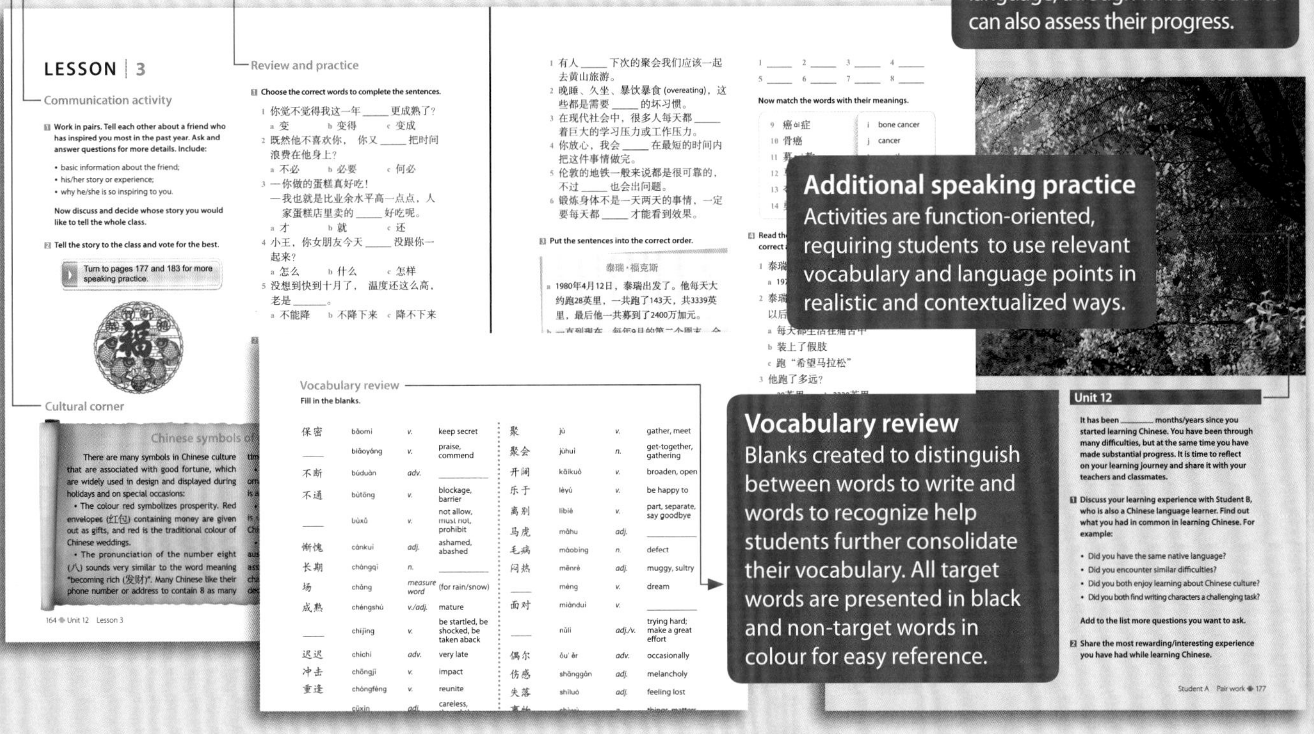

Additional speaking practice
Activities are function-oriented, requiring students to use relevant vocabulary and language points in realistic and contextualized ways.

Vocabulary review
Blanks created to distinguish between words to write and words to recognize help students further consolidate their vocabulary. All target words are presented in black and non-target words in colour for easy reference.

Contents

Grammar and Vocabulary	Pronunciation	Cultural Corner
• Expressing "not at all", "not even one", "not a single …" with 一……都/也 不/没…… • Emphasizing details of a past action using 是……的 • Showing direction of movement with 回/进/上/下 + 来/去 • Introducing an extreme case using 连……都/也…… • Words for job searching and internships	Giving encouragement	Tang poetry
• Indicating a very high degree of something with 不得了 • Repeated actions with 再 or 又 • Expressing "a little bit" using 一下 or 一点儿 • Indicating the beginning of an action or the start of a new state with 起来 • Words for interviews and CVs	Linking words for elaborating tones	Tips for job-hunting in China
• Introducing a new subject using 至于 • Comparative structures using 不如 • Expressing fractions and percentages with ……分之…… • Moderating positive adjectives with 还 • Travel planning	Expressing approximations	Harbin
• Verb + object as a separable compound • 通过 as a preposition • Introducing the agent or performer of an action using 由 • Disyllabic words that become monosyllabic in formal style • Welcome speeches and regulations	Welcoming people and giving good wishes	Collectivism vs. individualism
• Concessive clauses with 倒 • Expressing "doing well" with 好好 • Making deductions with 既然 • Stressing an extreme degree with 再……不过了 • Words for office work	Asking for opinions	Nature reserves and wildlife protection in China
• Indicating an extreme degree with ……死了 • Expressing wishes and hopes with 要是/如果……就好了 • Expressing emphasis using 可 • Justifying an opinion or decision using 反正 • Words for business events	Using 就 orally	Humility

Grammar and Vocabulary	Pronunciation	Cultural Corner
• Expressing "how come" with 怎么 • Emphasizing an inquiry with 到底/究竟 • Minimizing a situation with（只）不过/只（是）……罢了 • Indicating "not only..., but also..." with 不但/不只/不仅/不光……而且/还/也…… • Words for business complaints	Comforting someone and showing empathy	The square and the circle
• Comparing 后来 and 然后 • Expressing "no matter what/how/whether" with 无论/不论/不管……都…… • Expressing tones with adverbs 原来, 果然, 竟然 • Expressing personal judgments with 算（是） • Travelling and lifestyle	Using adverbs for different tones	Yunnan Province
• Expressing "seem to be" with 看起来 • Expressing "nearly" with 差点儿 • Exclamations with 多……啊 • Expressing "whether or not" with 是否 • Requirements of a competition	Showing confidence and giving encouragement	Four-character idioms in Chinese
• Continual repetition of an action with Verb 来 verb 去 • Indicating a continuing action with the complement 下去 • Talking about disposal of time/money/energy with 把 • Expressing "even if" with 即使……也…… • Argumentative discussions and writing	Showing objection and disagreement	The Four Great Inventions
• Expressing "as one pleases" with 想……就…… • Emphasizing a particular manner of carrying out an action using Verb 1着 + verb 2 • Emphasizing the reason for a result with 之所以……是因为…… • Expressing "to regard A as B" using 以……为…… • Life experience, feelings and hopes	Comforting and showing understanding	The modern "Marco Polo"
• Expressing an emphatic tone using 才……呢 • Expressing unnecessariness using 何必……呢 • Expressing "let alone" with 别说 A，就是 B，也/都…… • Indicating "constantly" or "non-stop" with 一直 or 不断 • Pains and gains, retrospection and expectations	Giving praise and showing admiration	Chinese symbols of good fortune

Classroom expressions

Classroom expressions used by teachers

Zhè shì yí gè cuòbiézì 这是一个错别字。	This character is incorrect.
Zhè liǎng gè zì fāyīn xiāngtóng dànshì yìsi bù yíyàng 这两个字发音相同，但是意思不一样。	These two characters sound the same, but their meanings are different.
Zhèli yǒuxiē cuò qǐng zǐxì jiǎnchá yíxià 这里有些错，请仔细检查一下。	There's something wrong here. Please check it carefully.
Zhè shì fēi zhèngshì zhèngshì yòngyǔ 这是非正式 / 正式用语。	This is an informal/a formal expression.
Qǐng zàojù 请造句。	Put these words into sentences.
Qǐng fùshù yíxià gùshi wénzhāng 请复述一下故事 / 文章。	Please retell the story/passage in your own words.
Qǐng kuàisù yuèdú wénzhāng ránhòu jiǎndān èyào de shuō-chū dàyì 请快速阅读文章，然后简单扼要地说出大意。	Please scan the passage and briefly summarize the main idea.
Qǐng bǐjiào zhǎochū xiāngtóng hé bùtóng zhī chù 请比较，找出相同和不同之处。	Please compare and contrast these two texts.
Duì zhè piān wénzhāng yǒu shénme gǎnxiǎng 对这篇文章有什么感想？	What did you think of the passage?
Qǐng jǔlì shuōmíng 请举例说明。	Please give an example.
Nǎ wèi tóngxué néng dàitóu fāyán 哪位同学能带头发言？	Who would like to speak first?
Nǐ huídá de hěn hǎo xiànzài ràng wǒmen tīngting biéde tóngxué yǒu shénme kànfǎ 你回答得很好，现在让我们听听别的同学有什么看法。	That's a good answer. Now let's hear what the others say.
Hái yǒu bǔchōng de ma 还有补充的吗？	Does anyone have anything else to add?
Jiélùn shì shénme 结论是什么？	What's your conclusion?
Xiànzài wǒ bǎ jīntiān shàngkè de nèiróng zǒngjié yíxià 现在我把今天上课的内容总结一下。	Now I'll summarize the content of today's lesson.

Classroom expressions used by students

Wèi shénme zhèli bù néng yòng zhège cí / zì 为什么这里不能用这个词/字？	Why can't I use this word/character here?
yǒu shénme qūbié ……有什么区别？	What's the difference between...?
Zhè jù huà gāi yòng zài shénmeyàng de chǎnghé 这句话该用在什么样的场合？	In what context can this sentence be used?
Qǐng zài duō gěi wǒmen yìdiǎnr zhǔnbèi de shíjiān 请再多给我们一点儿准备的时间。	Please give us a little more time to prepare.
Wǒ néng tántan wǒ gèrén de kànfǎ ma 我能谈谈我个人的看法吗？	Can I state my opinion?
Wǒ néng chā yí jù huà ma 我能插一句话吗？	Can I add/say something?
Wǒ xiān tīngting dàjiā zěnme shuō, ránhòu wǒ zài shuō, kěyǐ ma 我先听听大家怎么说，然后我再说，可以吗？	Could I listen to what the others say before I speak?
Tā shuō de zhèngshì wǒ xiǎng yào shuō de, wǒ tóngyì tā de guāndiǎn 他说的正是我想要说的，我同意他的观点。	What he said is just what I wanted to say. I agree with his point.
Wǒ bìng bú zhèyàng rènwéi, wǒ juéde 我并不这样认为，我觉得……	I don't agree. My opinion is...
Qǐng bǎ zuòyè de yāoqiú shuō de xiángxì yìdiǎnr 请把作业的要求说得详细一点儿。	Can you please explain the details of the assignment?

Places in *Discover China*

Huanghe River

黄河 (Huáng Hé) Huanghe River, or the Yellow River, the second-longest river in Asia and the sixth-longest in the world, called "the cradle of Chinese civilization"

Changjiang River

长江 (Cháng Jiāng) Changjiang River, or the Yangtze River, the longest river in Asia and the fourth-longest in the world

Yunnan

云南 (Yúnnán) Province in Southwest China

香格里拉县 (Xiānggélǐlā Xiàn) Shangri-La County, formerly Zhongdian County (中甸县 Zhōngdiàn Xiàn), renamed after the fictional land of Shangri-La featured in the 1933 James Hilton novel, *Lost Horizon*

梅里雪山 (Méilǐ Xuěshān) Mainri Snow Mountains, a mountain range in Yunnan, the highest peak of which, Kawagebo, rises 6740 metres above sea level and is considered sacred by Tibetan Buddhists

Historical timeline

兵马俑
Bīngmǎyǒng

青铜马
qīngtóngmǎ

BCE
300
CE

China
秦
Qín
汉 Hàn
三国
Sānguó

Europe/Middle East
Ancient Greece
Roman Empire (Western empire)

Americas
Olmec
Mayan Classic period

* This timeline does not include all dynasties and eras in China's history. The selected eras illustrate some notable contemporaneous periods in China and abroad.

RUSSIA
MONGOLIA
HEILONGJIANG
JILIN
LIAONING
NEI MONGOL ZIZHIQU (INNER MONGOLIA AUT.REG.)
GANSU
BEIJING SHI
TIANJIN SHI
HEBEI
SHANXI
SHANDONG
SHAANXI
HENAN
JIANGSU
ANHUI
SHANGHAI SHI
SICHUAN
HUBEI
CHONGQING SHI
ZHEJIANG
GUIZHOU
HUNAN
JIANGXI
FUJIAN
YUNNAN
GUANGXI ZHUANGZU ZIZHIQU (AUT.REG.)
GUANGDONG
TAIWAN
MACAO S.A.R.
HONG KONG S.A.R.
HAINAN
VIET NAM
LAOS
D.P.R. KOREA
R.O. KOREA
JAPAN
PHILIPPINES
YELLOW SEA
EAST CHINA SEA
SOUTH CHINA SEA
PACIFIC OCEAN
Harbin
哈尔滨 (Hā'ěrbīn) capital city of Heilongjiang Province
冰雪节 (Bīngxuějié) the annual Snow and Ice Festival, featuring grand ice and snow sculptures
唐三彩
Tángsāncǎi
1000
1500
1900
唐 Táng
辽 Liáo
宋 Sòng
元 Yuán
明 Míng
清 Qīng
Byzantine Empire
The Crusades
Ottoman Empire
The Middle Ages
Aztec Empire
Toltec
Inca Empire

Meet the characters

Mǎkè
Mark Johnson (马克) comes from Brisbane. Mark went on holiday to China after completing high school, and decided to stay and learn Chinese at a university in Beijing. Mark enjoys the outdoors, and he likes surfing and sailing.

Wáng Yù
Wang Yu (王 玉) was born in Beijing. She knows the others from university, where she studies music. She has played the piano since she was five. She likes cooking and sports including swimming and tennis.

Shǐdìfū
Steve Brown (史蒂夫), another classmate of Mark and Amanda's, comes from London. He works part-time for a UK-based magazine and is a keen photographer. He enjoys exploring different cultures, and meeting different people.

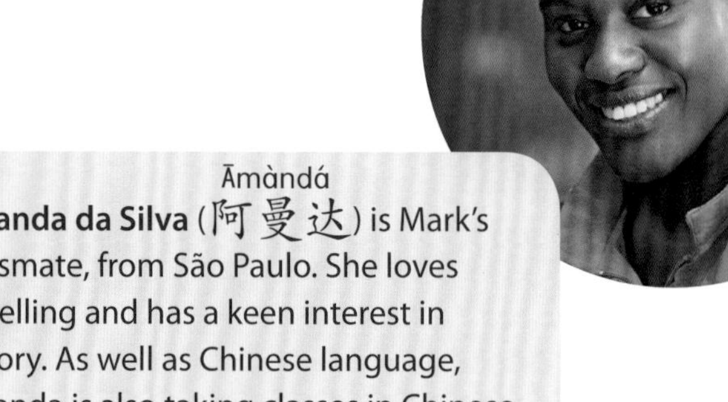

Āmàndá
Amanda da Silva (阿曼达) is Mark's classmate, from São Paulo. She loves travelling and has a keen interest in history. As well as Chinese language, Amanda is also taking classes in Chinese history at the university.

Jīn Yǒngmín
Kim Yeong-min (金 永民) is also studying Chinese at the university. He comes from Seoul. Like Wang Yu, Yeong-min is a musician, and plays guitar in a local band. He plans to study Chinese medicine after he finishes his courses in Chinese. Yeong-min likes to spend his free time reading and listening to music.

UNIT 1

Nǐ yídìng xíng
你一定行！

You can do it!

LESSON | 1

Vocabulary and listening

1 **Work in pairs. Talk about your winter break. Use the expressions in the box to help you.**

寒假过得怎么样？
假期去哪儿了？
对了……
你知道吗……
听说……

2 **Match the words to make phrases.**

1 招聘	a 经验
2 积累	b 要求
3 申请	c 实习生
4 符合	d 工作

3 **Mark and Yeong-min are catching up after the winter break. Listen to the conversation and check the topics they talk about.**

☐ 1 他们的朋友阿曼达和王玉在做什么
☐ 2 永民寒假做了什么
☐ 3 马克下个星期的面试
☐ 4 永民夏天的计划
☐ 5 他们的朋友史蒂夫在哪儿
☐ 6 永民最喜欢的游戏网站

马克：永民，寒假过得怎么样？

永民：挺好的。我回韩国去了，看了父母和朋友。在父母身边真幸福，我都吃胖了。你呢？假期去哪儿了？

马克：我哪儿也没去，就在学校学中文。我下个星期有一个面试。

永民：什么面试？你在找工作？

马克：只是一个实习生的职位。我想毕业以后留在中国工作，所以想利用暑假的时间实习，积累一点儿在中国的工作经验。

永民：你真棒，这么早就开始为找工作做准备了。是什么样的公司和职位呢？

马克：这是一家国际贸易公司，他们的客户服务部在招聘翻译。我喜欢跟人打交道，又了解一点儿中国文化，希望能符合他们的

要求。

永民：你的能力那么强，好好准备，一定没问题。

马克：谢谢你的鼓励。不过，听说申请这个职位的人不少，竞争很激烈，我一点儿信心都没有。

永民：放心吧，你一定行！对了，这些招聘信息，你是从什么地方看到的？

马克：在一个网站上。晚上我把链接发给你。对了，阿曼达回巴西去了，你知道吗？

永民：她给我发邮件了。唉，好多朋友都离开北京了。王玉也去美国留学了。

马克：是啊。不过，可以跟她们网上联系。最近我刚学了一句古诗："海内存知己，天涯若比邻"。

永民：你真行，连古诗都会了！

生词 New words

hánjià 寒假	winter break	fúhé 符合	accord with
xìngfú 幸福	happy; happiness	nénglì 能力	capacity, competence
miànshì 面试	interview	gǔlì 鼓励	encourage
shíxí 实习	internship	shēnqǐng 申请	apply; application
jīlěi 积累	accumulate	jìngzhēng 竞争	compete
gōngsī 公司	company	jīliè 激烈	fierce
zhíwèi 职位	position	xìnxīn 信心	confidence
guójì 国际	international	xìnxī 信息	information
kèhù 客户	client	wǎngzhàn 网站	website
zhāopìn 招聘	recruit	liànjiē 链接	link
fānyì 翻译	translator; translate		

4 Check the true statements.

☐ 1 永民寒假回韩国看了父母和朋友。

☐ 2 马克要面试的是一个实习生的职位。

☐ 3 马克想利用寒假的时间实习。

☐ 4 虽然竞争很激烈，可是马克对自己很有信心。

☐ 5 永民不知道阿曼达已经回国。

海内存知己
天涯若比邻

5 Choose the best answers.

1 马克打算毕业以后 ______。
a 留在中国工作　　b 去美国留学
c 在贸易公司做翻译

2 马克申请实习主要是为了 ______。
a 了解中国文化　　b 积累工作经验
c 和客户打交道

3 招聘信息，马克是在 ______ 看到的。
a 学校　b 一个网站上　c 朋友的邮件里

6 Predict what Mark and Yeong-min will do next.

马克：__________ 永民：__________

a 去巴西看阿曼达
b 到网上看一看有什么职位可以申请
c 为下个星期的面试做准备
d 申请去美国留学
e 在贸易公司当翻译
f 上网跟在别的国家的朋友们联系

1-5

7 You are going to hear a conversation between two classmates. Look at the words and predict what they are talking about.

世界500强的公司　运气好
校园招聘会　熟人

Now listen and write down the three ways to find a job.

找工作的方法	
1	
2	
3	

1-5

8 Work in pairs. Listen again and check your answers.

Now ask and answer the questions.

1 男同学为什么说自己运气好？
2 女同学让男同学别忘了她，是什么意思？
3 还有什么找工作的方法？

Pronunciation and speaking

1-6

1 Listen and repeat the sentences with a praising or encouraging tone.

1 你真棒，这么早就开始为找工作做准备了。
2 你的能力那么强，好好准备，一定没问题。
3 放心吧，你一定行！
4 你真行，连古诗都会了！

2 Work in pairs. Complete the conversations with a praising or encouraging tone.

1 A: 我这个学期选了六门课，而且都挺难的。
B: ______________________

2 A: 我明天有一个很重要的面试，我很紧张。
B: ______________________

3 A: 我刚学了一个新词叫"知己"。
B: ______________________

4 A: 我的中文水平能唱中文歌吗？
B: ______________________

3 Work in pairs. Talk about a position you would like to apply for. List your strengths and weaknesses, and encourage each other.

CHINESE TO GO

1-7

About me

Wǒ yìdiǎnr xìnxīn dōu méiyǒu
我 一点儿 信心 都 没有。
I have no confidence at all.

Wǒ xǐhuan gēn rén dǎ jiāodào
我 喜欢 跟 人 打 交道。
I am a people person.

LESSON 2

Reading and writing

1 Work in pairs. Look at the majors in the table below and talk about the potential job prospects.

专业	职位
管理	
英文	
经济	
历史	
新闻	

2 Work in pairs. Match the words with their meanings.

1 互联网	a link
2 网站	b website
3 链接	c home page
4 首页	d current page
5 搜索	e print
6 当前位置	f search
7 打印	g Internet

Now write down the meanings of the words.

网址：____________

网页：____________

3 Look at the meanings of the two-character words and complete the sentences.

经历: experience 简历: résumé 历史: history	The meaning of 历 is ____________.
能力: capacity 压力: pressure 风力: wind power	The meaning of 力 is ____________.
表演: perform 表现: display 表达: express	The meaning of 表 is ____________.
专业: major 行业: industry, walks of life 职业: profession	The meaning of 业 is ____________.
过程: process 全程: the whole trip 行程: itinerary	The meaning of 程 is ____________.

1-8

4 Mark is considering an internship at a company. Read the two web pages he has found and check the true statements.

- ☐ 1 马克要申请的职位工作地点在北京。
- ☐ 2 马克要申请的这家公司主要进口和销售儿童玩具和服装产品。
- ☐ 3 实习生不发工资。
- ☐ 4 申请人发送简历以后会在一周以后收到面试通知。
- ☐ 5 马克要申请的职位需要常常出差。
- ☐ 6 什么专业的人都可以申请这个职位。

网页一
rencaiwang.com

首页 职位搜索 公司搜索 打印

▶ 当前位置

亚深国际贸易有限公司

行　　业：进出口贸易
公司规模：100—150人
所在地区：中国大陆

亚深国际贸易有限公司是一家专门从事儿童玩具和服装产品进出口的公司。公司成立于2000年，在北京、重庆和深圳都设有分公司。

基本信息

职位名称		工作地点		发布日期	
	1. 客服实习生（2人）		深圳		三月二十八日
	2. 分公司销售经理（1人）		重庆		三月十五日

网页二
rencaiwang.com

首页 职位搜索 公司搜索 打印

▶ 当前位置

亚深国际贸易有限公司客户服务实习翻译（2人）

工作地点	深圳（需要经常出差）
工作内容	协助接待欧美客户，全程中英文口译 协助安排客户工作行程和参观游览活动
申请要求	在校大学生，英语专业、经济专业、管理专业优先 有英汉翻译或文秘工作经历者优先 有较强的沟通、表达能力
工资待遇	公司提供免费住宿和实习工资 实习期间表现优秀者，毕业后可正式进入公司工作
申请方式	请发简历到公司邮箱，一周内通知是否进入面试
联 系 人	文小姐

5 Complete the passage with the words in the box.

招聘　从事　口译　优先　待遇
表达　免费　进出口

亚深国际贸易有限公司主要 ______ 儿童玩具和服装的 ______ 贸易。现 ______ 中英文 ______ 实习生两名，要求申请人有比较强的沟通和 ______ 能力，有工作经历者 ______ 。 ______ 包括 ______ 住宿和实习工资。

6 Read the flyer Yeong-min found on the bulletin board and check the true statements.

☐ 1 国际交流中心为夏令营招聘实习生。
☐ 2 工作内容是协助夏令营的组织和管理工作。
☐ 3 除了免费吃、住以外，也提供生活补助。
☐ 4 其他学校的留学生也可以报名。
☐ 5 申请表应该用电子邮件发给王老师。

7 **Write an email to a student who worked as a volunteer last summer for the summer camp in Activity 7. Mention the following:**

1 Your basic background information;
2 Why the position interests you;
3 That you want to know more details about the workload, duties, benefits, etc.

国际交流中心招聘暑期志愿者

招聘人数：2名

工作项目：第四届国际中学生暑期夏令营

工作时间：7月15日—8月15日

工作地点：北京，哈尔滨

工作内容：协助国际交流中心完成国际中学生夏令营的组织和学生管理工作。

工作待遇：夏令营期间的吃、住、行费用由国际交流中心负责。另有每日生活补助。

申请要求：本校留学生，国籍不限；需中英文流利，有较强的沟通能力。

申请方式：请在3月30号前到留学生办公室找王老师填申请表；4月20日前通知面试。

联系方式：国际交流中心203室

电　　话：6235××××

生词 New words

shǒuyè	首页	home page
sōusuǒ	搜索	search
dǎyìn	打印	print
dāngqián wèizhì	当前位置	current page
yǒuxiàn gōngsī	有限公司	limited company
hángyè	行业	industry
jìn-chūkǒu	进出口	import and export
guīmó	规模	size, scale
zhuānmén	专门	specially
cóngshì	从事	be engaged in
értóng	儿童	children
wánjù	玩具	toy
chǎnpǐn	产品	product
chénglì	成立	establish
Chóngqìng	重庆	Chongqing
Shēnzhèn	深圳	Shenzhen
fēngōngsī	分公司	branch
xiāoshòu	销售	sell
jīnglǐ	经理	manager
dìdiǎn	地点	location
fābù	发布	issue, release
xiézhù	协助	help, assist
jiēdài	接待	receive (clients)
quánchéng	全程	the whole trip
kǒuyì	口译	interpret; interpreter
ānpái	安排	arrange
xíngchéng	行程	itinerary
yóulǎn	游览	tour
guǎnlǐ	管理	administer
zhuānyè	专业	major
yōuxiān	优先	be given priority
wénmì	文秘	secretary
jīnglì	经历	experience
gōutōng	沟通	communicate
biǎodá	表达	express
dàiyù	待遇	treatment, remuneration
zhùsù	住宿	get accommodation
qījiān	期间	period
zhèngshì	正式	formal
jiǎnlì	简历	résumé, CV
tōngzhī	通知	notice; notify
shìfǒu	是否	whether
xiàlìngyíng	夏令营	summer camp
bǔzhù	补助	subsidy
búxiàn	不限	no limit
liúlì	流利	fluent

Language in use

Expressing "not at all", "not even one", "not a single ..." with 一……都/也不/没……

1 Look at the sentences.

	Subject	一……	Noun	都/也	不/没……
明天的面试，	马克	一点儿	信心	都	没有。
昨天	他	一点儿	东西	也	没吃。
晚会上，	小李	一个	人	都	不认识。
刚到北京的时候，	他	一句	中文	也	不会说。
这些衬衫，	我	一件		也	不喜欢。

Now check the correct explanations.

- ☐ 1 一……都/也不/没…… is used to express "not at all", "not a single ..." or "not even one".
- ☐ 2 Both nouns and adjectives can appear before 都/也.
- ☐ 3 一点儿 modifies uncountable nouns while 一 + measure word precedes concrete nouns.
- ☐ 4 Sometimes, a noun or noun phrase can be moved to the beginning of the sentence in order to emphasize it.

2 Answer the questions with the words given.

1 哪门课你觉得最轻松？(压力)(一点儿压力也……)

2 感冒特别严重的时候，你是什么感觉？(一点儿力气也……)

3 你大学一年级的时候参加过招聘会吗？(一次……也……)

4 在你的家乡，如果是最重要的节日，商店是开门还是关门？(一家……也……)

Emphasizing details of a past action using 是……的

1 Look at the sentences.

1 你是什么时候来上海的？

2 他是在哪儿上的大学？

3 他是为了钱才跟她结婚的。

4 是我同屋帮我买的这张票。

5 马克打车去的机场。

Now check the correct explanations.

- ☐ 1 是……的 is used to emphasize the details of an action that took place in the past.
- ☐ 2 是……的 can emphasize the time, place, manner, purpose and agent of a particular action.
- ☐ 3 What the speaker wants to emphasize should be put between 是 and 的.
- ☐ 4 If there is an object of the verb, it can only follow 的, not precede it.
- ☐ 5 是 can be omitted, but 的 cannot.

2 Work in pairs. Ask each other about your most recent trip. Highlight the following information using 是……的.

- Where did you go?
- Who did you travel with?
- How did you get there?
- How did you book the tickets and hotel?

—你是怎么订的票？

—我是在网上订的票。

Showing direction of movement with 回/进/上/下+来/去

1 Look at the sentences.

	Verb	Object	Directional complement	
阿曼达已经	回	巴西	去	了。
她还会	回	中国	来	吗?
上课了，你们快	进	教室	去	吧。
你住几层?我可以	上	楼	去	找你。
你别站在那么高的地方，快	下		来。	

Now check the correct explanations.

☐ 1 回/进/上/下 can combine with either 来 or 去 to show the direction of movement.

☐ 2 来 and 去 serve as directional complements.

☐ 3 The location or destination is placed after 来/去.

☐ 4 来 indicates the action moves towards the speaker while 去 indicates the action moves away from the speaker.

2 Complete the conversations using directional complements.

1 A: 你住几层?
B: 我住十二层，你可以坐电梯 _______ 。
A: 算了，我不 _______ 了，我在楼下等你。你要几分钟能 _______ ?
B: 给我五分钟，我马上就 _______ 。

2 A: 我就不 _______ 了，只有几句话，我说完就走。
B: 都到门口了，怎么能不 _______ 呢?快 _______ 吧。

3 A: 儿子，你几点能 _______ 吃饭?
B: 我九点才能 _______ ，别等我了。

3 Work in pairs. Ask each other when you will next go back home and when you will come back to school. Write down the answers using directional complements.

Introducing an extreme case using 连……都/也……

1 Look at the sentences.

	连	Extreme case	都/也	Verb
你真行!	连	京剧	都	学会了。
学中文的人越来越多，	连	我奶奶	也	想学几句。
在北京三年了，可是我	连	一次长城	也	没去过。
她每天都去图书馆，	连	放假	都	去。
你听不听歌呀?怎么	连	这首歌	都	不知道?

Now check the correct explanations.

☐ 1 连……都/也…… means "even" and expresses surprise at unexpected events or information.

☐ 2 In order to talk about unexpected or surprising events, an extreme case is placed between 连 and 都/也.

☐ 3 In the structure, 连 is necessary, but 都/也 can be omitted.

2 Complete the sentences using 连……都/也…… to show that your friend is an expert about China.

1 我的朋友中文特别棒，她 ___________
___________________________ (古诗)

2 她什么中国菜都吃过，___________
___________________________ (云南菜)

3 中国的很多地方她都去过，_________
_________________ (我不认识的地方)

4 她对中国的传统文化和艺术非常了解，
_____________________ (古老的戏剧)

Turn to page 184 for grammar reference.

LESSON 3

Communication activity

1 Work in pairs. Choose three summer plans from the list below. Write down the pros and cons.

暑期计划	好处	坏处
去某大公司实习		
去小学生夏令营工作		
在快餐店打工		
去中国学中文、旅游		
在家休息		
去医院当志愿者		
其他 ______		

2 Work with another pair. Ask them about your choices. Elicit more pros and cons, and choose a plan.

3 Report your plan to the class and vote for the best one.

Turn to pages 172 and 178 for more speaking practice.

Review and practice

1 Complete the passage with the words in the box.

积累 安排 符合 激烈 信心 打交道
经历 职位 流利 招聘 搜索 游览
表达 通知 简历

真没想到两个月的实习这么快就过去了。半年以前，我在网上 ______ 暑期实习机会的时候，看到了这家国际贸易公司，他们当时正在 ______ 口译员。我把 ______ 发给他们以后，很快就收到了面试 ______。虽然我以前没有工作 ______，竞争也非常 ______，可是由于我的中文很 ______，沟通和 ______ 能力也比较强，所以经理觉得我 ______ 他们的要求。最后我很顺利地得到了实习 ______。我的工作，除了当翻译以外，也得协助经理 ______ 客户的参观 ______ 活动。这次实习让我 ______ 了很多跟客户 ______ 的经验。我有 ______，下次我一定会做得更好。

Cultural corner

Tang poetry

Taken from a poem by the early Tang-dynasty poet Wang Bo (649–676), 海内存知己，天涯若比邻 is often quoted by Chinese people at farewell parties. The line means that one can feel the presence of a close friend as if they lived next door, even if they live on the other side of the world. During the Tang Dynasty (618–907), poetry played an important part in Chinese cultural life, and a proliferation of poets and poems helped Tang poetry become established as an important influence in Chinese literature, culture and history. The legacy of the Tang poem is still felt in daily life in China today. Reciting Tang poems remains a part of Chinese children's education, and there is a famous Tang verse for every occasion, able to evoke a precise atmosphere or mood.

2 Choose the correct words to complete the sentences.

1 你还要在图书馆看书吗？你打算几点 _______ 啊？

a 回去宿舍　b 回宿舍去　c 去宿舍

2 每到考试他都会非常紧张，连听最喜欢的音乐 _______ 不能让他的压力小一点儿。

a 就　b 还　c 都

3 现在找工作越来越难了，不管是什么职位，竞争都特别 _______。

a 激烈　b 严重　c 强

4 为了让孩子变得更有信心，父母应该多 _______ 孩子。

a 表达　b 沟通　c 鼓励

5 学校安排留学生这个周末去山东 _______ 大明湖。

a 旅游　b 游览　c 参观

3 Work in pairs. Discuss the three issues below and rank them in terms of importance.

_______ 先努力工作再谈待遇

_______ 从小事做起

_______ 主动问问题

Now read the online discussion and answer the questions.

1 为什么方先生认为不应该一开始就问实习工资？

2 很多实习生不愿意做小事情的原因是什么？

3 张先生认为主动问问题跟工作进步有什么关系？

★我们喜欢这样的实习生★　收藏　回复

楼主

方先生
人事主管

先努力工作再谈待遇　举报　回复

经常有这样的大学生，来我们公司面试，第一句话就问：实习有工资吗？我们公司虽然提供实习工资，但是一个没有经验的学生，什么都还没开始做，就问待遇怎么样，这样的大学生，我一般都不会接受。

王小姐
项目经理

从小事做起　举报　回复

很多实习生觉得实习期间我们给他们安排的工作没有意思，学不到东西。其实，不应该这样想。事情一定会有，只是有大有小。不能因为是小事情就不愿意做。如果因为事情很小就不愿意做，或者不好好做，那么谁会放心让他们做重要的事情？

楼主

张先生

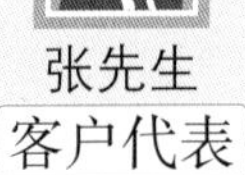

客户代表

主动问问题　举报　回复

很多实习生都不喜欢问问题。可是，如果你不知道公司的工作方法，也不知道怎么跟客户打交道，有的时候连你要找的人的联系方式都不知道，不问怎么能行呢？不懂的、不明白的，一定要问，没有谁一开始就什么都知道。在工作中，你问得越多，进步得越快。

4 Write a reply to the following post with your own suggestions.

举报　收起回复

我想利用暑假在学校打打工，赚点儿学费，也可以增加一点儿工作经验。可是我刚来不久，所以不太清楚去什么地方找打工的机会，也不知道我的英文够不够好。另外，打工的时候我应该注意些什么？你能不能给我一些建议？谢谢！

我也说一句

Vocabulary review

Fill in the blanks.

安排	ānpái	*v.*	________
________	biǎodá	*v.*	express
不限	búxiàn	*v.*	________
补助	bǔzhù	*n.*	subsidy
产品	chǎnpǐn	*n.*	________
________	chénglì	*v.*	establish
从事	cóngshì	*v.*	________
打印	dǎyìn	*v.*	________
待遇	dàiyù	*n.*	treatment, remuneration
当前位置	dāngqián wèizhì		current page
________	dìdiǎn	*n.*	location
儿童	értóng	*n.*	children
发布	fābù	*v.*	issue, release
翻译	fānyì	*n./v.*	translator; translate
分公司	fēngōngsī	*n.*	branch
符合	fúhé	*v.*	accord with
________	gōngsī	*n.*	company
沟通	gōutōng	*v.*	communicate
鼓励	gǔlì	*v.*	encourage
管理	guǎnlǐ	*v.*	________
规模	guīmó	*n.*	size, scale
国际	guójì	*adj.*	international
________	hánjià	*n.*	winter break
行业	hángyè	*n.*	industry
积累	jīlěi	*v.*	accumulate
激烈	jīliè	*adj.*	fierce
简历	jiǎnlì	*n.*	résumé, CV
接待	jiēdài	*v.*	receive (clients)
进出口	jìn-chūkǒu		import and export
经理	jīnglǐ	*n.*	________
经历	jīnglì	*n.*	experience
竞争	jìngzhēng	*v.*	compete
客户	kèhù	*n.*	________
口译	kǒuyì	*v./n.*	interpret; interpreter

链接	liànjiē	*v.*	link
流利	liúlì	*adj.*	fluent
面试	miànshì	*v.*	________
________	nénglì	*n.*	capacity, competence
期间	qījiān	*n.*	period
全程	quánchéng	*n.*	the whole trip
申请	shēnqǐng	*v./n.*	apply; application
实习	shíxí	*v.*	internship
________	shìfǒu	*adv.*	whether
首页	shǒuyè	*n.*	home page
搜索	sōusuǒ	*v.*	search
通知	tōngzhī	*n./v.*	notice; notify
玩具	wánjù	*n.*	________
网站	wǎngzhàn	*n.*	website
文秘	wénmì	*n.*	secretary
夏令营	xiàlìngyíng	*n.*	summer camp
销售	xiāoshòu	*v.*	sell
协助	xiézhù	*v.*	help, assist
________	xìnxī	*n.*	information
信心	xìnxīn	*n.*	confidence
行程	xíngchéng	*n.*	itinerary
________	xìngfú	*adj./n.*	happy; happiness
优先	yōuxiān	*v.*	be given priority
游览	yóulǎn	*v.*	tour
有限公司	yǒuxiàn gōngsī		limited company
招聘	zhāopìn	*v.*	recruit
正式	zhèngshì	*adj.*	________
职位	zhíwèi	*n.*	position
住宿	zhùsù	*v.*	get accommodation
专门	zhuānmén	*adv.*	specially
________	zhuānyè	*n.*	major
重庆	Chóngqìng	*n.*	Chongqing
深圳	Shēnzhèn	*n.*	Shenzhen

UNIT

2

Nǐ gǎn jué zěn me yàng

你感觉怎么样？

How did you feel?

LESSON 1

Vocabulary and listening

1 **Check the meanings of the words in the box and think about how you would use them.**

心情	吃不惯
对……满意	适应
困难　　暂时	复杂

Now work in pairs. Talk about how you felt when you were away from home for the first time.

— 第一次离开家的时候，我的心情很复杂。我很兴奋，但也很想家。

2 **Mark and Wang Yu are having a video chat to catch up. Listen to their conversation and answer the questions.**

1 马克对上个星期的面试感觉怎么样？
2 马克的工作经历复杂不复杂？
3 王玉对美国的感觉怎么样？
4 马克是怎么鼓励王玉的？

王玉：马克！上次你说的那家公司的面试进行得怎么样，要不要我再帮你练习一下？

马克：不用了，王玉，谢谢你。面试上个星期三就结束了，我正在等结果呢。

王玉：你感觉怎么样？

马克：还行吧，我对自己的表现还算满意。

王玉：都问了你一些什么问题？

马克：他们最感兴趣的是我作为一个外国人，为什么想留在中国工作。然后让我介绍一下以前的工作经历，还问了我将来的打算。总之，没有问特别复杂的问题。

王玉：工作经历你是怎么介绍的？

马克：我说我帮同学翻译过一些东西；在澳大利亚上高中的时候在一个老人院做过志愿者。

王玉：你有没有强调你的适应能力强、工作态度认真？

马克：我没直接说，但是他们应该能感觉到吧。面试快结束的时候，他们已经跟我谈到实习期间的待遇了。

王玉：应该机会很大！对了，你

拿的是学生签证，可以在中国工作吗？

马克：哎呀，我忘了问，你一提醒我又想起来了。明天我再写信问问吧。别光说我的事了，你对美国的生活感觉怎么样？

王玉：还是不太适应。我很想家，想得不得了。我这个中国胃吃不惯美国菜，加上学习压力大，英文又不够用……总之，心情挺复杂的。

马克：别担心，这些困难都是暂时的。我刚来北京的时候跟你感觉差不多，后来不是挺好的？我交了很多新朋友，也爱上了中国菜，现在都想留下来工作了。我想你一定能很快适应新生活！

生词 New words

mǎnyì	满意	satisfy
zuòwéi	作为	as
jiānglái	将来	future
zǒngzhī	总之	in sum
fùzá	复杂	complicated
lǎorényuàn	老人院	retirement home
qiángdiào	强调	emphasize
shìyìng	适应	adapt to
tàidu	态度	attitude
tándào	谈到	talking about
qiānzhèng	签证	visa
wàng	忘	forget
tíxǐng	提醒	remind
bùdéliǎo	不得了	extremely
wèi	胃	stomach
chī bú guàn	吃不惯	not get used to eating
jiāshang	加上	plus
xīnqíng	心情	mood, feelings
kùnnan	困难	difficulty
zànshí	暂时	temporary
hòulái	后来	later on
jiāo péngyou	交朋友	make friends
àishang	爱上	fall in love

3 Check the true statements.

☐ 1 王玉以前帮马克练习过面试。

☐ 2 马克觉得自己在面试中的表现还不错。

☐ 3 面试时，马克直接强调了自己工作态度认真。

☐ 4 马克已经问过签证的事情了。

☐ 5 虽然王玉很想家，但是她很快就适应了美国的生活。

4 Choose the best answers to the questions.

1 马克的面试是什么时候结束的？
 a 这个星期三 b 上个星期三
 c 三个星期以前

2 面试的公司对马克的什么最感兴趣？
 a 以前的工作经历 b 将来的打算
 c 想留在中国工作的原因

3 面试快结束的时候，公司和马克谈到了什么？
 a 面试的结果 b 实习期间的待遇
 c 签证的事情

5 Match the people with the facts.

1 马克

2 王玉

a 帮同学翻译东西
b 学习压力大
c 吃不惯美国菜
d 爱上中国菜
e 在老人院做过志愿者
f 出国后心情很复杂
g 交了很多新朋友
h 外语水平还不够好

6 You are going to hear a telephone conversation. Look at the words and predict what the conversation is about.

应聘 广告 行业 心理学 专业
推销 门票

Now listen and put the topics in the order you hear them.

______ 工资待遇
______ 面试结果
______ 自己的优点
______ 以前的工作经历
______ 专业和职位的关系

7 Work in pairs. Listen again and check your answers.

Now ask and answer the questions.

1 王助理觉得心理学专业和广告行业的关系大不大？

2 李天亮为什么要说推销门票的事情？

Pronunciation and speaking

1 Listen to the sentences. Notice how the underlined words help emphasize the tone.

1 还是不太适应。我很想家，想得不得了。我这个中国胃吃不惯美国菜，加上学习压力大，英文又不够用……总之，心情挺复杂的。

2 我刚来北京的时候跟你感觉差不多，后来不是挺好的？我交了很多新朋友，也爱上了中国菜，现在都想留下来工作了。我想你一定能很快适应新生活！

Now read aloud.

2 Work in pairs. Tell each other how you feel about learning Chinese. Use the underlined words in Activity 1 to make your sentences sound natural.

CHINESE TO GO

After an interview

Nǐ gǎnjué zěnmeyàng
你 感觉 怎么 样？
How do you feel (about...)?

Hái xíng ba
还 行 吧。
Not too bad.

Jīhuì yīnggāi hěn dà
机会 应该 很 大！
I think you have a pretty good chance of success!

LESSON 2

Reading and writing

1 Work in pairs. Talk about three jobs you could be good at, and explain why.

— 我认为我能胜任 ______ 的工作，因为我过去 ______，锻炼了 ______ 能力。
— 因为我曾经 ______，养成了 ______ 的好习惯。
— 因为我多次 ______。
— 因为我的专业是 ______。
— 因为我富有 ______。

2 Look at the words on the left and write down the meanings of the words on the right.

同情: sympathetic
责任: responsible
幽默: humorous
心: heart
感: sense

同情心: ______
责任心: ______
责任感: ______
幽默感: ______

帮助: help
于: towards, to

有助于: ______

求: ask
申请: apply for
推荐: recommend
职位: position, job
信: letter
感谢: thank

求职信: ______
申请信: ______
推荐信: ______
感谢信: ______

3 Work in pairs. Read Mark's résumé and discuss how a résumé in China differs from one in your home country.

马克
Mark Johnson

联系我

电话：010-6345XXXX
地址：北京外国语大学留学生楼XXX室

个人简历

基本资料

国籍	年龄	性别
澳大利亚	21	男
学历	兴趣爱好	
在校大学生	旅游，冲浪，中国功夫	

工作经历

4 Read Mark's application letter for the internship on page 32 and check the true statements.

☐ 1 马克的专业是经济学，明年毕业。
☐ 2 马克常常为同学做商务口译。
☐ 3 马克在老人院做志愿者的时候，工作主要是照顾老人。
☐ 4 马克认为自己在中国的学习、生活经历对他的工作会很有帮助。
☐ 5 马克有一些从事商务的朋友。

求职信

尊敬的文小姐：

您好。感谢您抽时间阅读我的求职信。

我叫马克，来自澳大利亚，是北京外国语大学现代汉语专业的留学生，将于明年毕业。我希望毕业以后留在中国工作，所以想利用暑假的时间积累一些相关的工作经验。我对贵公司客户服务翻译实习生的工作很有兴趣，我认为自己可以在短时间内适应并胜任这份工作。

我的母语是英文，目前的专业是中文，辅修经济。在过去的两年里，我多次帮助我的同学翻译各类文章。尽管我没有做过正式的商务接待工作，但是我在澳大利亚的朋友来中国进行商务考察时，我曾经帮助他们安排在中国的行程。

我性格开朗，热爱运动和旅行；喜欢和各种各样的人打交道，富有同情心和责任感。上高中时，我曾经在布里斯班的一家老人院做过两年的志愿者，主要帮助他们整理资料、做会议记录，并且组织了很多活动。在这份工作中，我锻炼了自己的组织、策划和沟通能力，养成了做事认真、仔细的好习惯。在中国学习、生活的这几年，我既学到中国历史文化方面的很多知识，也对东西方文化上的差异有了更多的理解。我认为这些都有助于我胜任贵公司客服翻译的工作。

我非常希望能够得到贵公司这份工作的实习机会，也相信这会为我将来的工作打下坚实的基础。随信附上个人简历一份。

期待您的答复。

此致

敬礼！

申请人：马克

2014年3月4日

5 Answer the questions.

1 马克为什么要申请这份工作？

2 马克是学什么的？

3 马克有哪些工作经历？

4 什么事情能说明马克富有同情心和责任感？

5 老人院的工作经历对马克来说重要吗？为什么？

6 在中国的这几年，马克的收获大不大？

生词 New words

xuélì 学历	academic qualification	zérèn 责任	responsibility
qiúzhíxìn 求职信	application letter	céngjīng 曾经	ever
gǎnxiè 感谢	thank heartily	Bùlǐsībān 布里斯班	Brisbane
chōu shíjiān 抽 时间	make time	zhěnglǐ 整理	sort out, clean
guì 贵	honourable	huìyì 会议	meeting, conference
shèngrèn 胜任	competent at (a job)	jìlù 记录	record
mǔyǔ 母语	mother tongue	bìngqiě 并且	and
mùqián 目前	for the time being	zǔzhī 组织	organize
fǔxiū 辅修	minor	cèhuà 策划	plan
guòqù 过去	past	yǎngchéng 养成	cultivate (habits)
duōcì 多次	many times	zǐxì 仔细	careful
wénzhāng 文章	article	jì 既…… yě 也……	both … and …
jǐnguǎn 尽管	even though		
kǎochá 考察	investigate	chāyì 差异	differences
kāilǎng 开朗	extrovert	suí 随	go with
fùyǒu 富有	be rich in	fù 附	attach
tóngqíng 同情	sympathize	qīdài 期待	look forward to

6 Complete the passage with the words in the box.

热爱　将于……毕业　富有　认为
目前　有助于　曾经　进行……考察
并且　来自　多次

马克是一位 ______ 澳大利亚的留学生。他性格开朗，______ 运动和旅行；他 ______ 同情心和责任感。上高中时，他 ______ 在布里斯班的一家老人院做过志愿者。______ 他正在北京外国语大学学习。在过去的两年中，他 ______ 帮助他的同学翻译各类文章，______ 协助接待他的朋友来中国 ______ 商务 ______。马克 ______ 2015年 ______。为了积累工作经验，他申请了一家公司的实习翻译职位。马克 ______ 自己的知识、能力和经历都 ______ 他胜任这份实习工作。

7 Read about Mark's work experience.

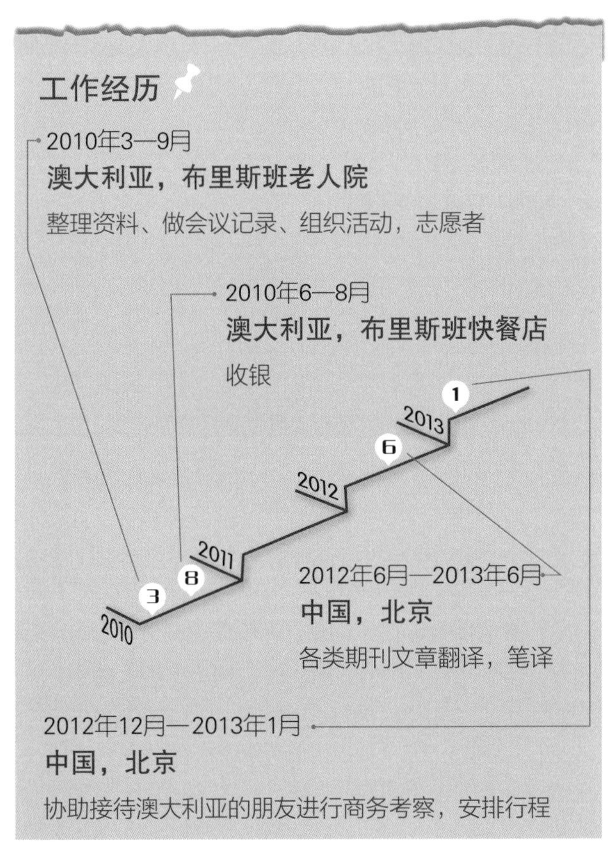

工作经历
2010年3—9月
澳大利亚，布里斯班老人院
整理资料、做会议记录、组织活动，志愿者
2010年6—8月
澳大利亚，布里斯班快餐店
收银
2013
1
6
2012
2011
8
3
2010
2012年6月—2013年6月
中国，北京
各类期刊文章翻译，笔译
2012年12月—2013年1月
中国，北京
协助接待澳大利亚的朋友进行商务考察，安排行程

Now answer the questions.

1 在这些工作经历中，哪一个是马克在求职信中没有谈到的？他为什么没有强调这个经历？

2 马克协助接待他的朋友进行商务考察，这算不算他的工作经历？能不能写在简历中？

8 Write your own résumé. Use Mark's résumé in Activities 3 and 7 to help you.

Language in use

Indicating a very high degree of something with 不得了

1 Look at the sentences.

	Adj. / Verb	得	不得了
广州的夏天	热	得	不得了。
暑假大家都回家了，我一个人留在宿舍里，	寂寞	得	不得了。
快到春节的时候，大大小小的商店都	热闹	得	不得了。
我想我妈妈做的饭	想	得	不得了。
他喜欢这个新游戏	喜欢	得	不得了。

Now check the correct explanations.

☐ 1 不得了 is used to indicate a very high degree of something.

☐ 2 得 preceding 不得了 introduces 不得了 as a complement.

☐ 3 As a complement, 不得了 can be used to modify either an adjective or an emotional verb.

☐ 4 The adjective or verb that is modified by 得不得了 should express negative, not positive, meaning.

2 Answer the questions using 不得了.

— 你还记得你小时候最喜欢的玩具吗？你有多喜欢它？

— 我小时候有一个熊猫玩具，我喜欢它喜欢得不得了，每天睡觉都要抱着它。

1 你们学校里的超市，哪家比较便宜，哪家比较贵？

2 你这个学期选的课中，哪门课最容易，哪门课最难？

3 你觉得什么饮料最好喝？你喝得多吗？

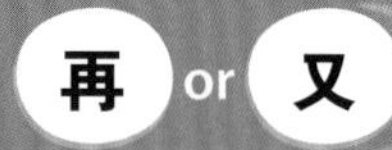

Repeated actions with 再 or 又

1 Look at the sentences.

	再/又	Verb phrase	
我可以	再	帮你模拟一下面试。	
你得	再	给那家公司打个电话。	
你们下次	再	来香港，	一定要跟我联系。
我昨天	又	去了学校附近的那家中餐馆，	他家做的菜都好吃得不得了。
你怎么	又	买了一件白衬衫？	
明天	又	是星期六了。	

Now check the correct explanations.

☐ 1 Both 再 and 又 can serve as adverbs meaning "again", thus indicating the repetition of an action or activity.

☐ 2 再 refers to a future event. It indicates that an action will occur, and it will be a repeat of an earlier action.

☐ 3 If there is a modal verb in the sentence, 再 should be placed before the modal verb.

☐ 4 又 indicates that the repeated action has already taken place.

☐ 5 又 can also be used to indicate an action which can be expected to recur in the future.

2 Complete the sentences with 再 or 又.

1 这部电影，我两年以前看过一遍，去年暑假 _______ 看了一遍，我打算今年暑假 _______ 看一遍。

2 我第一次去北京是高中毕业的时候，去年和我姐姐一起 _______ 去了一次，要是将来有机会，我还想 _______ 去一次。

3 中文课上个星期五刚考完试，这个星期五 _______ 要考试了。

Expressing "a little bit" using 一下 or 一点儿

1 Look at the sentences.

	Verb	一下/一点儿	Object	
请你	介绍	一下	你的专业。	
我能不能	看	一下	那个电脑?	
你太累了，好好	休息	一下		吧。
我早上	吃了	一点儿	东西，	所以现在不太饿。
他	听说过	一点儿	你哥哥的事。	
你们想	喝	一点儿	什么?	我有咖啡和可乐。

Now check the correct explanations.

☐ 1 一下 and 一点儿 can both be used to moderate a statement to mean "a little bit".

☐ 2 一点儿 is used to express that an action is carried out to a minor extent or "a little bit"; therefore it refers to the verb itself rather than the object of the verb.

☐ 3 一下 is often used to make a suggestion, a request or an order.

☐ 4 一点儿 can be used as a qualifier to modify the object of the verb and denote that the action performed on it was minor.

2 Complete the sentences with 一下 or 一点儿.

1 这件事情，你再给我 _______ 时间，让我再想一想。
2 你不知道布里斯班在哪儿，上网搜索 _______ 就知道了。
3 我今天忘了带手机，能不能借用 _______ 你的手机？我想给我父母打个电话。
4 我刚去超市买了 _______ 蔬菜和水果，刚回来。
5 我今天午饭吃得很少，只吃了 _______ 面包，喝了 _______ 牛奶。

3 Work in pairs. Ask your partner for help by making three requests using 一下.

— 我不认识这个字，你能不能看一下这是什么字？

Indicating the beginning of an action or the start of a new state with 起来

1 Look at the sentences.

	Verb 起 (object) 来/ Adj. 起来
他们一见面就	吵了起来。
你一说我就	想起来了。
一看见巧克力没有了，那个孩子马上就	哭了起来。
她一进屋就	听起音乐来。
外面	下起雪来了。
过了四月，天气就慢慢地	热起来了。

Now check the correct explanations.

☐ 1 起来 is used after an action verb or an adjective to indicate the beginning of an action or the start of a new state.

☐ 2 If the verb takes an object, the object can be inserted between 起 and 来 or be placed after 起来.

☐ 3 Even though 起来 still serves as a complement, its literal meaning of "upward movement" as a directional complement has been lost.

2 Work in pairs. Ask and answer the questions using 起来.

1 你小时候最怕什么动物？看见这种动物，你会怎么样？
2 你有没有一想起来就生气的事情？
3 你很难过的时候，有什么办法可以让你高兴起来？
4 在你的家乡，到了几月天气会慢慢冷起来？过了几月，天气又会慢慢热起来？

Turn to page 185 for grammar reference.

LESSON 3

Communication activity

Choose a job ad below. Apply by revising your résumé in Activity 8, Lesson 2 accordingly.

招聘

职位：暑期小学英文老师2名
工作地点：XX小学
工作时间：七月初至八月底，周一至周五上午8点到下午3点
申请人要求：英文专业或英文为母语，喜欢孩子，有教学工作经验。
具体工作待遇及工作内容请联系刘小姐。

诚聘

因本公司业务发展需要，现招聘以下人员：
1. 中英翻译 1名
2. 客户服务 3名
3. 市场经理 1名

要求大学本科文化水平，有相关经验。以上人员一经录用，工资待遇面议，待遇从优，包食宿。
联系人：钱先生

诚聘

梦飞国际教育公司

经理助理 1名

女性，年龄25岁以下，办事认真，责任心强，有文秘工作经验，懂英文且会开车者优先。

清风国际旅行社
因业务发展

销售代表 3名

男性，要求沟通能力强，会英文、有销售工作经验者优先。需经常出差。

导游 5名

高中或大学毕业，形象好，中英文流利，喜欢旅游，有责任心。

Now work in pairs.

- Prepare a list of interview questions for the position your partner is applying for.
- Act out the job interviews.

Turn to pages 172 and 178 for more speaking practice.

Review and practice

1 Choose the correct words to complete the sentences.

1 你 ______ 宿舍的条件满意吗？
a 为　b 对　c 让

2 她从小就 ______ 戏剧和表演，希望自己将来能当一名演员。
a 热爱　b 爱上　c 有兴趣

3 我 ______ 在国际交流夏令营做过两年的志愿者。
a 经常　b 从来　c 曾经

4 他妹妹性格活泼 ______，既喜欢帮助别人，又喜欢跟各种各样的人打交道。
a 开心　b 开放　c 开朗

5 上高中的时候，我住在家里，每天早睡早起。可是上了大学以后，我慢慢 ______ 了晚睡晚起的习惯。
a 养成　b 造成　c 变成

Cultural corner

Tips for job-hunting in China

The days are long gone when it was easy for someone from overseas to find a desirable position in China, and when there was a big gap between the salaries of non-national and local Chinese employees. Whilst expatriates can still expect to easily find jobs teaching or tutoring English, if you are looking for a corporate job, be prepared for fierce competition, a low entry-level salary, and high living expenses in big cities like Beijing, Shanghai and Guangzhou, where jobs are concentrated. If you have a special skill or work experience in China, you have a competitive edge. Knowledge of Chinese language and culture may not be a requirement, but is definitely a major advantage.

2 Complete the passage with the words in the box.

复杂	作为	认真	满意	组织
强调	感觉到	一点儿	一下	流利

大家都知道，______留学生，在中文还不是特别______的时候，要用中文写简历、写求职信、进行面试是很不容易的。在这里我可以跟大家谈谈我的______经验。首先要写好简历和求职信。然后可以请朋友帮你模拟______面试。到面试的时候，你就不会紧张了。我在面试中，一共回答了四个问题，都不是很______。我主要介绍了自己做志愿者时______过的各种活动。这些例子既可以说明我做事______、仔细，也可以让他们______我的策划、沟通能力很强。另外，我也______了自己很有责任心。总之我对自己的表现还算______。

3 Read the sentences and work out the meanings of the underlined words.

1 这本书的开头很有意思，可是越看越没有意思了，结尾我已经不想看了。
2 你昨天发给我的邮件，怎么只有你的姓名和联系方式，没有正文啊？
3 我应该称呼她"王秘书"还是"王小姐"？
4 那家公司正在招聘英语翻译，什么专业背景的人都可以申请，英语好就行。

开头 _____ 结尾 _____ 正文 _____
称呼 _____ 背景 _____

Now read paragraphs a–h and put them in the correct order.

1 _____ 2 _____ 3 _____ 4 _____
5 _____ 6 _____ 7 _____ 8 _____

怎样写求职信

a 信的开头要向收信人问好，称呼应该正式，然后清楚地说明自己想申请的职位。

b 一封好的求职信会给招聘的人留下很好的印象，所以在工作申请中常常起到很大的作用。写求职信的目的是让对方了解自己、相信自己可以胜任，要根据不同职位来写。

c 也可以说明你为什么想申请这个职位，或者这个职位对你将来的发展有什么好处。

d 最后写上"此致"、"敬礼"，还有你的名字和日期。

e 信的正文可以从自我介绍开始，可以多介绍一些专业背景、专业和申请的职位有什么关系、你的兴趣，等等。

f 总之，要让招聘的人感觉无论是你的专业知识、申请原因还是你的工作经历，都让你能够胜任你申请的职位。

g 除了自我介绍和申请原因以外，正文的主要内容还应该包括你过去的工作经历。要选择和你申请的职位相关的工作经历，并且要强调你的工作能力、态度、责任心，等等。

h 信的结尾要表达你非常希望得到这个工作机会，希望对方阅读你的简历，并表示期待对方的答复。

4 Complete the table according to the passage in Activity 3.

开头	称呼，问好
正文	自我介绍，专业背景
结尾	希望得到工作机会
最后	此致敬礼，名字，日期

5 Choose one position from the Communication activity on page 36 and write an application letter.

Vocabulary review

Fill in the blanks.

爱上	àishang	*v.*	fall in love
并且	bìngqiě	*conj.*	______
不得了	bùdéliǎo		extremely
策划	cèhuà	*v.*	plan
______	céngjīng	*adv.*	ever
差异	chāyì	*n.*	______
吃不惯	chī bú guàn	*v.*	not get used to eating
抽时间	chōu shíjiān		make time
多次	duōcì	*adv.*	______
辅修	fǔxiū	*v.*	minor
附	fù	*v.*	attach
复杂	fùzá	*adj.*	______
富有	fùyǒu	*v.*	be rich in
______	gǎnxiè	*v.*	thank heartily
贵	guì	*adj.*	honourable
过去	guòqù	*n.*	______
______	hòulái	*n.*	later on
______	huìyì	*n.*	meeting, conference
记录	jìlù	*v./n.*	record
既……也……	jì...yě...	*conj.*	both ... and ...
加上	jiāshang	*v.*	plus
将来	jiānglái	*n.*	______
交朋友	jiāo péngyou		make friends
______	jǐnguǎn	*conj.*	even though
开朗	kāilǎng	*adj.*	extrovert
考察	kǎochá	*v.*	investigate
困难	kùnnan	*n.*	______
老人院	lǎorényuàn	*n.*	retirement home

满意	mǎnyì	*v.*	satisfy
母语	mǔyǔ	*n.*	mother tongue
______	mùqián	*n.*	for the time being
期待	qīdài	*v.*	look forward to
签证	qiānzhèng	*v./n.*	visa
强调	qiángdiào	*v.*	emphasize
求职信	qiúzhíxìn	*n.*	application letter
胜任	shèngrèn	*v.*	be competent at (a job)
______	shìyìng	*v.*	adapt to
随	suí	*v.*	go with
态度	tàidu	*n.*	______
谈到	tándào		talking about
提醒	tíxǐng	*v.*	remind
同情	tóngqíng	*v.*	sympathize
______	wàng	*v.*	forget
胃	wèi	*n.*	stomach
文章	wénzhāng	*n.*	article
______	xīnqíng	*n.*	mood, feelings
学历	xuélì	*n.*	academic qualification
养成	yǎngchéng	*v.*	cultivate (habits)
暂时	zànshí	*n.*	temporary
责任	zérèn	*n.*	responsibility
整理	zhěnglǐ	*v.*	sort out, clean
______	zǐxì	*adj.*	careful
总之	zǒngzhī	*conj.*	in sum
组织	zǔzhī	*v.*	organize
作为	zuòwéi	*prep.*	as
布里斯班	Bùlǐsībān	*n.*	Brisbane

UNIT 3

Ràng nín de lǚxíng méiyǒu hòugùzhīyōu
让您的旅行没有后顾之忧！

We can help you plan a worry-free trip!

LESSON 1

Vocabulary and listening

1 Look at the words and their meanings.

购	make a purchase	卧铺	berth
处	place	团体	group, team
务	matters, affairs	送	deliver

Now work out the meanings of the words in the word map.

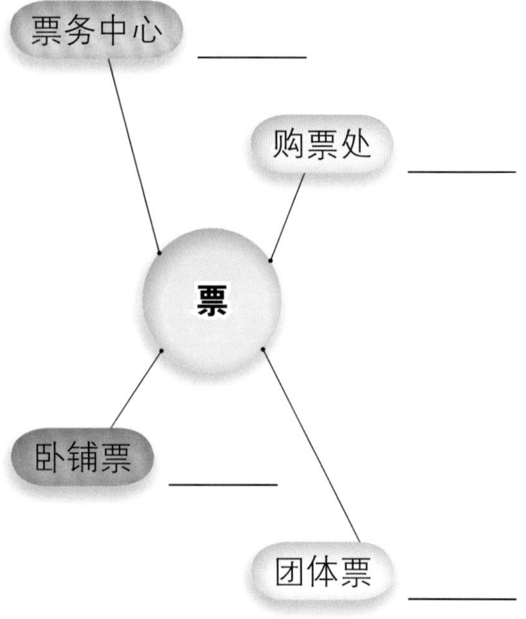

Now write down more words with 票.

2 Yeong-min is checking with a travel agent about tickets to Harbin for the summer camp. Listen to their conversation and answer the questions.

1 永民主要问了哪些问题？
2 最后客服把永民的电话转给谁了？
3 你觉得这家旅行社的服务怎么样？

客服：您好。清风旅行社票务中心。有什么可以帮您？

永民：您好，我是北京外国语大学的。我们学校有一个十五人左右的团要在七月中从北京去哈尔滨。我想问一下那个时候的机票和火车票大概都是多少钱？

客服：您稍等，我帮您查一下。请问您贵姓？

永民：我姓金。

客服：金先生，因为七月是旅游旺季，所以机票基本上是全价。至于火车票，选择就比较多了。您可以选普通列车或者动车，卧铺票或者座票。

永民：不好意思，能不能麻烦您详细解释一下？

客服：金先生，是这样的：普通列车从北京到哈尔滨需要10到20个小时不等，卧铺票价大约是硬座票价的两到三倍。硬座当然不如卧铺舒服，但是价钱便宜多了。动车是高速列车，最快的8个小时就到哈尔滨。动车只有座票，不过座位比普通列车要舒服；动车一等座的票价差不多是飞机票全价的一半，二等座还要便宜大约三分之一。

永民：火车票还真不贵。不过我要跟

生词 New words

shǒuzé 守则	rules	jǐnjí 紧急	urgent
tīngcóng 听从	listen to and obey	yíngyuán 营员	camper
zūnshǒu 遵守	abide by, observe (the rules)	yǒuhǎo 友好	friendly
zuòxī 作息	work and rest	xiāngchǔ 相处	get along
wùpǐn 物品	item, thing	hùxiāng 互相	each other
guìzhòng 贵重	valuable	zhīchí 支持	support
diūshī 丢失	get lost	fāyáng 发扬	carry on (spirit)
bàogào 报告	report	tuánduì jīngshén 团队 精神	team spirit
yǐnshí 饮食	food and drink	huǒjǐng 火警	fire department
wèishēng 卫生	hygiene	yīliáo 医疗	medical
qǐngjià 请假	ask for time off	jíjiù 急救	give first aid
wánchéng 完成	complete, accomplish	wǔxiū 午休	lunch break
zìxí 自习	self-study	chángxiù 长袖	long sleeves
rènhé 任何	any	fángshàishuāng 防晒霜	sun cream
gōngkè 功课	homework	màozi 帽子	hat
zhíbān 值班	be on duty	tàiyángjìng 太阳镜	sunglasses
jījí 积极	active; actively	yàopǐn 药品	medicine
kèwài 课外	extracurricular	xǐshù yòngpǐn 洗漱 用品	toiletries
tèshū 特殊	special	shǒubiǎo 手表	watch
dāndú 单独	alone, by oneself	sǎn 伞	umbrella
shúxī 熟悉	get familiar with	língyòngqián 零用钱	petty cash
chángyòng 常用	frequently used	rénmínbì 人民币	Renminbi

5 Complete the passage with the words in the box.

遵守　听从　参加　管理　通知
支持　报告　相处　完成　行动

营员应该 ______ 老师的安排，______ 作息时间，按时上课，按时 ______ 作业。夏令营期间，应该 ______ 好自己的物品，如果发现丢失，要向领队 ______。也要积极 ______ 各种活动，如果有特殊原因不能参加，需要提前 ______ 领队。不要单独 ______，记好常用号码，跟其他营员要友好 ______、互相 ______。

6 Check if the following actions are appropriate, according to the rules of the camp.

1 你发现钱包丢了，马上给父母打电话，两天后才告诉领队。

2 你上课时觉得身体不舒服，马上告诉了老师。

3 上课的时候你努力说中文，回宿舍以后你就不说中文了。

4 星期三下午的安排是去参观历史博物馆。你以前去过，所以你就单独去见朋友了。

5 你跟同学在外面遇到紧急情况，你马上给110打电话。

6 你下午1点钟的时候在教室里看书。

7 Think of a place to go for the weekend. List five necessities you should bring and explain why.

Now write a short passage based on your list.

Language in use

Verb + object as a separable compound

1 Look at the sentences.

	Verb		Object	
我昨天晚上只	睡	了四个小时的	觉。	
王主任将给大家	致	欢迎	辞。	
你给大家	唱	一首英文	歌	吧。
他会	跳	印度	舞。	
我每个星期	跑	两次	步。	

Now check the correct explanations.

☐ 1 "Verb + object" (VO) compounds are verbs which are composed of a verb and an object.

☐ 2 A VO compound is a single word, whose English translation is usually also one word, e.g. 睡觉 = sleep; 唱歌 = sing.

☐ 3 VO compounds can be separated by inserting the aspectual particles 了, 过, 着, but not by duration, frequency, measure words or number.

☐ 4 Because VO compounds already contain an object, they cannot be followed directly by another object. For this reason, *我要见面他 is ungrammatical, and the correct sentence is 我要跟他见面.

2 Underline the separable verbs in the sentences.

1 毕了业，你打算去哪儿工作？
2 上个月我们放了三天假。
3 这门课这个学期一共要考三次试。
4 夏天太热了，我有时候一天洗好几次澡。
5 明天我就不去跟他见面了，我上个星期已经跟他见过面了。

通过 as a preposition

1 Look at the sentences.

	通过	Method	
	通过	各种语言实践活动，	大家的中文水平有了很大的提高。
大家的中文水平	通过	各种语言实践活动	有了很大的提高。
	通过	研究，	人们发现喝茶对身体很好。
人们	通过	研究	发现喝茶对身体很好。
	通过	他的大学同学，	我们联系到了他。
我们	通过	他的大学同学	联系到了他。

Now check the correct explanations.

☐ 1 通过 as a preposition indicates that a certain method is used to achieve a desired outcome.

☐ 2 The correct structure is "通过 + method + subject + verb phrase" or "Subject + 通过 + method + verb phrase".

☐ 3 The method introduced by 通过 should be expressed in a verb phrase.

2 Complete the sentences.

1 通过研究，科学家们发现 ____________ ____________。
2 现代生活不能没有网络。人们通过网络 __________，也通过网络 __________。
3 通过实习，马克 __________________。

3 Work in pairs. Ask and answer the questions.

1 如果不上中文课，只通过聊天学习中文，你觉得能学会吗？
2 如果别人想了解你，他们可以通过什么方式了解你？

Introducing the agent or performer of an action using 由

1 Look at the sentences.

Object	由	Agent	Verb
夏令营订票的事情	由	永民	负责。
生病的同学	由	助理	带着去看医生。
明天开会的时间到底	由	谁	决定？
电影《少林寺》	由	李连杰	主演。
参观游览活动全都	由	领队	安排。

Now check the correct explanations.

☐ 1 由 as a preposition is used to introduce an agent who performs a certain action.

☐ 2 The structure is "由 + agent + object + verb".

☐ 3 The agent introduced by 由 should be a noun or a pronoun.

2 Work in pairs. Think about the division of housework within a family and discuss.

1 你认为在一个家庭里，这些事情应该由谁负责？

2 在你的家里，这些事情由谁负责？

收拾屋子　打扫洗手间　扔垃圾
洗衣服　洗碗　买菜　做饭
修理草坪 (lawn)　照顾宠物

3 Work in pairs and talk about the travel arrangements of your last trip.

上次去 ______ 旅行：

______ 票是由 ______ 订的；

______ 是由 ______ 决定的；

______ 是由 ______ 负责的；

______ 是由 ______ 安排的。

Disyllabic words that become monosyllabic in formal style

1 Look at the sentences.

	Disyllabic words	
贵重物品丢失	应 (该)	及时向领队报告。
	如 (果)	有特殊原因不能上课，要事先请假。
任何问题都	可 (以)	向老师询问。
尽量只说中文，少说	或 (者)	不说其他语言。
他	已 (经)	不再是总统了。

Now check the correct explanations.

☐ 1 In written Chinese or formal speech, some disyllabic words may appear in their monosyllabic forms.

☐ 2 The monosyllabic forms may also appear in oral Chinese or in an informal style of writing.

☐ 3 These words can be modal verbs, conjunctions or adverbs.

2 Find out the meanings of the underlined monosyllabic words and figure out their disyllabic forms.

1 咖啡虽好，多饮伤身。

2 去哈尔滨的同学，可找钱老师报名。

3 越来越多的外国人到中国工作或居住。

4 你看过《世界因你不同》这本书吗？

Turn to page 188 for grammar reference.

LESSON 3

Communication activity

Work in pairs. Put together a brochure for the Chinese students at your university's summer camp. Include:

- A brief introduction to your university;
- An introduction to the nearby area, including places of interest, local restaurants, things to do in the summer, etc.;
- A daily schedule for the campers;
- Summer camp rules;
- Important contacts;
- A list of things the campers should bring.

Present your brochure to the class and vote for the best one.

Turn to pages 173 and 179 for more speaking practice.

Cultural corner

Collectivism vs. individualism

While the concept of individualism is deeply rooted in Western societies, collectivism is firmly associated with Chinese and other Asian cultures. In collectivism, the emphasis is placed on people's interdependence, rather than on their independence. Priority is given to the group, the community, or the country rather than to individuals or individual rights. The collective good often triumphs over individual benefit. Children are encouraged to respect rules and obey adults, especially in school, where individual creativity is typically not the focus of education. During the modernization of China, people's awareness of the importance of individuality increased, and many started to criticize traditional collectivism, especially its effects on the education of young people. However, a collectivist approach is still very prevalent.

Review and practice

1 Choose the correct words to complete the sentences.

1 这所大学的留学生 ______ 世界各地。
a 而来 b 从来 c 来自

2 我们请王校长致欢迎辞 ______ 宣布开营。
a 并 b 而 c 但

3 我们已经成功地 ______ 了三届中文演讲比赛。
a 举办 b 办理 c 进行

4 今年世界地球日的 ______ 是"低碳 (low-carbon) 经济，绿色发展"。
a 题目 b 主题 c 话题

5 去年我们在法国南部 ______ 了一个愉快的夏天。
a 通过 b 经过 c 度过

2 Complete the paragraph with the words in the box.

欢迎	宣布	代表	表示	介绍
长足	正式	丰富多彩	远道而来	

在开营仪式上，王主任首先 ______ 北京外国语大学国际交流中心向 ______ 的各国同学表示 ______。然后，他向同学们 ______ 了北京外国语大学的情况，并 ______，他相信通过 ______ 的语言实践活动，大家的汉语水平一定会取得 ______ 的进步。最后，他 ______ 国际中学生夏令营 ______ 开营。

3 Complete the sentences with the words in the box.

一定	及时	按时
尽量	提前	积极

1 你们要 ______ 上课，不能迟到。
2 上课的时候，______ 要 ______ 参加讨论。
3 不管在哪儿，都应该 ______ 只说中文，不说英文或其他语言。
4 如有贵重物品丢失，应该 ______ 向领队或助理报告。
5 如有特殊情况不能上课，需要 ______ 向老师请假。

4 Read the book club rules below. Match the words with their meanings.

1 交友	a member (of an organization)
2 会员	b member fees
3 非法	c associate with
4 会费	d illegal

书友会守则

一　书友会的目的是“通过阅读交友”。

二　书友会每周举行两次与读书相关的活动。

三　参加书友会的会员应遵守书友会守则，并积极参加书友会组织的活动。

四　参加活动时，会员不可从事任何非法活动。

五　如有特殊情况不能参加书友会的活动，要提前通知书友会。

六　书友会每月为会员推荐十本书，会员要尽量读完三到四本。

七　会员之间应友好相处、互相帮助、互相支持。

八　会员应按时交会费（每月30元）。

九　会员的个人信息如有变化，应及时通知书友会。

活动安排时间表

周三晚上	19:00—21:00	新书推荐，新书讨论，会员聚餐
周六上午	10:00—12:00	书与电影，老书再读，书与音乐

Now check the true statements.

- ☐ 1 书友会的目的是让会员在读好书的同时也能认识更多的朋友。
- ☐ 2 书友会会员每个月都得读完十本书。
- ☐ 3 书友会的会费每年交一次。
- ☐ 4 会员如果不能参加活动应该早一点儿通知书友会。
- ☐ 5 这个星期三的活动可能是看电影。
- ☐ 6 星期六的活动可能是看电影，这部电影应该跟一本书有关。

5 Make a list of the activities you would like to organize for the student's club at your university. Write a schedule.

______ 俱乐部活动安排时间表

星期	时间	活动

Now write six rules for the club. Use formal expressions and adverbials expressing restriction or emphasis that you have learnt in Lesson 2.

Vocabulary review

Fill in the blanks.

报告	bàogào	*v./n.*	______
长袖	chángxiù	*n.*	long sleeves
______	chángyòng	*adj.*	frequently used
单独	dāndú	*adj.*	______
当	dāng	*prep.*	when
______	diūshī	*v.*	get lost
对外汉语	duìwài Hànyǔ		Chinese for speakers of other languages
发言	fāyán	*n./v.*	speech; give a speech
发扬	fāyáng	*v.*	carry on (spirit)
防晒霜	fángshàishuāng	*n.*	sun cream
丰富多彩	fēngfù-duōcǎi	*adj.*	rich and colourful
各位	gèwèi	*pron.*	everyone
功课	gōngkè	*n.*	homework
贵重	guìzhòng	*adj.*	______
______	hùxiāng	*adv.*	each other
火警	huǒjǐng	*n.*	fire department
积极	jījí	*adj./adv.*	active; actively
急救	jíjiù	*v.*	give first aid
______	jiǎng	*v.*	tell, speak
届	jiè	*measure word*	session, class (for meetings, graduating classes, etc.)
紧急	jǐnjí	*adj.*	urgent
举办	jǔbàn	*v.*	host, hold
开营	kāiyíng	*v.*	open (a summer camp)
课外	kèwài	*n.*	extracurricular
良多	liángduō	*num.*	quite a lot
零用钱	língyòngqián	*n.*	petty cash
______	màozi	*n.*	hat
陪	péi	*v.*	______
请假	qǐngjià	*v.*	ask for time off
人民币	rénmínbì	*n.*	Renminbi
______	rènhé	*pron.*	any
______	sǎn	*n.*	umbrella

实践	shíjiàn	*n.*	practice
手表	shǒubiǎo	*n.*	______
守则	shǒuzé	*n.*	rules
熟悉	shúxī	*v.*	get familiar with
所	suǒ	*measure word*	(for institutions)
太阳镜	tàiyángjìng	*n.*	sunglasses
特殊	tèshū	*adj.*	special
听从	tīngcóng	*v.*	listen to and obey
______	tōngguò	*prep.*	via, through
团队精神	tuánduì jīngshén		team spirit
完成	wánchéng	*v.*	______
卫生	wèishēng	*n.*	hygiene
午休	wǔxiū	*v.*	lunch break
物品	wùpǐn	*n.*	item, thing
洗漱用品	xǐshù yòngpǐn		toiletries
______	xiàmiàn	*n.*	following
相处	xiāngchǔ	*v.*	get along
宣布	xuānbù	*v.*	______
药品	yàopǐn	*n.*	medicine
医疗	yīliáo	*v.*	medical
仪式	yíshì	*n.*	ceremony
饮食	yǐnshí	*n.*	food and drink
营员	yíngyuán	*n.*	camper
______	yǒuhǎo	*adj.*	friendly
远道而来	yuǎndào' érlái		coming from far away
朝夕相处	zhāoxī-xiāngchǔ		be together day and night
______	zhīchí	*v.*	support
值班	zhíbān	*v.*	be on duty
致辞	zhìcí	*v.*	make a speech
主任	zhǔrèn	*n.*	______
______	zhǔtí	*n.*	theme, topic
助理	zhùlǐ	*n.*	assistant
自习	zìxí	*v.*	self-study
遵守	zūnshǒu	*v.*	abide by, observe (the rules)
作息	zuòxī	*v.*	work and rest

Review 1

Vocabulary

1 Match the words to make phrases.

1 制订	美食
2 申请	要求
3 品尝	活动
4 组织	工作
5 符合	经验
6 积累	方案

2 Write two words with each of the characters below.

1 品 ______ ______

2 职 ______ ______

3 守 ______ ______

4 急 ______ ______

5 相 ______ ______

6 历 ______ ______

7 自 ______ ______

3 Circle the odd words out.

1 仔细 开朗 积极 曾经

2 招聘 医疗 面试 求职

3 搜索 住宿 链接 首页

4 组织 策划 整理 差异

5 支持 暂时 鼓励 同情

6 后顾之忧 避暑胜地 团队精神 丰富多彩

4 Choose the correct words to complete the sentences.

1 贵重物品丢失，应该赶快向警察_____。

a 报告 b 发言 c 请示

2 _____时候你都应该提醒自己注意安全。

a 任何 b 全部 c 所有

3 我们应该_____。

a 鼓励 b 鼓励互相 c 互相鼓励

4 感谢你_____时间为我们整理会议记录。

a 抽 b 做 c 给

5 这次招聘活动我们是请专业人士_____的。

a 策划 b 制订 c 讨论

6 因为没有奖学金，所以我得_____去中国留学。

a 自由 b 免费 c 自费

7 本地的小吃很特别，你应该_____一下。

a 品尝 b 经历 c 体会

8 非常_____大家对我的鼓励。

a 欣赏 b 感谢 c 支持

5 Match the words with their opposites.

1 暂时	a 普通
2 特殊	b 长期
3 开朗	c 便宜
4 贵重	d 到达
5 出发	e 过去
6 输入	f 输出
7 团体	g 个人
8 将来	h 内向

Grammar

1 Choose the correct words to complete the sentences.

1 这件衣服我 _____ 在网上买 _____。

a 是……了 b 是……的

c 是……

2 李经理让你明天 _____ 给那家公司打个电话。

a 再 b 又 c 还

3 永民，金老师让你订 _____ 去哈尔滨的火车票。

a 一点儿 b 一些 c 一下

4 没想到这首歌 _____ 挺难唱的。

a 更 b 又 c 还

5 我和中文兴趣小组的朋友们每个星期 _____。

a 两次见面 b 见两次面 c 不见面

6 他只来过伦敦三次，却对伦敦熟悉 _____ 不得了。

a 得 b 的 c 地

7 你怎么又跟妹妹 _____ 了？

a 吵起架来 b 吵架起来

c 吵起来架

8 招聘实习生的事情 _____ 销售部负责。

a 对 b 为 c 由

2 Complete the sentences with the words in the box.

回……来	回……去	进来
进去 上来	上去 下来	下去

1 —外面太冷了，你要不要 _____？

—没事儿，外面空气好，我一会儿再 _____。

2 —毕业以后，你还打算 _____ 上海 _____ 吗？

—上海虽然是我的家乡，不过我更喜欢北京。

—嗯，我也打算继续呆在北京。

3 —你还是别 _____ 了，我站在上面也看不清远处的那些山。我马上就 _____。

—那你快 _____ 吧，我就不 _____ 了。

4 —下个月是你爷爷的生日，你别忘了 _____ 香港 _____ 给爷爷过生日。

—放心，我一定回去，机票都买好了。

3 Complete the dialogues with the words given.

1 —跟旅行社旅游价钱贵不贵？行程安排怎么样？

—_____________________ (至于)

2 —是中文语法复杂还是英文语法复杂？

—_____________________ (不如)

3 —李连杰是谁？没听说过。

—你在开玩笑吗？_____________________ (连……都……)

4 —你参加过中文夏令营吗？

—没有，_____________________ (一……都没……)

4 Rewrite the sentences by changing the monosyllabic words to disyllabic ones.

1 事虽小，影响大。

2 他已开始行动。

3 如有问题，请与客服部联系。

4 航班因大雨取消。

5 出国旅行应注意些什么？

Integrated skills

1-24

1 Listen to the conversation and choose the correct answers to the questions.

1 王宇刚开始打算应聘的是什么职位？

a 旅游顾问　b 市场策划　c 新闻策划

2 王宇在大学的专业是什么？

a 新闻　b 旅游　c 中文

3 张小姐最有可能在哪个部门工作？

a 市场部　b 人力部　c 客服部

4 张小姐认为王宇能不能胜任旅游顾问的职位？

a 能　b 不能　c 不清楚

5 张小姐为什么建议王宇申请市场部的新职位？

a 因为王宇有相关的工作经验。

b 因为王宇的专业符合要求。

c 因为王宇对市场策划特别有兴趣。

6 市场部的职位试用期间工资一个月多少钱？

a 三千　b 四千　c 两千

2 Look at the pictures. Choose your favourite city.

a

b

c

d

Now work with a partner. Take turns to ask and answer the questions about your cities.

1 什么季节去最好？有什么好玩的活动？

2 可以去什么地方逛街？

3 可以去什么地方散步？

4 应该品尝什么美食？

5 可以去什么地方欣赏音乐？

6 最有名的博物馆和广场分别是什么？

3 **Complete the passage with the correct words in the box.**

遵守　适应　任何　流利　丰富多彩
友好　鼓励　相处　互相　吃不惯

去年夏天，我参加了一个北京的中文夏令营。去以前我担心自己不能 ______ 北京的生活，特别是怕自己 ______ 中餐，可是没想到，到了北京我一点儿问题都没有。营员们都很 ______，大家都 ______ 营员守则，也 ______ 帮助，所以都 ______ 得非常好。夏令营的老师和助理都很热情，我们遇到 ______ 困难都可以找他们帮忙。为了提高我们的中文水平，老师 ______ 我们尽量只用中文交流。虽然开始的时候觉得很难，可是慢慢地我发现我的中文越来越 ______ 了。除了学中文以外，夏令营还给我们安排了 ______ 的活动。比方说，参观博物馆，去哈尔滨旅游。对我来说，参加中文夏令营是一次非常难忘的经历。

4 **A Chinese educational organization is going to host an English summer camp in your city. You are recommending activity ideas to help the students improve their English and understand local culture. Write an email to the organization. Include:**

1 活动的内容或名字

2 活动对提高英文水平有什么帮助

3 活动对了解当地的文化有什么好处

Enjoy Chinese

草：grass

菜：vegetable, greens

药：medicinal herbs

The radical 艹 originally meant "grass". It then evolved to mean all plants except trees. Therefore, characters that have the 艹 radical are usually related to plants. Can you figure out why the following characters share the 艹 radical?

花：flower

蒜：garlic

茶：tea

荒：waste, barren

苦：bitter

茂：luxuriant, lush

UNIT 5

Wǒ yídìng jìnlì' érwéi
我一定尽力而为！

I will try my best !

LESSON 1

Vocabulary and listening

1 Match the words to make phrases.

1 举行	a 机会
2 把握	b 客户
3 接待	c 事情
4 商量	d 玩具
5 制作	e 晚宴

2 Match the questions with the best responses.

1 你一定能做好。	a 谢谢你的关心。
2 听说你病了，我很担心你。	b 谢谢你的信任。
3 有压力才有动力。	c 嗯，有道理。
4 晚会上唱什么歌呢？	d 我再好好想想。

Now work in pairs. Ask and answer.

3 Mark's company is about to receive visitors from abroad. His manager, Tang Yu, is talking to him about the arrangements. Listen to their conversation and answer the questions.

1 公司接下来的两周要接待什么客人？
2 唐经理让马克主要负责什么工作？
3 唐经理问了马克什么问题？

马克：唐经理，您有事找我？
唐雨：马克，来，沙发这边坐。怎么样，实习的第一个星期还习惯吧？
马克：谢谢您的关心。我很喜欢我的工作，一来就跟同事学到了很多东西。
唐雨：那就好。有问题及时跟同事们交流。接下来的两周我们要接待一个从澳大利亚来的考察团，这次将由你全程陪同，并且负责主要的翻译工作。
马克：哦……我一定尽力而为。
唐雨：不过也不用紧张，客服部的同事会全力配合你的工作。我看过你的简历，我对你有信心。
马克：谢谢您的信任。压力的确不小，但对我来说倒是个难得的锻炼机会，我会好好把握。
唐雨：好的。还有两件事想问问你的意见。我们打算为考察团举行一个欢迎晚宴，你认为西餐还是中餐比较合适？
马克：我觉得既然他们来了中国，应该希望尝到地道的中国菜吧？
唐雨：有道理。另外，我们想送他们每人一点儿纪念品，你有什么建议吗？
马克：我认为不用送太贵重的礼物。对了，我在公司看到过一只用环保材料制作的玩具熊猫，不但代表我们公司的环保理念，而且具有中国特色，当礼物再合适不过了。您觉得怎么样？
唐雨：嗯，这个建议也不错。这样

吧，关于这个代表团的事情，在周五的例会上我们再具体商量一下。

马克：好的，唐经理。我也再好好想想有没有其他事情需要注意。要是没别的事我先去忙了。

唐雨：好的。

生词 New words

shāfā	沙发	sofa, couch	wǎnyàn	晚宴	dinner banquet
péitóng	陪同	accompany	jìrán	既然	since
fùzé	负责	take charge of	cháng	尝	taste
ò	哦	oh (expressing understanding)	zhī	只	(for certain animals)
jìnlì' érwéi	尽力而为	try one's best to finish a task	huánbǎo	环保	environmentally friendly
quánlì	全力	full strength	cáiliào	材料	material
pèihé	配合	cooperate	zhìzuò	制作	manufacture, make
xìnrèn	信任	trust	búdàn	不但	not only
dào	倒	nevertheless	lǐniàn	理念	belief
nándé	难得	rare, hard to get	jùyǒu	具有	have (an abstract quality)
hǎohǎo	好好	making a great effort	tèsè	特色	special feature
bǎwò	把握	grasp, seize	lìhuì	例会	regular meeting
jǔxíng	举行	host, hold	shìqing	事情	matter, affair

4 Check the true statements.

- ☐ 1 马克主动找唐经理谈自己的实习。
- ☐ 2 马克负责考察团所有的事情。
- ☐ 3 马克觉得安排中餐晚宴更合适。
- ☐ 4 马克觉得礼物一定要非常贵重才行。
- ☐ 5 马克实习的公司具有环保理念。

5 Complete the sentences with the words in the box.

具体　全程　全力　好好　及时

1 唐经理让马克有问题______告诉同事。
2 考察团将由马克______陪同。
3 马克会______把握这个难得的机会。
4 公司客服部的同事们会______配合马克的工作。

6 Choose all possible answers to the questions.

1 唐经理为什么要马克负责考察团的陪同和翻译?
- a 因为马克对澳大利亚的情况很熟悉。
- b 因为唐经理对马克很有信心。
- c 因为马克的工作经验很丰富。

2 关于这个任务，马克觉得怎么样?
- a 他觉得有压力。
- b 他觉得机会难得。
- c 他会尽自己最大的努力。

3 马克为什么推荐用环保材料做的玩具熊猫作为礼物?
- a 因为它很贵重。
- b 因为它能代表公司的环保理念。
- c 因为它具有中国特色。

7 You are going to hear a conversation about a wedding. Underline the main issues you expect to be discussed.

- ☐ a 要不要去参加婚礼
- ☐ b 谁会参加婚礼
- ☐ c 和参加婚礼的人关系怎么样
- ☐ d 参加婚礼送什么
- ☐ e 送什么礼物合适
- ☐ f 应该送多少钱的红包

Now listen and check the three issues discussed.

8 Listen again and answer the questions.

1 小王为什么建议马克参加婚礼?
2 送红包有什么好处?
3 根据小王的解释，怎么决定送多少钱的红包?

Now work in pairs and check your answers.

Pronunciation and speaking

1 Listen to the sentences asking for advice.

1 我有两件事想问问你的意见。
2 我们打算请朋友吃饭，你觉得四川菜合适还是云南菜合适?
3 我想在北京买一点儿纪念品送给朋友。你有什么建议吗?
4 我想送他一本中文字典当生日礼物，你觉得怎么样?

Now say the sentences aloud.

2 Complete the conversations with the sentences in Activity 1.

1 — ____________________
— 哪两件事? 你说吧，我帮你出主意。

2 — ____________________
— 既然你的朋友是四川人，就准备四川菜吧。

3 — ____________________
— 这个吧，如果是我的朋友，我会送一件有中国书法的上衣。

3 Work in pairs. Ask for and give advice on the following issues.

1 面试穿什么衣服
2 要不要去中国留学
3 父亲节送什么礼物给爸爸

CHINESE TO GO

1-28 Adapting to a new environment

hái xíguàn ma ……还 习惯 吗?	How are you coping with …?
Wǒ yídìng jìnlì'érwéi 我 一定 尽力而为。	I will try my best.
Wǒ huì hǎohǎo bǎwò 我 会 好好 把握。	I'll seize the opportunity.

LESSON | 2

Reading and writing

1 **Work in pairs. Check the words which usually appear in business writing.**

- ☐ 日记　☐ 博客　☐ 留言条
- ☐ 请柬　☐ 通知　☐ 会议记录
- ☐ 行程　☐ 安排　☐ 简历广告

2 **Look at the meanings and complete the table.**

1-29

负责 means ______________.	负责人: person who is in charge, director
留言: leave a message	留言条 means ______________.
会议: meeting, conference	会议室 means ______________.
总结: summary	工作总结 means ______________.
邀请: invite	邀请信 means ______________.
未: not yet 完成: finish	未完成 means ______________.
版本: version	英文版 means ______________.

Now work in pairs and check your answers.

3 **Match the formal expressions with their informal meanings.**

1 需	a 打算
2 并	b 安排
3 未	c 需要
4 拟	d 没有
5 定	e 在
6 于	f 而且

Now work in pairs. Make sentences with the formal expressions.

4 **Read the note on page 72 and complete the sentences.**

谢月给马克的留言条里提到了三件事情：

1 让马克找 ______________。
2 让马克翻译 ______________。
3 让马克给她发 ______________。

5 **Choose the correct answers to the questions.**

1 谢月给马克写留言条的原因是什么？
 a 马克现在不在办公室，她不能当面告诉他这些事情。
 b 马克听不懂谢月说的话，她觉得写出来会更清楚。
 c 马克这两天一直收不到谢月的电子邮件。

2 马克给谢月发电子邮件，应该写什么内容？
 a 关于澳大利亚考察团的事情
 b 翻译好的英文请柬
 c 公司的中文请柬

3 马克可能什么时候给谢月发电子邮件？
 a 7月3日上午10点15分
 b 7月3日下午3点15分
 c 7月2日上午9点15分

留言条

马克：

唐经理让你回来后去她办公室，主要是布置澳大利亚考察团的任务。另外，公司请柬需要制作一个英文版本，麻烦你翻译一下，桌上的中文请柬供你参考。最晚请在明天中午之前用邮件发给我，谢谢！

谢月

7月2日 10:15

会议通知

客户服务部拟于7月5日（本周五）召开每月例会，会议安排如下：

时间：上午9:50开始签到，10:00正式开始

地点：总经理办公室旁边的大会议室

参加人员：客服部全体员工

会议内容：

1) 由各小组负责人汇报本月工作的完成情况和下月的工作计划；需包括对未完成工作的分析，并提出具体的改进建议；

2) 由唐经理做客服部的工作总结；

3) 布置澳大利亚考察团的接待准备工作；

4) 集体讨论客户对新的电子客服系统的反馈。

亚深（深圳）客户服务部　7月2日

生词 New words

liúyán	留言	leave a message
tiáo	条	note
bùzhì	布置	arrange for
qǐngjiǎn	请柬	invitation card
bǎnběn	版本	version
gōng	供	for
cānkǎo	参考	refer to
zuìwǎn	最晚	the latest
zhīqián	之前	time before
nǐ	拟	propose
zhàokāi	召开	call (a meeting)
rúxià	如下	as follows
qiāndào	签到	sign in
quántǐ	全体	the whole, all
yuángōng	员工	employee, staff
huìbào	汇报	report
wèi	未	not yet
fēnxī	分析	analyze
gǎijìn	改进	improve
zǒngjié	总结	summarize; summary
xìtǒng	系统	system
fǎnkuì	反馈	feedback
chéngyì	诚意	sincerity
zī dìng yú	兹定于	scheduled for
gōngqǐng	恭请	humbly invite
jièshí	届时	at that time

請柬

亚深国际贸易有限公司深圳分公司

诚意邀请

尊敬的 ____________（先生 / 女士）

兹定于 ___ 年 ___ 月 ___ 日（周 ___）___ 时

举行 ______________________

恭请届时光临！

地址：________　　电话：________

总经理：李树青

____ 年 ____ 月 ____ 日

6 **Read the notice about the meeting on page 72 and check the true statements.**

1 客服部每个月只开一次会。

2 9点55分去签到也来得及。

3 开会地点是总经理办公室。

4 每个员工都要汇报本月工作的完成情况。

5 考察团的接待准备工作是这次例会的内容之一。

6 新的电子客服系统很受客户欢迎。

7 **Read the note below and complete the table.**

> 永民：
>
> 7月5号（周五）中午12点我们要举办一个欢迎宴会，欢迎国际夏令营的学生和相关客人，地点在第二餐厅。钱老师让我告诉你，以国际交流中心王云青主任的名义制作一份请柬，并在明天下午4点以前用电子邮件发给钱老师。谢谢！
>
> 小文
>
> 7月3号 11:18

欢迎宴会

时间	
地点	
举办单位	
邀请的人员	
请柬签名人	

Now write a formal invitation card based on the information and the invitation card on this page.

Language in use

Concessive clauses with 倒

1 Look at the sentences.

Clause 1 (negative)	Clause 2 (倒 positive)
这次任务的确不轻，	但对我来说倒真是个难得的锻炼机会。
他说中文，发音虽然不太准确，	说得倒很流利。
这间屋子真够小的，	不过倒挺干净。

Clause 1 (倒 positive)	Clause 2 (negative)
这次机会倒真是难得，	不过我觉得压力太大了。
他说中文，说得倒还流利，	可发音不太准确。
这间屋子倒是干净，	不过实在是太小了。

Now check the correct explanations.

☐ 1 倒 serves as an adverb marking a turning point or concession in the sentence.

☐ 2 If clause 1 expresses a negative comment, clause 2 uses 倒 to introduce a positive comment.

☐ 3 If clause 1 uses 倒 to show a concession to introduce a positive comment, clause 2 should also express a positive comment.

☐ 4 Clause 2 often contains 不过/但是/可是.

☐ 5 The comments in clause 2 are what the speaker wants to emphasize or highlight.

2 Work in pairs. Ask and answer the following questions using 倒.

1 你收到过的礼物中，你不太喜欢的是什么，为什么？

2 有没有一部电影，你对它的看法跟周围的人不一样？哪里不一样？

Expressing "doing well" with 好好

1 Look at the sentences.

	好好 + verb phrase
这是一次难得的锻炼机会，	我会好好把握的。
嗯，这个建议不错，	我再好好想想。
身体不舒服，你就别工作了，	还是好好休息吧。
他唱得也太难听了，	应该回家再好好练练。
	我们要好好利用这次机会为客户提供更好的服务。

Now check the correct explanations.

☐ 1 好好 as an adverbial modifies the verb phrase which follows it, meaning "doing something thoroughly" or "doing something as well as possible".

☐ 2 Sometimes modal verbs like 想/会/应该/得/要 are used after 好好 to emphasize the tone or the attitude of the speaker.

☐ 3 In colloquial expressions, the second 好 changes to "hāo" and an "er" sound is added, pronounced as "hǎohāor".

2 Complete the conversations using 好好.

1 —马上就要考完试了。你有什么打算？
—我已经想好了，等考完试了，我要先 ______，再 ______，最后还要 ______。

2 —大夫，我最近老觉得没什么精神，每天都累得不得了。
—你觉得累就是因为你不 ______，不 ______，也不 ______。你需要改变你的生活习惯。

Making deductions with 既然

1 Look at the sentences.

Clause 1(既然)	Clause 2
我觉得既然他们到中国来，	应该希望尝到地道的中国菜吧。
既然那所大学已经接受他了，	他就不会去别的大学了。
既然他们都这么忙，	我猜他们没时间跟咱们见面了。

	Clause 1(既然)	Clause 2
A: 我不进去了，我走了。	B: 既然都来了，	那就进去坐一会儿吧。
A: 这件衣服你穿真好看。	B: 既然你也觉得好看，	那我就买啦。

Now check the correct explanations.

☐ 1 The conjunction 既然 is used in clause 1 to restate a known fact, reason or premise.

☐ 2 Clause 2, as the main clause, presents a logical inference or suggestion deduced from the fact, reason or premise in clause 1.

☐ 3 Clause 2 often has 那 or 就, meaning "then" to show the inference or suggestion is natural and logical.

☐ 4 If there is a subject in clause 2, the subject goes after 那 or 就.

☐ 5 Clause 2 sometimes contains a rhetorical question indicated by 为什么 to show a strong questioning tone.

2 Complete the sentences.

1 —火车票已经卖光了，怎么办啊？
—既然 ________，那 ______________。

2 —这本书马上要还，可是我现在得去上课，来不及去图书馆了。
—既然 ________，那 ______________。

3 既然吸烟对健康特别不好，那 ________？

Stressing an extreme degree with 再……不过了

1 Look at the sentences.

	再……不过了
把玩具熊猫送给客户	再合适不过了。
他对她有意思，这	再明显不过了。
这种巧克力	再受欢迎不过了。
他不来麻烦我，就	再好不过了。
把工作交给马克，经理	再放心不过了。

Now check the correct explanations.

☐ 1 再……不过了 is used to stress an extreme degree, and means "nothing is more ... than".

☐ 2 The words inserted between 再 and 不过了 can be either adjectives or emotional verbs.

☐ 3 The adjectives or emotional verbs usually have negative meanings.

2 Work in pairs. Ask and answer the questions using 再……不过了.

1 怎么过夏天最舒服？

2 你看过电影《哈利·波特》(*Harry Potter*)吗？哪个演员演得最好？

3 你为家人做什么事情，会让他们很高兴？做什么事他们最高兴？

4 很多人说做饭很难，你觉得呢？

Turn to page 190 for grammar reference.

LESSON 3

Communication activity

Work in pairs. You are helping a group of Chinese teachers who are attending a conference in your city.

Student A: You are a tour guide. Leave a note for your partner and ask him/her to get back to you to discuss your responsibilities.

Student B: You are a translator. Discuss the following with your partner:

- where you should take the teachers to have dinner on the first and the last nights;
- the places where you should take them for a half-day tour. Include details about what they will see and what activities they can do;
- what gifts and souvenirs to buy for the teachers.

Turn to pages 174 and 180 for more speaking practice.

Review and practice

1 Choose the correct words to complete the sentences.

1 我们马上要 ______ 一个从加拿大来的考察团。

a 接受　b 接待　c 收到

2 —小唐，这次美国客户的接待工作主要由你负责。

—经理，您放心，我 ______ 尽力而为。

a 好好　b 的确　c 一定

3 我知道你能力很强，我对你有 ______。

a 信心　b 信任　c 相信

4 这家国际公司的发展 ______ 是"服务与创新"。

a 意见　b 想法　c 理念

5 你的建议很有 ______，我会再跟其他同事商量商量。

a 理由　b 优点　c 道理

Cultural corner

Nature reserves and wildlife protection in China

By 2010, China had established around 2500 nature reserves nationwide. The most famous include Wolong in Sichuan Province (for pandas), Shennongjia in Hubei Province (for golden monkeys), and Changbai Mountain in Northeast China (for Siberian tigers). But many of the smaller reserves suffer from lack of funding, poor management and weak law enforcement. The biggest challenge facing wildlife conservation in China is the conflict between environmental protection and economic growth.

Experts agree that to maintain nature reserves successfully, committed financial support from national and local governments is required as well as extensive wildlife protection laws, successful implementation of such laws, and cooperation between the government and other domestic or international organizations. In recent years, the Chinese government nevertheless has made ambitious plans to revive nature reserves and strengthen wildlife protection, and there has been substantial progress.

2 Complete the passage with the words in the box.

把握　纪念品　难得　任务　制作　配合
建议　关心　接下来　举办　负责

7月5日　星期二　晴

今天唐经理找我谈了一些工作上的事情。她首先很 ______ 地问了我实习第一周的情况，然后她告诉我 ______ 的两周我们要接待一个澳大利亚考察团，由我 ______ 陪同工作和主要的翻译工作。尽管会有客服部的同事们 ______ 我的工作，我还是觉得 ______ 非常重。不过，我觉得这是一次 ______ 的锻炼机会，我一定会好好 ______。另外，我还 ______ 公司 ______ 的欢迎宴会选用中餐，把用环保材料 ______ 的玩具熊猫作为 ______ 送给考察团的客人。

3 Complete the sentences with the words in the box.

交代　制作　召开　总结　分析
参考　提出　布置　完成

1 请你 ______ 这份请柬 ______ 一份新的请柬。
2 经济系拟于本周四下午三点 ______ 全系大会，请全系师生准时参加。
3 天亮，你休假之前别忘了跟马克 ______ 一下电子客服系统的事情。
4 昨天的公司大会上，人事部的同事们 ______ 了一些很有用的建议。
5 上个星期刘经理 ______ 给你的任务，你 ______ 得怎么样了？
6 这两天真忙，不但要 ______ 上个月的工作情况，还要 ______ 客户的反馈意见。

4 Read the notice and check the true statements.

☐ 1 通知是国际交流中心主任发出的。
☐ 2 例会一般在每月月末召开。
☐ 3 只有交流中心的老师们需要参加这个会议。
☐ 4 国际交流中心今年夏天只有三个项目。
☐ 5 助理被聘用以后需要参加培训。

Now work in pairs. Write down the meanings of the words.

短期：__________　　暑期：__________
进展：__________　　培训：__________

会议通知

国际交流中心拟于5月30日（下周三）召开每月例会，会议安排如下：

1 **时间：** 下午4:00—5:30
2 **地点：** 国际交流中心大会议室
3 **参加人员：** 国际交流中心全体老师和各项目学生助理
4 **会议内容：**
   1) 由各项目的负责老师汇报各项目的进展情况。
   2) 由王主任布置暑期三个项目的具体准备工作，包括国际中学生夏令营项目、大学生社会实践项目、短期语言培训项目。
   3) 讨论项目助理的培训办法。

请大家提前做好准备并准时参加。

国际交流中心主任办公室
5月25日

5 Write an email to Yeong-min and Xiaowen on behalf of Mr Qian, notifying them of the meeting in Activity 4.

Vocabulary review

Fill in the blanks.

把握	bǎwò	*v.*	grasp, seize
版本	bǎnběn	*n.*	version
______	búdàn	*conj.*	not only
布置	bùzhì	*v.*	arrange for
材料	cáiliào	*n.*	______
______	cānkǎo	*v.*	refer to
尝	cháng	*v.*	______
诚意	chéngyì	*n.*	sincerity
倒	dào	*adv.*	nevertheless
反馈	fǎnkuì	*v.*	feedback
______	fēnxī	*v.*	analyze
负责	fùzé	*v.*	take charge of
改进	gǎijìn	*v.*	______
供	gōng	*v.*	for
恭请	gōngqǐng	*v.*	humbly invite
好好	hǎohǎo	*adv.*	making a great effort
环保	huánbǎo	*adj.*	environmentally friendly
汇报	huìbào	*v.*	report
______	jìrán	*conj.*	since
届时	jièshí	*v.*	at that time
尽力而为	jìnlì'érwéi		try one's best to finish a task
举行	jǔxíng	*v.*	host, hold
具有	jùyǒu	*v.*	______
理念	lǐniàn	*n.*	belief
例会	lìhuì	*n.*	regular meeting
留言	liúyán	*v.*	leave a message
难得	nándé	*adj.*	rare, hard to get
拟	nǐ	*v.*	propose
______	ò	*interj.*	oh (expressing understanding)
陪同	péitóng	*v.*	accompany
配合	pèihé	*v.*	cooperate
签到	qiāndào	*v.*	sign in
请柬	qǐngjiǎn	*n.*	invitation card
全力	quánlì	*n.*	full strength
______	quántǐ	*n.*	the whole, all
如下	rúxià		as follows
沙发	shāfā	*n.*	______
______	shìqing	*n.*	matter, affair
特色	tèsè	*n.*	______
条	tiáo	*n.*	note
晚宴	wǎnyàn	*n.*	dinner banquet
未	wèi	*adv.*	______
______	xìtǒng	*n.*	system
信任	xìnrèn	*v.*	______
员工	yuángōng	*n.*	employee, staff
召开	zhàokāi	*v.*	call (a meeting)
之前	zhīqián	*n.*	time before
______	zhī	*measure word*	(for certain animals)
制作	zhìzuò	*v.*	manufacture, make
兹定于	zī dìng yú		scheduled for
总结	zǒngjié	*v./n.*	summarize; summary
最晚	zuìwǎn	*adv.*	the latest

UNIT 6

Nǐmen liǎng gè pèihé de hěn hǎo
你们两个配合得很好！

You two make a good team!

LESSON 1

Vocabulary and listening

1 Work in pairs. Check the topics which are appropriate for small talk between two colleagues.

☐ 1 天气	☐ 5 最喜欢的电视节目
☐ 2 收入	☐ 6 兴趣爱好
☐ 3 专业	☐ 7 家庭
☐ 4 工作经历	☐ 8 老家

Now give one or two examples for each topic.

你是什么地方人？
听说你是对外汉语专业高材生。

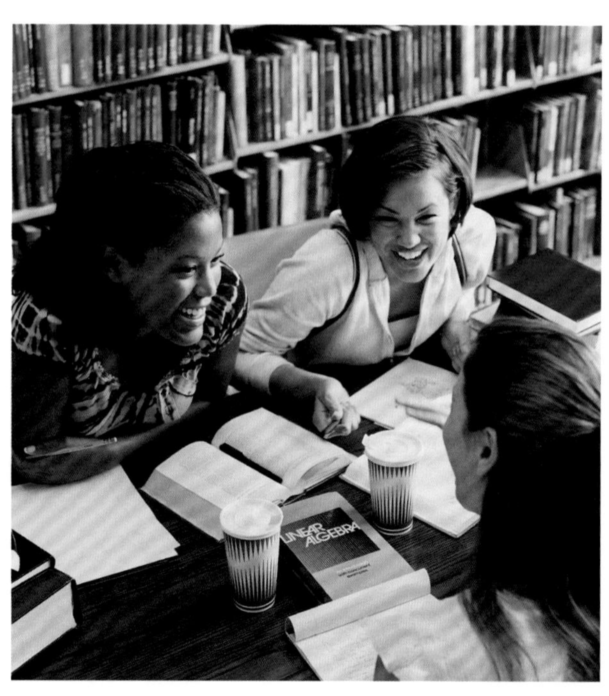

1-30 **2 After the welcome dinner, Mark is talking with his colleagues. Listen to the conversation and answer the questions.**

1 马克在欢迎晚宴上的表现怎么样？
2 周详是学什么的？
3 谢月在公司的哪两个部门工作过？
4 他们打算晚上去做什么？

谢月：马克，你今天表现不错啊！
马克：谢谢，其实我当时都紧张死了，就怕没听清楚或者翻译得不准确，漏掉了重要的信息。
谢月：是吗？没看出来啊。
马克：那就好。多亏周详事先帮我准备资料，要不然我今天的表现肯定很糟糕。
周详：你太谦虚了，马克。同事之间互相帮忙是应该的。
谢月：是啊，你们两个配合得很好！
周详：谢谢夸奖。马克，我真佩服你，中文学得这么好！要是我的英文能说得跟你的中文一样就好了。
马克：你的英文已经很好了啊！我还想跟你学习外贸知识呢！
谢月：是啊，周详是外贸专业的高材生。你们俩正好可以取长补短，共同进步。
马克：我们更应该向你和公司的其他前辈学习。实践经验可比书本知识重要多了。
周详：马克说的一点儿没错。对了，谢月，你一来公司就是在客服部吗？
谢月：不是，我刚来的时候是在销售部，但是后来发现自己更适合做客服，于是不

到一年就转到这边来了。

周详：是这样啊。如果有机会，我也想去销售部学习学习。

谢月：是吗？那过一段时间我推荐你过去实习吧。

周详：那太好了！

谢月：怎么样，你们俩累不累？还有兴致去唱卡拉OK吗？

马克：现在吗？周详，看你的，你去我就去。

周详：反正明天是周末，也不着急睡觉。走吧，唱完歌我请大家吃夜宵。

3 Check the true statements.

- ☐ 1 马克做翻译的时候不太紧张。
- ☐ 2 做翻译的时候，周详和马克互相帮助。
- ☐ 3 马克想跟谢月学习外贸知识。
- ☐ 4 谢月以前在销售部工作了一年多。
- ☐ 5 马克自己本来不是很想去唱卡拉OK。
- ☐ 6 谢月请马克和周详先去唱歌再去吃夜宵。

4 Complete the sentences.

1 马克做翻译的时候怕自己翻译得 ______。
2 谢月夸奖马克和周详配合得 ______。
3 周详佩服马克中文说得 ______。
4 周详希望自己说英文能说得 ______。

生词 New words

sǐ 死	extreme	gāocáishēng 高材生	top student
zhǔnquè 准确	accurate, precise	qǔcháng-bǔduǎn 取长补短	complement one another
lòudiào 漏掉	miss	gòngtóng 共同	together
kàn chūlai 看出来	discern, make out	qiánbèi 前辈	senior
duōkuī 多亏	owing to; fortunately	yúshì 于是	thereupon
zāogāo 糟糕	terrible	guò 过	over
qiānxū 谦虚	modest, humble	xìngzhì 兴致	mood to enjoy
kuājiǎng 夸奖	praise, compliment	jiù 就	as soon as; (if…) then; only, just
pèifú 佩服	admire	fǎnzhèng 反正	anyway, all the same
wàimào 外贸	foreign trade	yèxiāo 夜宵	night snack or refreshment

5 Choose the correct answers to the questions.

1 谢月说她没看出来马克紧张是因为 ______。

a 马克表现得很紧张

b 马克的表现很不错

c 马克事先做了很多准备

2 谢月说自己后来“转到这边来了”，指的是转到 ______；她说要推荐周详“过去实习”，是指去 ______ 实习。

a 客服部 b 销售部 c 总经理办公室

3 谢月离开销售部是因为 ______。

a 她不喜欢销售部的同事

b 公司安排她去客服部

c 自己不太适合做销售

6 You are going to hear a conversation between Mark and his colleagues. Listen and put the topics in the order you hear them.

问好 介绍 专业
女朋友 为什么转行

1 ______ 4 ______

2 ______ 5 ______

3 ______

7 Listen again and check the true statements.

☐ 1 周乐杰不喜欢跟人打交道。

☐ 2 马克是根据周乐杰的工作猜他的专业。

☐ 3 马克并没有因为周乐杰的问题生气。

Now answer the questions.

4 马克是什么时候认识周乐杰的？

5 周乐杰和女朋友是怎样认识的？

6 周乐杰觉得帮小王介绍女朋友怎么样？

7 小王为什么不让周乐杰问马克的工资？

Pronunciation and speaking

1 Listen to the sentences with 就.

1 其实我当时紧张得要死，就怕没听清楚。

2 —我没看出来你紧张啊。
—那就好。

3 她一来公司就在客服部了。

4 她不到一年就转到这边来了。

5 看你的，你去我就去。

6 要是我的英文能说得跟你的中文一样就好了。

7 我寒假哪儿也没去，就在学校学中文。

8 你这么早就开始为找工作做准备了？

9 面试上个星期三就结束了。

10 至于火车票，选择就比较多了。

11 我一来公司就跟同事学到了很多东西。

Now match them to the explanations by writing the numbers in the table.

a	就 means “only” or “just”, with an emphatic tone.	
b	就 means “then”, indicating a logical connection.	
c	就 indicates earliness.	
d	一……就…… means “as soon as”, showing two events in quick succession.	

2 Work in pairs. Talk about the most pleasant topics for small talk and make a list.

Now act out a conversation between two people meeting for the first time.

CHINESE TO GO

Reassurances

Méi kàn chūlái a 没 看 出来 啊。	No one could tell.
Shuō de yìdiǎnr méi cuò 说 的 一点儿 没 错。	That’s absolutely right.
Kàn nǐ de 看 你 的。	It’s up to you.

LESSON | 2

Reading and writing

1 Match the words with their meanings.

1 附件	a forward
2 查看	b download
3 下载	c document
4 文件	d attachment
5 另存为	e save as
6 打印	f print
7 收件箱	g sent mails
8 已发邮件	h inbox
9 回复	i view
10 转发	j reply

2 Look at the meanings of the characters and write down the meanings of the words.

邀请：invite	邀: invite
	请: invite, ask politely
寻求: _______	寻: search
	求: seek, find
祝愿: _______	祝: wish
	愿: hope, wish
查看: _______	查: review, check
	看: look, see
引导: _______	引: lead
	导: guide

Now work in pairs. Talk about the features of these words and think of similar two-character words.

3 Match the words to make phrases.

1 主持	a 合作
2 接待	b 会议
3 寻求	c 来宾
4 回顾	d 历史
5 欣赏	e 音乐

Now write three sentences using any of the above phrases.

1-34

4 Read the email Zhou Xiang sent to Mark on page 84 before the welcome dinner and complete the sentences.

在周详给马克的电子邮件里，他一共告诉马克三件事情：

1 晚宴的 _______ 和 _______ 在附件里。

2 总经理致辞的 ____________________。

3 如果需要帮助 ____________________。

邮箱

mail.com 邮箱 邮箱首页 | 设置

反馈建议 | 帮助中心 | 退出

写信
收信
通讯录

收件箱
星标邮件
群邮件
草稿箱
已发送
已删除 [清空]
垃圾箱
日历 | 记事本
附件夹

«返回 | 回复 | 转发 | 删除 | 举报 | 拒收 | 标记为... | 移动到...

文件

发件人：周详
时　间：7月10日
收件人：马克
附　件：附件1：晚宴流程及分工
附件2：总经理致辞（提纲）

马克：

附件是后天晚宴要用到的两份文件，一份是晚宴的分工和流程，一份是总经理致辞的提纲。总经理这次发言的时间不长，也不准备用讲稿，所以只有一个大概的内容。你还需要什么资料，马上告诉我，我来帮你找。

附件（2个）

晚宴流程及分工　查看　下载　　总经理致辞（提纲）　查看　下载

总经理致辞（提纲）

文件　编辑　格式　查看　帮助

晚宴欢迎辞（提纲）

一、开场白

“从澳大利亚远道而来的各位代表，来自深圳的业界同仁，女士们，先生们，大家晚上好！我代表亚深公司深圳分公司的全体员工，向前来我公司考察的澳大利亚代表团表示最热烈的欢迎！”

二、简单回顾亚深公司的发展历史；着重介绍深圳分公司现阶段的主要业务和国际合作伙伴。

三、介绍公司今后两年在澳大利亚的发展业务、寻求合作伙伴的计划。祝愿考察团在中国的考察大有收获。

四、结束语

“最后，我提议：为我们的友谊和将来的合作，为在座各位先生、女士的健康干杯！”

晚宴流程及分工

文件　编辑　格式　查看　帮助

澳大利亚考察团欢迎晚宴流程

时间： 2014年7月12日18:30-22:00
地点： 深圳酒店一楼宴会厅
接待： 客服部接待组
翻译： 马克
主持： 唐雨

18:30　参加晚宴的来宾开始入场，由接待组引导就座
18:45　澳大利亚代表团成员和公司主要领导就座
19:00　主持人介绍公司领导及重要来宾
19:10　总经理致欢迎辞
19:20　澳大利亚代表团致答谢辞
19:30　晚宴正式开始，中间穿插民乐演奏供来宾欣赏
22:00　晚宴结束

生词 New words

fùjiàn 附件	attachment	
hòutiān 后天	the day after tomorrow	
wénjiàn 文件	document, file	
fēngōng 分工	divide work; division of labour	
liúchéng 流程	programme	
tígāng 提纲	outline	
jiǎnggǎo 讲稿	speech notes, script	
xiàzǎi 下载	download	
kāichǎngbái 开场白	opening note	
yèjiè tóngrén 业界同仁	colleagues	
rèliè 热烈	warm	
huígù 回顾	review, retrospect	
jiēduàn 阶段	phase	
yèwù 业务	business	
hézuò 合作	cooperate	
huǒbàn 伙伴	partner	
jīnhòu 今后	from now on	
xúnqiú 寻求	seek, explore	
zhùyuàn 祝愿	wish	
tíyì 提议	propose	
yǒuyì 友谊	friendship	
zàizuò 在座	be present	
gānbēi 干杯	empty one's glass	
zhǔchí 主持	host	
láibīn 来宾	guest	
rùchǎng 入场	enter	
yǐndǎo 引导	guide	
jiùzuò 就座	be seated	
dáxiè 答谢	acknowledge, return thanks	
mínyuè 民乐	Chinese folk music	

5 Choose all the correct answers to the questions.

1 哪些情况需要马克做翻译？
- a 主持人介绍公司领导及重要来宾
- b 总经理致欢迎辞
- c 澳大利亚代表团致答谢辞

2 马克可能还需要什么资料？
- a 代表团成员、公司领导、重要来宾的名单
- b 公司的发展史
- c 深圳分公司现阶段的主要业务和合作伙伴

3 举办欢迎晚宴的主要目的是什么？
- a 祝愿考察团在中国考察顺利
- b 介绍公司领导及重要来宾
- c 介绍公司业务、寻求合作伙伴

6 Read the email from Xiaowen and complete the schedule.

7 Write an outline for Ms Wang's speech for the competition. Use the speech on page 84 to help you.

永民：

钱老师让我转告你，演讲比赛定在本月最后一个星期五下午1至4点。由你负责全程带领参赛的学生，我负责安排评委和观看比赛的师生就座，钱老师主持比赛。比赛开始的时候王主任会有简短致辞，比赛结束后也由王主任为学生发奖，最后全体拍照留念。钱老师让你做一份演讲比赛的分工及流程说明，做好以后用电子邮件发给他。有不清楚的地方可以随时给我打电话。

祝好！

小文

夏令营中文演讲比赛分工及流程

带领参赛学生	
	小文
主持	
致辞及发奖	
1:00	参赛学生、评委、观众入场
1:20	
1:30	比赛开始
3:30	
3:45	集体照
4:00	结束

Language in use

Indicating an extreme degree with ……死了

1 Look at the sentences.

	Adj. + 死了
我翻译的时候都要	紧张死了。
这两天	热死了。
别穿那件衣服，	难看死了。
我们宿舍的网速	慢死了。
坐地铁	挤死了。
到现在还没吃饭呢，	饿死我了。
搬家	累死我了。
找到这么好的工作，他一定	高兴死了。
见到她最喜欢的明星让她	兴奋死了。

Now check the correct explanations.

☐ 1 死了 is used as a degree complement to intensify the adjectives preceding it, indicating an extreme degree of the adjective in question.

☐ 2 死了 is similar to "deadly …" or "…to death" in English. For example, 冷死了 means "deadly cold".

☐ 3 Usually the adjectives preceding 死了 have negative meanings, but 死了 can also be used to show positive emotions, e.g. 高兴, 开心, 兴奋.

☐ 4 If the speaker uses 死了 to express that they personally are affected to an extreme degree, 我 can be inserted between 死 and 了.

2 Work in pairs. Answer the following questions using 死了.

1 你喜欢冬天还是夏天？为什么？
2 你最不喜欢的电影或小说是哪一部，为什么？
3 你在学中文的时候，觉得最困难的地方是什么？
4 最近一个月，你最开心的事情是什么？

Expressing wishes and hopes with 要是/如果……就好了

1 Look at the sentences.

(要是/如果) clause	就好了
要是我的英文能说得像你这样	就好了。
如果在伦敦也能吃到地道的西安小吃	就好了。
我会游泳	就好了。
要是你没邀请他们	就好了。
这套房子要是有三个卧室	就好了。

Now check the correct explanations.

☐ 1 要是/如果……就好了 is a structure in the subjunctive mood which expresses a wish or hope.

☐ 2 要是/如果……就好了 means "It would be great, if only …".

☐ 3 要是/如果 cannot be omitted.

2 Complete the conversations.

1 —没想到今天会堵车堵得这么厉害。我们真不应该打车。
—是啊，要是 ______ 就好了。

2 —这张沙发太舒服了，就是太贵了！
—嗯，如果 ______ 就好了。

3 —你的脚怎么了？
—我昨天练功扭了脚。要是 ______ 就好了。

3 Work in pairs. Talk about something you want to invent using the following expression.

要是能发明一种 ____________ 就好了，就可以 ____________。

Expressing emphasis using 可

1 Look at the sentences.

Subject	可	Verb phrase
实践经验	可	比书本上的知识重要多了。
你	可	别忘了买牛奶回来。
我家	可	没有钱换新车。
她	可	不是你以前认识的李安安了。
我	可	知道上下班时间挤地铁是什么感觉了。

Subject	可	Adj. + 了
他的狗	可	聪明了。
香港	可	好玩儿了。

Now check the correct explanations.

☐ 1 可 is used to emphasize a statement. Without 可, the meaning of the statement does not change, but the tone of the statement is weakened.

☐ 2 The emphatic 可 is a conjunction.

☐ 3 The emphatic 可 is mainly used in a colloquial context.

☐ 4 可……了 can also be employed to intensify an adjective. It is similar to 很, but its tone is slightly stronger.

2 Complete the conversations using 可.

1 —你有空吗，下午陪我去趟邮局吧？
—不行啊，我今天 ________________。

2 —昨天我见到小李了，他好像变了。
—现在的小李 ________________。

3 —他把房子和车都卖了，把工作也辞了，就是为了做一次环球 (around the world) 旅行。
—________________。

Justifying an opinion or decision using 反正

1 Look at the sentences.

	反正+justification
A: 这么晚了还去唱歌吗？	B: 去，反正明天是周末，也不着急睡觉。
A: 明天的聚会，我不太想去。	B: 那你就别去了，反正聚会也不一定有意思。
A: 要不咱们去吃披萨？	B: 行啊，反正对我来说吃什么都一样。
A: 我明天就去上海了，可能没有时间跟你见面了。	B: 没关系，反正我也挺忙的，咱们有机会下次再见吧。

Now check the correct explanations.

☐ 1 反正 as a modal adverb means "anyway" or "anyhow".

☐ 2 The clause involving 反正 indicates a reason to support the speaker's subjective attitude or judgment of a situation which usually involves options or choices.

☐ 3 反正 can only appear at the very beginning of a clause.

2 Complete the conversations with different answers.

1 —这件衣服很好看，不过挺贵的，你说我买不买？
—________________，反正你赚钱多。
—________________，反正这样的衣服到处都有卖的。

2 —我是星期六还是星期天做作业呢？
—星期六还要做作业？休息休息吧，反正 ________________。
—反正 ________________，早点儿做完，就轻松啦。

Turn to page 192 for grammar reference.

LESSON 3

Communication activity

1 Work in groups of three. Plan an event for a group of high school principals from China visiting your university next week.

- **Student A:** You are the vice principal who will be hosting the event. Write an outline of a welcome speech.
- **Student B:** You are the assistant to the vice principal. Write an email calling for a meeting to discuss the event. Include the meeting agenda in your email, the division of labour and the programme for the event.
- **Student C:** You are a teacher who used to live in China. Prepare the itinerary for the visitors.

Now act out the meeting.

2 Present the email, the itinerary and the speech outline to the class and vote for the best one.

Turn to pages 174 and 180 for more speaking practice.

Review and practice

1 Complete the sentences with the correct words.

1 开会的时候我紧张死了，就 _______ 总经理对我的报告不满意。
   a 恐怕　　b 怕

2 不是所有的人都 _______ 做销售工作。
   a 适合　　b 合适

3 你太 _______ 了，就算没有我的帮助，你也一定做得很好。
   a 骄傲　　b 谦虚

4 你是学销售的，他是学外贸的，你们俩 _______ 可以互相学习学习。
   a 正好　　b 幸好

5 我爸 _______ 好的时候就会给我们表演几段京剧。
   a 兴趣　　b 兴致

Cultural corner

Humility

The Chinese have always placed great importance on humility, or being humble, and it has been considered to be a characteristic of the Chinese for many centuries. In *The Analects* Confucius considers humility with its qualities self-discipline, modesty and unpretentiousness, and teaches us how to learn humility in order to ask for help or advice, whatever our status or education. Lao Tze also points out that one's title is not enough to command respect, but one's humility which should guide others. The common metaphor he uses is that of water, which runs deep and low but gives strength to others in the way it conforms to the laws of nature.

Even today it's considered impolite to boast, so it's still common to respond to a compliment or praise with a self-deprecating response. If you commend your host on the wonderful dinner you've been served, the reply might be "No, it's nothing". Accepting compliments is considered impolite. Even someone who has all the trappings of wealth and power would claim their business isn't doing very well, in order to show humility.

2 **Complete the passage with the words in the box.**

当时　现在　刚来　后来　未来
两年后　第一年　今后　过段时间

我 ______ 的时候也是什么都不懂，于是就一边向公司的前辈学习，一边努力工作。______ 想一想，自己在公司的 ______ 真是特别辛苦，______ 几乎每个周末都在加班，好像有做不完的工作。______ 自己通过实践慢慢地熟悉了业务，经验也多了，______ 我当上了客服部的经理。______ 要不要一直在客服部工作下去，我还没有想好，不过，我打算 ______ 去读MBA，我相信多学点儿东西一定会对我 ______ 的发展有很大的帮助的。

3 **Read the thank-you speech and put the parts into the correct order.**

____ a 在开场白中向对方表示感谢
____ b 再次感谢并祝愿对方
____ c 提及对方的致辞
____ d 向大家问好
____ e 介绍自己方面的情况并表达对对方的回应

Now check the true statements.

☐ 1 考察团不清楚亚深公司的情况。
☐ 2 考察团的公司都是从事玩具制造的。
☐ 3 考察团认为中国经济的发展很快、市场的潜力很大。
☐ 4 考察团对他们这次在中国的考察很有信心。

澳大利亚代表团的答谢辞

由马克翻译整理

尊敬的李总经理、尊敬的各位来宾：

非常感谢亚深公司深圳分公司为我们举办这一欢迎宴会，我代表我们澳大利亚考察团的全体同仁对贵公司热情的款待和周到的安排表示衷心的感谢。

通过李总经理的介绍，我们了解到贵公司的发展历史、现阶段的主要业务以及国际合作伙伴的情况，特别是贵公司希望在澳大利亚寻求合作伙伴的强烈愿望。

我们这个考察团的代表来自跟外贸相关的多个行业，包括从玩具制造到进出口运输的30多家公司。随着中国经济的快速发展，我们越来越感觉到中国市场的巨大潜力以及与中国公司合作的重要性。我们都希望能借此次考察之机探讨与中国公司——特别是像亚深公司这样的大公司——合作的可能性。虽然我们的中国之行才刚刚开始，但是我们相信这次考察一定会有巨大的收获。

最后，我想再次感谢李总经理为我们安排的晚宴，也祝愿亚深公司今后有更大的发展。

谢谢！

代表团团长埃里克

4 **Write a complete welcome speech for the communication activity based on the outline your group has worked out. Include the following:**

- 开场白
- 你们学校的历史
- 学校以前跟中国的合作情况以及将来的计划
- 结束语

Vocabulary review

Fill in the blanks.

答谢	dáxiè	*v.*	acknowledge, return thanks
多亏	duōkuī	*v.*	owing to; fortunately
____	fǎnzhèng	*adv.*	anyway, all the same
分工	fēngōng	*v./n.*	divide work; division of labour
附件	fùjiàn	*n.*	attachment
____	gānbēi	*v.*	empty one's glass
高材生	gāocáishēng	*n.*	top student
共同	gòngtóng	*adv.*	____
过	guò	*v.*	____
合作	hézuò	*v.*	cooperate
____	hòutiān	*n.*	the day after tomorrow
回顾	huígù	*v.*	review, retrospect
伙伴	huǒbàn	*n.*	____
讲稿	jiǎnggǎo	*n.*	speech notes, script
阶段	jiēduàn	*n.*	phase
今后	jīnhòu	*n.*	____
____	jiù	*adv.*	as soon as; (if)…then; only, just
就座	jiùzuò	*v.*	be seated
开场白	kāichǎngbái	*n.*	opening note
看出来	kàn chūlai		discern, make out
夸奖	kuājiǎng	*v.*	____
来宾	láibīn	*n.*	guest
流程	liúchéng	*n.*	programme
漏掉	lòudiào	*v.*	miss

民乐	mínyuè	*n.*	Chinese folk music
佩服	pèifú	*v.*	admire
谦虚	qiānxū	*adj.*	modest, humble
前辈	qiánbèi	*n.*	senior
取长补短	qǔcháng-bǔduǎn		complement one another
热烈	rèliè	*adj.*	warm
入场	rùchǎng	*v.*	enter
____	sǐ	*adj.*	extreme
提纲	tígāng	*n.*	outline
提议	tíyì	*v.*	____
外贸	wàimào	*n.*	foreign trade
____	wénjiàn	*n.*	document, file
下载	xiàzǎi	*v.*	____
兴致	xìngzhì	*n.*	mood to enjoy
寻求	xúnqiú	*v.*	seek, explore
业界同仁	yèjiè tóngrén		colleagues
业务	yèwù	*n.*	business
夜宵	yèxiāo	*n.*	night snack or refreshment
引导	yǐndǎo	*v.*	guide
____	yǒuyì	*n.*	friendship
于是	yúshì	*conj.*	____
在座	zàizuò	*v.*	be present
糟糕	zāogāo	*adj.*	terrible
主持	zhǔchí	*v.*	host
祝愿	zhùyuàn	*v.*	wish
____	zhǔnquè	*adj.*	accurate, precise

UNIT 7

Gùkè yǒngyuǎn shì duì de

顾客 永远 是 对 的!

The customer is always right!

LESSON 1

Vocabulary and listening

1 **Look at the words to describe the service in a shop. Which are the most important to you?**

态度　诚恳　热情　折扣
送货时间　讲信用　道歉

2 **Match the words to make phrases.**

1 取得	a 上司
2 处理	b 问题
3 请示	c 谅解

4 找	d 信用
5 接	e 电话
6 讲	f 借口

2-2

3 **Mark has got some problems at work. Listen to the conversation and answer the questions.**

1 马克碰到了什么问题？
2 谢月给了马克什么建议？
3 马克下一步应该怎么办？

4 **Check the true statements.**

☐ 1 马克的公司不讲信用，要取消客户的订单。
☐ 2 工厂不能按时完成订单是因为工人不够。
☐ 3 马克向客户提出了解决办法。
☐ 4 谢月认为这全是马克的责任。
☐ 5 谢月认为只要态度诚恳地向客户道歉，问题就一定能解决。

谢月：马克，办公室就剩你了。你怎么还不走，打算加班吗？
马克：唉，加班也不一定能解决问题啊。
谢月：愿意和我说说吗？
马克：是这样的，昨天我接到工厂的电话，说有个订单无法按时完成。我直接给订单的客户发邮件说了这个情况，没想到他们非常生气，批评我们不讲信用，还说要取消订单。我是不是闯祸了？
谢月：别着急，先冷静一下。究竟是什么原因导致工厂不能按时完成订单？
马克：据说是因为最近劳务市场上请不到合格的工人。
谢月：这倒是有可能。那你在邮件中有没有提出什么解决办法？
马克：没有，我只是解释了一下情况。
谢月：这也不能全怪你，处理这种问题的确需要经验。如果我是客户，我会认为你不过是在找借口罢了。
马克：那我现在该怎么办呢？
谢月："顾客永远是对的。"你不仅要态度诚恳地向客户道歉，还要提出解决办法，比如缩短送货时间或者给客户一些折扣等等。但是，具体怎么处理你应该请示唐经理。记住，以后遇到类似的问题，一定要马上请示你的上司。
马克：太谢谢你了……你觉得唐经理会原谅我吗？
谢月：别担心了，先下班吧。

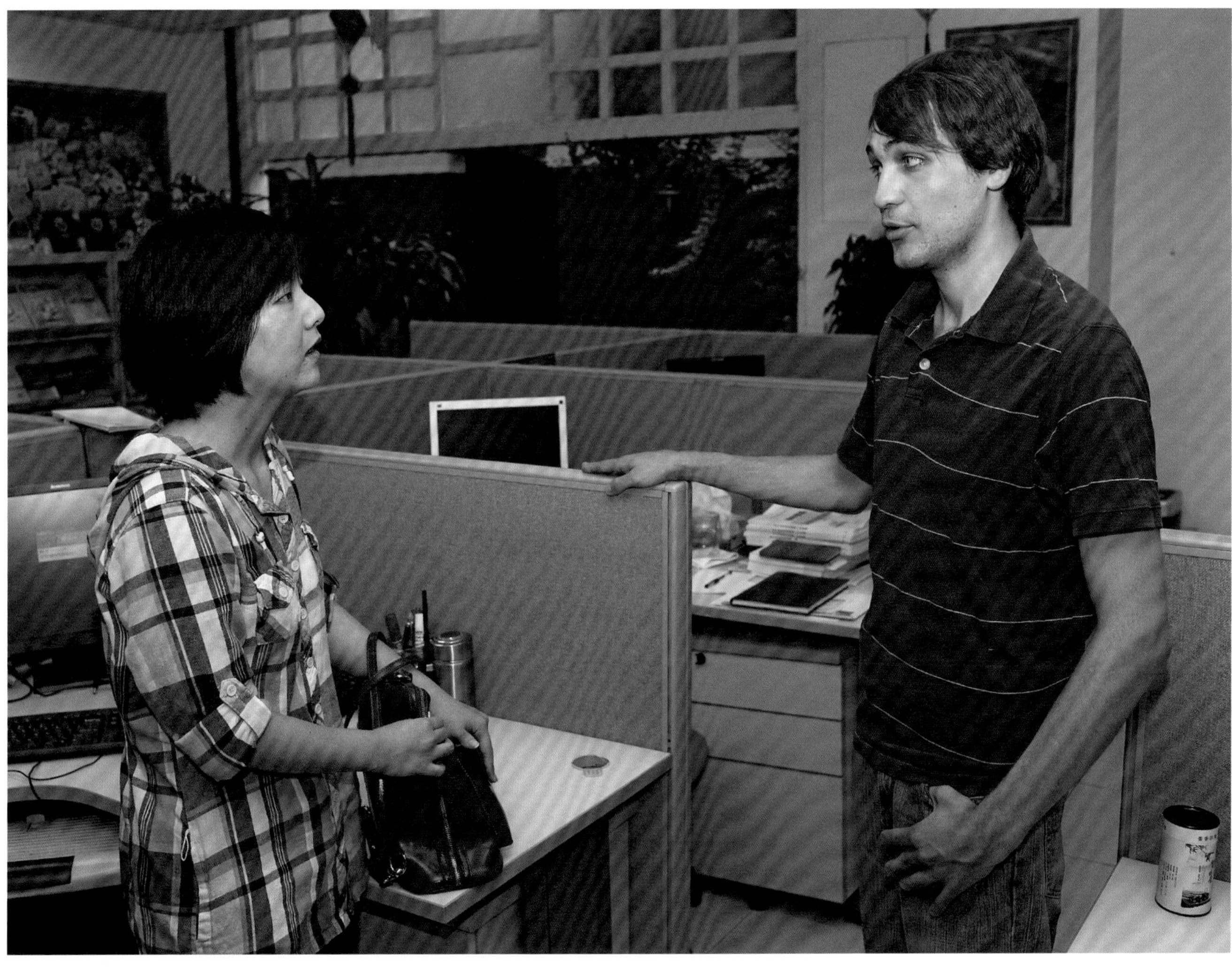

生词 New words

shèng	剩	remain, be left
jiābān	加班	work overtime
jiějué	解决	solve
gōngchǎng	工厂	factory
dìngdān	订单	order (form)
wúfǎ	无法	be unable, be incapable
pīpíng	批评	criticize, blame
jiǎng xìnyòng	讲 信用	care about one's trustworthiness
chuǎnghuò	闯祸	make trouble
lěngjìng	冷静	calm; cool down
jiūjìng	究竟	what on earth, what exactly
dǎozhì	导致	cause
láowù	劳务	labour
shìchǎng	市场	market
qǐng	请	hire
hégé	合格	qualified
gōngrén	工人	worker
guài	怪	put the blame on
búguò … bàle	不过……罢了	just, only
jièkǒu	借口	excuse
gùkè	顾客	customer
yǒngyuǎn	永远	forever
chéngkěn	诚恳	sincere
dàoqiàn	道歉	apologize
suōduǎn	缩短	shorten
sònghuò	送货	deliver goods
lèisì	类似	similar
qǐngshì	请示	ask for opinion (of one's superior)
shàngsi	上司	supervisor
yuánliàng	原谅	forgive

5 **Put the events in the order they took place.**

____ a 客户非常生气

____ b 马克接到工厂的电话

____ c 劳务市场工人不足

____ d 马克向谢月请教

____ e 马克给客户发邮件

____ f 工厂发现无法按时完成订单

2-3

6 **You are going to hear a conversation between Mark and Zhou Xiang about their internship. Predict what they will say they do not enjoy.**

☐ 1 常常加班

☐ 2 常常出差

☐ 3 没有意思

☐ 4 压力很大

☐ 5 麻烦很多

☐ 6 成就感很小

☐ 7 老板难相处

☐ 8 同事难相处

☐ 9 客户难沟通

☐ 10 实习工资低

Now listen and check your answers.

2-3

7 **Listen again and check the true statements.**

☐ 1 马克需要继续处理上次订单的事情。

☐ 2 马克在帮加拿大客户订机票和酒店。

☐ 3 如果客户早一点儿跟马克的公司联系，机票就不会这么难订了。

☐ 4 马克今天下午花了三四个小时忙一件事情。

☐ 5 下班的时候，马克还没订好客户的机票。

Pronunciation and speaking

1 **Listen and repeat the sentences showing care or expressing reassurance.**

1 出什么事儿了？愿意跟我说说吗？

2 别着急，先冷静一下。

3 如果我是你的话，可能也会这么处理的。

4 这件事儿也不能都怪你。

5 别担心，问题肯定会解决的。

Now choose the correct sentences to complete the conversations.

1 — 怎么办，订单出了问题，可是客户那边的电话总是打不通！

— ______________________ 我们一起想想还有没有别的办法。

2 — ______________________

— 事情是这样的，我不小心把应该发给经理的信发给客户了。

3 — 我想先请示经理再给客户答复，可是经理突然出差了，这两天联系不到他。现在客户那边非常着急。

— ______________________

2 **Work in pairs. Talk about something that has been bothering you recently. Reassure each other and offer some suggestions.**

我同屋总是听很吵的音乐！

CHINESE TO GO

2-5

Consolations

Yuànyì gēn wǒ shuōshuo ma 愿意 跟 我 说 说 吗？	Do you want to talk about it with me?
Zhè dàoshi yǒu kěnéng 这 倒是 有 可能。	That's quite possible.
Bié zháojí xiān lěngjìng yíxià 别 着急， 先 冷静 一下。	Relax and calm down a bit first.

LESSON 2

Reading and writing

1 Work in pairs. Compare handwritten letters with emails and complete the table.

	手写的信	电子邮件
好处		
坏处		

2 Match the words to make phrases.

1 回不完的	a 功课
2 做不完的	b 资料
3 打不完的	c 邮件
4 查不完的	d 电话

Now work in pairs. Talk about what happened and how you felt when you were extremely busy.

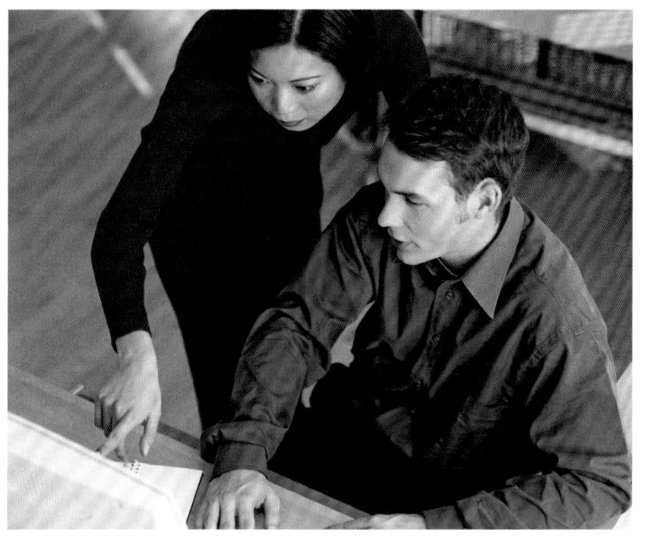

3 Look at the meanings of the words and complete the sentences.

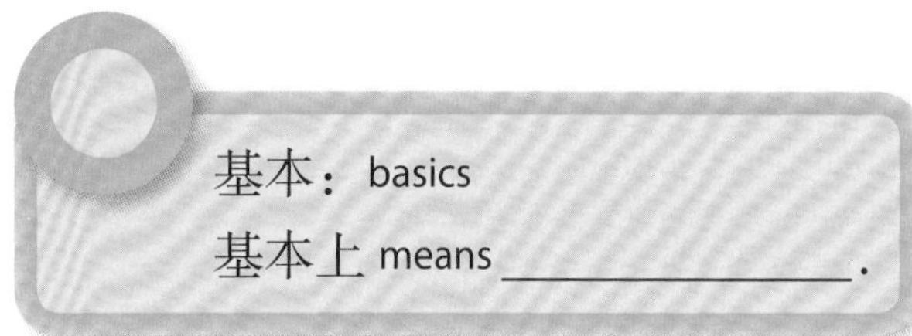

基本：basics

基本上 means ________________.

随便: random; with no limit on scope or amount

随时 means ________________.

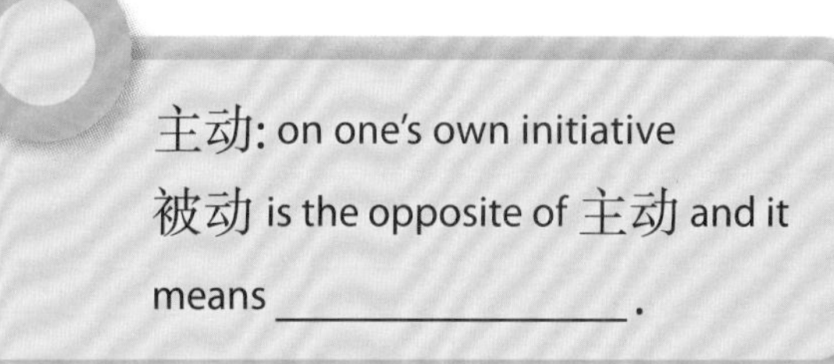

主动: on one's own initiative

被动 is the opposite of 主动 and it means ________________.

2-6

4 Read the letter on page 96 and complete the sentences.

马克在信中说到哪些事情？

1 为什么要____________________。

2 ____________________很忙碌。

3 每天都在____________________。

4 公司的____________________。

5 业余时间____________________。

6 ____________________照片。

7 问一问____________________。

王玉：

你好！

现在大家都习惯发邮件和上网聊天，基本上都不写信了，可我还是觉得手写的信有意思，还可以练练字。

我在深圳的公司已经实习一个月了。上班跟上学的感觉很不一样。我每天早出晚归，有查不完的资料，回不完的邮件，打不完的电话；同事们还经常来问我跟英语和文化差异有关的问题。下班后脑子也停不下来，总是很兴奋！可我觉得自己变聪明了，因为每天的忙碌给了我很多学习新东西的机会。

比如，上周我第一次出差，陪客户参观工厂。从订酒店、订票、安排行程到翻译，一切都要自己来。尽管有点儿手忙脚乱，可是做这些事情很锻炼我的能力。

我觉得自己非常幸运，公司里的老板和同事都对我特别好，我有什么问题都可以随时请教他们。就在昨天，因为经验不足，我在工作中犯了一个不小的错误，而老板不但没有批评我，而且给了我很好的建议，这让我特别感动。我真希望毕业以后能继续在这家公司工作。

业余时间我经常跟同事去唱卡拉OK，我现在已经会唱好几首中文歌了！等你回来，我们一起去唱歌吧！

随信寄去一张我自己拍的照片，是深圳的街景。我非常喜欢这个城市，因为它充满了活力。

你在美国怎么样？是不是交了很多新朋友？有空的时候也给我写写信吧。

祝一切顺利，心想事成！

你的朋友：马克

7月24日于深圳

生词 New words

shǒuxiě	手写	handwrite
xìn	信	letter
nǎozi	脑子	brain
xīngfèn	兴奋	excited
cōngming	聪明	smart
mánglù	忙碌	busy
yíqiè	一切	everything
zìjǐ lái	自己来	do by oneself
shǒumáng-jiǎoluàn	手忙脚乱	in a flurry, in a rush
xìngyùn	幸运	lucky
suíshí	随时	anytime
qǐngjiào	请教	ask for help (from one's seniors)
bùzú	不足	not enough
fàn	犯	commit (an error, crime)
cuòwù	错误	mistake, error
gǎndòng	感动	touch
jì	寄	mail
chōngmǎn	充满	be filled with
huólì	活力	energy
xīnxiǎng-shìchéng	心想事成	May all your wishes come true!

5 Choose all the correct answers to the questions.

1 马克为什么要手写这封信?
  a 他更习惯用手写信。
  b 他觉得挺有意思的。
  c 他想练练写字。

2 马克为什么说"下班后脑子也停不下来"?
  a 一下班马克就很兴奋。
  b 下班后他可能还在想工作上的事情。
  c 下班以后还有同事问他跟英文有关的问题。

3 上周马克做了什么事情?
  a 出差
  b 订酒店、订机票、安排行程
  c 翻译

4 马克出了错，他的上司是怎样处理的?
  a 给他建议
  b 批评他
  c 不让他继续工作

6 Choose four words from the box to describe Mark's feelings.

感受	忙碌	做不完	停不下来
兴奋	充实	手忙脚乱	很锻炼人
幸运	感动	充满	活力

• 感受:

马克已经实习一个月了，他的感受特别多，所以他写信跟朋友分享这些感受。

7 Read Mark's journal and check the true statements.

问题解决了

……

昨天跟谢月谈了以后，虽然心里还是非常担心，但是知道应该怎么做了，所以今天一到公司就马上向唐经理请示具体的处理办法。我很诚恳地告诉唐经理这件事情是由于我经验不足导致了客户的不满。唐经理听了以后建议我马上给客户打电话，告诉他们我们公司会尽量缩短送货时间，争取在十月底以前将货品送到客户的手中。我向客户道了歉，并提出这个解决办法。他们听了以后很满意。这让我既高兴又感动，我没想到唐经理和客户最后都原谅了我。

☐ 1 跟谢月的谈话让马克明白了自己应该怎么做。

☐ 2 向经理汇报时，马克没有为自己的错误找借口。

☐ 3 客户并不接受缩短送货时间的解决办法。

☐ 4 唐经理原谅了马克，但客户不愿意原谅他。

8 Write a letter to your best friend about a difficulty you have encountered. Include the following:

• 问题是什么
• 你向谁求助了
• 问题是否解决了
• 你的感受如何

Language in use

Expressing "how come" with 怎么

1 Look at the sentences.

你怎么还没走？打算加班吗？
他的女朋友怎么没来？
那个订单不是已经确认过了吗？怎么还有问题？
今年夏天的天气怎么这么奇怪？
他怎么那么容易忘事儿？

Now check the correct explanations.

☐ 1 怎么 is a question word used to ask for a reason or explanation.
☐ 2 怎么 has a similar tone and connotation to "how come" in English. It not only asks "why", but also expresses a tone of surprise.
☐ 3 怎么 always appears at the beginning of a sentence, after the subject.

2 Work in pairs. Ask and answer questions about the following scenarios using 怎么.

1 在去北京的飞机上你突然看见了你小时候的朋友。
2 下午三点了，你发现你的室友还没吃午饭。
3 上课已经十分钟了，可是班里一半的同学都没到。
4 在你最喜欢的咖啡店里，你点了你每天都喝的咖啡，可是店员告诉你咖啡涨价了。

Emphasizing an inquiry with 到底 / 究竟

1 Look at the sentences.

Subject	到底/究竟 + question forms
	究竟是什么原因导致工厂不能按时完成订单？
那我现在	到底应该怎么办呢？
你	到底能不能来开会？
老板，你	到底卖不卖？
我们	到底要请张教授还是请王教授？
这种病毒 (virus)	究竟是从动物身上来的还是从人身上来的？

Now check the correct explanations.

☐ 1 到底 and 究竟 express an incredulity or intensity similar to the phrase "on earth". They are adverbs used to emphasize the question or to press the other speaker to give an answer or tell the truth.
☐ 2 到底 and 究竟 can precede the subject of the sentence.
☐ 3 到底 and 究竟 emphasize three question forms: questions beginning with wh-words; questions posed by a verb; and questions which offer an "either ... or ... " alternative.
☐ 4 到底 and 究竟 cannot be used in an embedded question.
☐ 5 究竟 is more formal than 到底.

2 Work in pairs. Talk about the discrepancies between the two messages about the same event using 到底.

大家好：

这个星期五我们公司要在明珠酒店为美国纽约来的客户举办一个欢迎宴会。欢迎大家都来参加。有问题请跟客服部的王风联系。

赵成功（经理）

大家好：

这个星期六我们公司要在东方酒店为美国纽约来的客户举办一个欢迎宴会。欢迎大家都来参加。要是有问题，请联系客服部的王风。

张光希（总经理）

Minimizing a situation with （只）不过/只（是）……罢了

■1 Look at the sentences.

	不过/只不过/只/只是	Verb phrase	罢了	
你的这些解释	不过	是在找借口	罢了。	
她	不过	是个孩子，		当然会犯错误。
他	只不过	开个玩笑	罢了，	你怎么那么生气？
你快来吧，	只	是一顿饭	罢了，	花不了你太多时间。

Now check the correct explanations.

☐ 1 不过/只不过/只/只是……罢了 is a structure used to minimize or downplay the thing, the situation, or the number it modifies.

☐ 2 不过/只不过/只/只是 means "merely".

☐ 3 罢了 is a modal particle expressing a minimizing tone.

☐ 4 罢了 should always appear at the end of the clause; it cannot be omitted.

■2 Complete the conversation using 不过/只不过/只/只是……罢了 and the given words.

A: 你 ______________，怎么这么多天不去上课呢？（跟……分手）

B: 你又没有女朋友，你懂什么。

A: 可是我能明白你的感受。其实我早就知道她不喜欢你了，我没告诉你，______________。（难过）

B: 我总是想着我们在一起时的那些快乐的事情。

A: 你会把她忘了的，______________。（需要）

Indicating "not only ..., but also ..." with 不但/不只/不仅/不光……而且/还/也……

■1 Look at the sentences.

Subject	不但/不只/不仅/不光 + adj./verb phrase	而且/还/也 + adj./verb phrase
老板	不但没有炒我的鱿鱼，	而且还给了我很好的建议。
他	不但听了我的烦恼，	而且给我出了很多主意。
你	不光要态度诚恳地跟客户道歉，	还要商量解决办法。
他	不但会说中文，	而且说得特别流利。
那家公司	不仅工作环境很好，	而且也为员工提供了非常好的待遇。

Now check the correct explanations.

☐ 1 不但……而且…… is the most commonly used structure to express "not only ..., but also ...".

☐ 2 There are some other structures which can be used to express the same meaning. 不但 can be replaced with 不仅/不只/不光; 而且 with 还/也.

☐ 3 而且 cannot be used in conjunction with 还 or 也.

☐ 4 Besides adjectives and verb phrases, noun phrases can also follow 不但/不只/不仅/不光 and 而且/还/也. Therefore, a sentence like 他会说不但法文，而且中文 is acceptable.

■2 Answer the questions using 不但/不只/不仅/不光……而且/还/也……

1 如果你是公司经理，你想招什么样的职员？

2 如果你是公司的员工，你想要什么样上司？

Turn to page 193 for grammar reference.

LESSON 3

Communication activity

1 Write a letter to a customer service representive about a recent purchase. Complain about one or more of the following:

- quality of the product;
- problems with delivery;
- poor after-sales services.

Now work in pairs. In turns, act out a telephone conversation between the salesperson and the customer about how to solve the problem.

2 Work with another pair. Act out the telephone conversation again.

Turn to pages 175 and 181 for more speaking practice.

Review and practice

1 Choose the correct words to complete the sentences.

1 他对咖啡太有研究了，一说到咖啡他就 ______。

a 不停下来　b 停不下来　c 不能停

2 这份实习工作虽然非常辛苦，每天都从早忙到晚，但是让我感到特别 ______。

a 充满　b 丰富　c 充实

3 听到他唱出那首歌，我一下子就被 ______ 了。

a 感动　b 感觉　c 感受

4 从看房子、刷墙、买家具到搬家，______ 都要自己来。

a 所有　b 任何　c 一切

5 尽管他犯了错，可是他的上司 ______ 没批评他，______ 还原谅了他。

a 不是……而是……

b 不但……而且……

c 不只……连……

Cultural corner

The square and the circle

Of all geometric shapes, the square (方) and the circle (圆) are especially prominent in Chinese culture. Ancient Chinese people believed that the sky was round, and the earth square, so the word 方圆 can refer to "neighbourhood" or "vicinity". The figurative meaning of the square is often associated with rule, principle and appropriateness, as the word 方正 (upright and righteous) indicates. The round shape is related to perfection or fulfilment. For example, 圆满 indicates that something is satisfactory, 圆梦 means a dream has been fulfilled, and 团圆 refers to a reunion of family or friends. The two shapes illustrate the complexity of Chinese social life: on the one hand, Chinese culture stresses integrity and proper behaviour, but on the other hand it also emphasizes the importance of flexibility and avoiding conflict in social interaction (see the meaning of 圆通).

2 Complete the sentences with the words in the box.

批评　道歉　棘手　谅解　市场
合格　无法　导致　讲信用

1 家庭生活中最 ______ 的问题可能就是孩子的教育。
2 那家旅行社也太不 ______ 了，已经定好的行程，怎么能随便改变呢？
3 他说他永远 ______ 原谅出卖朋友的人。
4 他的新书受到来自周围人的各种各样的 ______。
5 不管她怎么努力，都无法取得女儿的 ______。
6 他最喜欢说："如果 ______ 有用，还要警察做什么？"
7 这些不 ______ 的产品，一件都不能进入 ______。
8 过度开发和过度放牧 ______ 草原沙化越来越严重。

3 Complete the passage with the words in the box.

不足　充实　分享　实在
手忙脚乱　错误　继续　随时
感动　很锻炼人　忙碌

马克在写给王玉的信中 ______ 了很多他实习以后的感受。他觉得上班和上学的感觉 ______ 是不一样。工作让他既 ______ 又 ______：一方面每天都有做不完的事情，一方面每天都在学习新东西。虽然有的时候他会 ______，可是他觉得工作中的事情 ______。不管是老板还是同事都对马克很好，他可以 ______ 向他们请教。尽管他由于工作经验 ______ 犯了 ______，可是上司并没有让他离开公司。这让他非常 ______。他希望毕业以后还能 ______ 在这家公司工作。

4 Read the email and check the true statements.

«返回　回复　转发　删除　举报　拒收　移动到...

发件人：　王思聪
时　间：　X月X日
收件人：　唐经理

唐经理：

您好！

我是北京新艺有限公司市场部的业务员。一个月前我们公司从你们亚深公司订购了一批儿童服装。但是货到后，我们发现数量与我们之前的订单有一些差别。我已经几次与贵公司客服部的人员进行沟通，而他们只说他们会跟贵公司的工厂方面联系，看看究竟是哪里出了差错。但是一个星期过去了，问题还是没有解决。我给您写信是希望您能尽快处理这件事情，并给我们一个满意的答复。

谢谢。

王思聪

☐ 1 新艺公司从亚深公司订购的货物是儿童玩具。
☐ 2 亚深公司发给新艺公司的货物数量不对。
☐ 3 亚深公司的客服部还没找到出问题的原因。
☐ 4 新艺公司觉得亚深公司不讲信用。
☐ 5 王思聪给唐经理写信是因为她觉得亚深公司客服部处理问题的速度太慢了。

Now match the words with their meanings.

1 业务员	a batch
2 批	b mistake
3 数量	c reply
4 差错	d salesman
5 答复	e amount

5 Write an email to your friend and include the following:

- 一件很有趣的事情
- 一段不开心的经历
- 问候这位朋友最近的情况

Vocabulary review

Fill in the blanks.

不过……罢了	búguò...bàle		just, only
不足	bùzú	*adj.*	not enough
诚恳	chéngkěn	*adj.*	sincere
充满	chōngmǎn	*v.*	______
闯祸	chuǎnghuò	*v.*	make trouble
______	cōngming	*adj.*	smart
错误	cuòwù	*n.*	mistake, error
导致	dǎozhì	*v.*	cause
道歉	dàoqiàn	*v.*	______
订单	dìngdān	*n.*	order (form)
犯	fàn	*v.*	commit (an error, crime)
感动	gǎndòng	*v.*	touch
工厂	gōngchǎng	*n.*	______
______	gōngrén	*n.*	worker
顾客	gùkè	*n.*	customer
______	guài	*v.*	put the blame on
合格	hégé	*adj.*	______
活力	huólì	*n.*	energy
______	jì	*v.*	mail
加班	jiābān	*v.*	______
讲信用	jiǎng xìnyòng		care about one's trustworthiness
解决	jiějué	*v.*	solve
借口	jièkǒu	*n.*	excuse
究竟	jiūjìng	*adv.*	what on earth, what exactly
劳务	láowù	*n.*	labour
类似	lèisì	*v.*	similar
冷静	lěngjìng	*adj.*	calm; cool down
忙碌	mánglù	*adj.*	busy
脑子	nǎozi	*n.*	brain
批评	pīpíng	*v.*	criticize, blame
______	qǐng	*v.*	hire
请教	qǐngjiào	*v.*	ask for help (from one's seniors)
请示	qǐngshì	*v.*	ask for opinion (of one's superior)
上司	shàngsi	*n.*	supervisor
剩	shèng	*v.*	______
市场	shìchǎng	*n.*	market
手忙脚乱	shǒumáng-jiǎoluàn		in a flurry, in a rush
手写	shǒuxiě	*v.*	______
送货	sònghuò	*v.*	deliver goods
______	suíshí	*adv.*	anytime
缩短	suōduǎn	*v.*	shorten
无法	wúfǎ	*v.*	be unable, be incapable
心想事成	xīnxiǎng-shìchéng		May all your wishes come true!
______	xìn	*n.*	letter
兴奋	xīngfèn	*adj.*	______
幸运	xìngyùn	*adj.*	lucky
______	yíqiè	*pron.*	everything
永远	yǒngyuǎn	*adv.*	______
原谅	yuánliàng	*v.*	forgive
自己来	zìjǐ lái		do by oneself

UNIT 8

Yúnnán zhēn shì gè hǎo dìfang
云南真是个好地方！

Yunnan is amazing!

LESSON 1

Vocabulary and listening

1 Work in pairs. Talk about what a typical office job is like.

白领　典型　收入
享受　体面　压力

Now ask and answer the questions.

1 在现代社会中，为什么人们都觉得压力很大？
2 只有在度假或旅游时才能“享受生活”吗？

2 Work out the meanings of the idioms.

如：like, as
画：painting, picture

风景如画：________

名：fame,
虚：vain, fake
传：spread

名不虚传：________

3 Steve meets Da Liu during his holiday in Yunnan. Listen to the conversation and answer the questions.

1 大刘是本地人吗？他以前是做什么的？
2 史蒂夫喜欢不喜欢云南？
3 史蒂夫和大刘接下来要做什么？

史蒂夫：你好，我叫史蒂夫，你怎么称呼？

大刘：叫我大刘吧。你的中文真棒！是第一次来丽江吗？

史蒂夫：谢谢，大刘，我是第一次来云南，昨天刚从昆明到了丽江。云南真是个好地方！你是本地人吗？能住在这里真是再幸福不过了！

大刘：我不是本地人。七年前我来旅游，来了就不想走了。后来就辞了职，搬到丽江来了。

史蒂夫：那你过去是做什么的？

大刘：我以前在上海工作，是个典型的白领。工作看着体面，其实压力大得不得了，常常失眠。我那时总怀疑这是不是自己想要的生活。来丽江旅游的时候，忽然体会到了享受生活的感觉……我问自己，为什么不能换一种生活方式呢？我实在是讨厌原来的生活了。

史蒂夫：嗯，我采访过一个老师，她也是放弃了北京的生活，去内蒙古教书。

大刘：原来你是记者啊，是来采访的吗？

史蒂夫：我是来度假的。早就听说云南风景如画，是摄影爱好者

	的天堂，果然名不虚传。
大刘：	你觉得丽江怎么样？
史蒂夫：	丽江是个很美的小城，不过商业化的程度比我想象中的高。下一步去哪儿我还没想好，你有什么建议吗？
大刘：	你算是问对人啦！你等着，我去拿张地图，然后跟你说说云南你必须去、不去会后悔的地方。
史蒂夫：	太好了，一会儿请你喝啤酒！

4 Listen again and check the true statements.

- ☐ 1 史蒂夫以为大刘是云南本地人。
- ☐ 2 大刘在丽江已经住了七年了。
- ☐ 3 史蒂夫曾经采访过一个北京的老师。
- ☐ 4 史蒂夫是来丽江采访的。
- ☐ 5 史蒂夫为云南之行做了很好的计划。

5 Choose the correct answers to the questions.

1 大刘对以前的工作有什么不满意？
  a 不体面　　b 薪水不高　　c 压力大

2 史蒂夫对丽江的印象怎么样？
  a 他觉得丽江很美。
  b 他没想到丽江的商业化程度这么高。
  c 他来了就不想走了。

生词 New words

Lìjiāng	丽江	Lijiang
Yúnnán	云南	Yunnan Province
Kūnmíng	昆明	Kunming
cízhí	辞职	quit one's job
diǎnxíng	典型	typical
báilǐng	白领	white-collar worker
tǐmiàn	体面	decent, respectable
shīmián	失眠	insomnia
huáiyí	怀疑	doubt, suspect
hūrán	忽然	all of a sudden
tǐhuì	体会	experience
xiǎngshòu	享受	enjoy
shízài	实在	indeed, truly
tǎoyàn	讨厌	dislike, loathe
fàngqì	放弃	give up
yuánlái	原来	as it turns out to be
fēngjǐng rú huà	风景如画	picturesque landscape
shèyǐng	摄影	take a photograph; photography
àihàozhě	爱好者	hobbyist, enthusiast, fan
tiāntáng	天堂	heaven
guǒrán	果然	sure enough
míngbùxūchuán	名不虚传	live up to one's name
chéngdù	程度	degree
xiǎngxiàng	想象	imagine
bìxū	必须	must
hòuhuǐ	后悔	regret
píjiǔ	啤酒	beer

6 Draw a timeline of Da Liu's life noting the key events that have changed it.

→ 过去 → 七年前 → 现在

7 Steve is talking to another tourist in Lijiang. Predict what questions Steve will ask.

Now listen and write down the three questions. Check the reasons why they are asked.

1 ______________________________

2 ______________________________

3 ______________________________

- ☐ a 这是游客之间常问的一个问题。
- ☐ b 史蒂夫想知道这个游客有多长时间的假期。
- ☐ c 史蒂夫觉得丽江并不清静。
- ☐ d 史蒂夫觉得这个游客不应该到这儿来。
- ☐ e 史蒂夫想知道这个游客对商业化和传统文化关系的看法。
- ☐ f 史蒂夫对商业化影响的态度不太乐观。

8 Listen again and check the correct statements.

- ☐ 1 这里的吵闹跟大城市一样。
- ☐ 2 这是一个令人愉快的地方。
- ☐ 3 这座城市的历史超过五百年。
- ☐ 4 这里有重视商业发展的传统。
- ☐ 5 由于商业化程度太高，这里的传统和文化已经被破坏了。
- ☐ 6 这里的自然环境将来一定会受到破坏。

Pronunciation and speaking

1 Listen to the sentences. Notice how the tone of each sentence is changed by the underlined word.

1 工作看着体面，其实压力大得不得了。
2 我忽然体会到享受生活的感觉。
3 我实在是讨厌原来的生活了。
4 原来你是记者啊，是来采访的吗？
5 听说这里风景如画，果然名不虚传。

Now say the sentences with the appropriate tones.

2 Choose the correct underlined words from Activity 1 and put them in the right places to complete the sentences.

1 a 他看起来 b 像大学刚毕业，c 已经 d 工作五年了。
2 a 他们说你 b 没去上课，c 你 d 在宿舍里啊。
3 a 早上 b 出门天气还好好的，c 就 d 开始下雨了。
4 a 这些衣服我 b 能明天再洗吗？ c 我现在 d 累了。
5 a 到了香港 b 我 c 才明白，d "的士"就是出租车啊。

3 Work in pairs. Act out a conversation between two tourists meeting at a scenic spot that you are familiar with. Include the following topics:

- 假期 • 风景 • 游客对环境的影响

CHINESE TO GO

2-10

Making acquaintances

Nǐ zěnme chēnghu 你 怎么 称呼？	How should I address you?
Jiào wǒ …… ba 叫 我 …… 吧。	You can call me …
Nǐ suànshì wènduì rén la 你 算是 问对 人 啦！	You have asked the right person!

LESSON 2

Reading and writing

1 **Number the words according to how weak(1) or strong(5) their tones are.**

__十分　__挺　__最　__有点儿

Now complete the sentences.

a ________________ 挺危险。

b ________________ 十分危险。

c ________________ 最危险。

d ________________ 有点儿危险。

2 **Work in pairs. Talk about your favourite holiday destinations for different seasons.**

Use the words in the box to help you.

阳光	懒	最爱
季节	停止	散步

3 **Look at the meanings of the words and complete the sentences.**

傣族: Dai ethnic group　　傣家菜 means ____________________.

孔雀: peacock
跳舞: dance　　孔雀舞 means ____________________.

神: god, deity, divine　　神山 means ____________________.

2-11

4 **Read the postcards on page 108 and complete the table.**

史蒂夫的明信片

从哪里	寄给谁	提到的地方或特别的东西
	永民	昆明，石林，________
丽江		香格里拉，梅里雪山
	阿曼达	
		雨崩村，__________

永民：

我现在在云南昆明。昆明无论什么季节都是温暖如春，所以也叫“春城”。图片上就是著名的“石林”。这里好吃的东西特别多，我的最爱是傣家菜。傣族是云南的一个少数民族，他们的孔雀舞非常美。傣族还有一种乐器叫“葫芦丝”，声音很有特点，你一定会喜欢！

史蒂夫

于云南昆明

王玉：

你在美国一切都好吗？我现在在云南丽江，一个十分可爱的小城。在这里，生活可以很懒、很慢，时间似乎都停止了。要是你也在这儿就好了，我们可以一起享受阳光，一起发呆……

在丽江我碰到了一群又一群来自大城市的年轻人，他们常常提到的一个词是“慢生活”，你听说过吗？

史蒂夫

于云南丽江

阿曼达：

很久没有你的消息了，希望你回巴西后一切顺利！我现在在云南中甸，也就是传说中的“香格里拉”。这里的一切都带着藏族的宗教和文化色彩，跟外面的世界很不一样。明天我就要出发去梅里雪山了，心里非常激动。希望这座“神山”能给我带来好运气！

史蒂夫

于云南中甸

马克：

我在云南已经两个星期了，很多地方还来不及去，可惜今天就要离开了。这一趟印象最深的是骑马去梅里雪山背后的雨崩村。虽然有的地方路很窄，有点儿危险，我的高原反应也挺厉害，但是到雨崩之后，我觉得实在太值得了！竟然真的有这么一个世外桃源！

史蒂夫

于云南昆明机场

生词 New words

jìjié 季节	season	shífēn 十分	very	Zhōngdiàn 中甸	Zhongdian	Yǔbēng Cūn 雨崩村	Yubeng Village
wēnnuǎn-rúchūn 温暖如春	as warm as springtime	lǎn 懒	lazy	Xiānggélǐlā 香格里拉	Shangri-La	zhǎi 窄	narrow
Shílín 石林	the Stone Forest	sìhū 似乎	seemingly; as if	Zàngzú 藏族	Tibetan ethnic group	wēixiǎn 危险	dangerous; danger
zuì'ài 最爱	favourite	tíngzhǐ 停止	stop	sècǎi 色彩	colour	gāoyuán fǎnyìng 高原反应	altitude sickness
Dǎizú 傣族	Dai ethnic group	fādāi 发呆	stare blankly, daydream	jīdòng 激动	excite	jìngrán 竟然	surprisingly
kǒngquèwǔ 孔雀舞	peacock dance	qún 群	group, flock	shénshān 神山	holy mountain	shìwài-táoyuán 世外桃源	a Shangri-La
húlusī 葫芦丝	cucurbit flute	niánqīngrén 年轻人	young people	láibují 来不及	have no time		
shēngyīn 声音	sound, voice	tídào 提到	mention	tàng 趟	(for trips)		
tèdiǎn 特点	feature	xiāoxi 消息	news	qí 骑	ride (a horse/ a bike)		

5 Check the true statements.

☐ 1 昆明的冬天非常冷。

☐ 2 丽江的生活节奏吸引了很多老年人。

☐ 3 中甸和传说中的很不一样，这让史蒂夫觉得很激动。

☐ 4 去雨崩村的路有点儿危险。

☐ 5 云南值得去的地方太多了，史蒂夫觉得两个星期时间是不够的。

6 Complete the sentences.

“神山”指的是云南的梅里雪山，据说看见“神山”的人会有好运气。

1 “春城”指的是 ______________，因为这里 ______________________。

2 “慢生活”是说在 ______________ 那样的生活，可以 ______________。

3 “世外桃源”是指像 ______________ 那样的地方，也许很难找到，但很值得去。

7 Work in pairs. Write one sentence to highlight the main features of each place.

1 昆明 ______________________________

2 丽江 ______________________________

3 中甸 ______________________________

4 雨崩村 ____________________________

8 Write a travel journal for Steve's blog. Include the three places Steve mentions in his postcards that impress you most.

《云南游记》

- 到了哪些地方
- 遇到了什么人
- 有什么难忘的经历
- 心情怎么样
- 有什么感受

Language in use

Comparing 后来 and 然后

1 Look at the sentences.

Past event 1	后来 + past event 2
七年前，我到云南来旅游，来了就不想走了。	所以后来就辞职，搬到丽江来了。
我刚来的时候是在销售部，	但是后来发现自己更适合做客服。
大概三年前我在一次聚会上见过他，	后来就再也没见过他了。

Action 1	然后 + action 2
你等着，我去拿张地图，	然后给你说说你必须去的地方。
我们还是先去吃饭，	然后再去看电影吧。
她先抱了抱那个孩子，	然后又亲了亲他的小脸。

Now check the correct explanations.

☐ 1 后来 refers to a certain period of time long ago in the past.

☐ 2 后来 can only be used to give the sequence of past events. It is similar to "afterwards" or "later on" in English.

☐ 3 然后 is used together with 先，最后 to indicate the sequence of actions.

☐ 4 Both 后来 and 然后 can be used to indicate the sequence of actions in the future.

2 Work in pairs. Talk about the schools you went to using ……年以前……后来……再后来……现在…….

3 Work in pairs. Tell each other a simple recipe using 先……然后……最后…….

Expressing "no matter what / how / whether" with 无论/不论/不管……都……

1 Look at the sentences.

无论/不论/不管 + circumstances	都 + result
昆明无论什么季节	都是温暖如春。
这一时期的艺术无论是音乐还是绘画	都达到了前所未有的高度。
不论在哪个行业工作，	都应该认真负责。
不管是冬天还是夏天，	这里的游客都多得不得了。
不管你讨厌不讨厌她，	你都得去采访她。

Now check the correct explanations.

☐ 1 无论，不论 and 不管 mean "no matter what / how / whether", and appear in the first part of the sentence to introduce the circumstances.

☐ 2 都 appears in the second part of the sentence to emphasize that the result will not change.

☐ 3 无论，不论 and 不管 are always used with wh-questions, questions which offer "either ... or ..." alternatives (是 X 还是 Y), or questions in the "verb-not-verb" form.

☐ 4 The progression of the three in terms of formality is 无论，不论 and 不管. 无论 can only be used in colloquial speech, and 不管 only in formal writing.

2 Complete the sentences using 无论 / 不论 / 不管……都…….

1 ____________，都辛苦得不得了。

2 ____________，都得参加新生欢迎会。

3 无论是太阳能还是风能，____________。

4 无论是哪一门外语，____________。

Expressing tones with adverbs 原来, 果然, 竟然

1 Look at the sentences.

	原来
教室里这么热，	原来是空调坏了。
我听说你会说法文，	原来你不会啊。

	果然
听你的口音，我就觉得你是上海人，	我果然猜对了。
吃了朋友推荐的药以后，	他的病果然很快就好了。

	竟然
什么？	你竟然没见过熊猫？
只不过两年没见，	他竟然不记得我是谁了。

Now check the correct explanations.

☐ 1 原来 is used for recently discovered information. The tone is that of sudden realization.

☐ 2 果然 is used to indicate that the fact or the situation is unexpected from the speaker's point of view, or is an unusual situation.

☐ 3 竟然 is used to confirm that the fact indeed corresponds to the previous statement, assumption or expectation.

☐ 4 All three adverbs can only appear after the subject.

2 Complete the sentences with 原来, 果然 or 竟然.

1 天气预报说有暴风雪，______ 就下起雪来了。

2 早上还是晴天，没想到中午 ______ 下起雨来。

3 他学中文才一年就说得这么好，______ 是天天跟中国朋友聊天的结果。

4 这个学期一开学我就知道我会非常忙，______ 现在连吃午饭的时间都没有。

5 ______ 你一直在骗 (deceive) 我！我 ______ 相信了你这么多年，我真是太傻了！

Expressing personal judgments with 算(是)

1 Look at the sentences.

Topic	算(是) + judgment
你	算(是)问对人啦。
他不来麻烦我们	就算(是)帮了我们的忙了。
他只不过请我看了场电影，	不算(是)约会吧。
在我去过的地方中，西安	算(是)历史比较悠久的城市。
这个宾馆的条件	还算(是)比较好的。

Now check the correct explanations.

☐ 1 算 means "to be considered as" or "to count as". As a verb, it introduces the speaker's subjective judgment about a person, a thing or an event.

☐ 2 算 prevents a judgment, positive or negative, from sounding absolute.

☐ 3 Adverbs like 就, 也 and 还 often follow 算(是).

☐ 4 是 is optional.

2 Work in pairs and discuss the following questions.

1 一个只在网络上写文章、从来没出过一本书的人，能算是作家吗？

2 什么样的工作算是好工作？什么样的工作不算好工作？

3 怎样的生活方式才算是健康的生活方式？

Turn to page 195 for grammar reference.

LESSON 3

Communication activity

Work in groups of four.

Student A: You are an office worker who wants to quit their job, but you are not sure what to do next. Ask your friends for help. Listen to their suggestions and choose the best one.

Students B, C and D: You are friends of Student A. Each choose one idea from below, and explain to Student A why it is good.

1 Staying with the current job while searching for his/her genuine passion for life.
2 Taking one year off and travelling around the world.
3 Starting his/her own business.

Now act out a group conversation and present your solution to the class. Vote for the best one.

Turn to pages 175 and 181 for more speaking practice.

Cultural corner

Yunnan Province

Yunnan is a province located in the furthest southwestern part of China. Its capital and largest city is Kunming. The region is very mountainous and rich in natural resources, and there is a great diversity of plant life. 34% of Yunnan's population is made up of ethnic groups, the largest percentage among all Chinese provinces, with the Yi and Bai peoples being the most significant. The Old Town of Lijiang and the South China Karst are recognized as UNESCO World Heritage sites. Yunnan cuisine is a mixture of Han Chinese and ethnic ingredients and cooking styles, with emphasis on spices, plants and mushrooms. Yunnan also has several tea-growing regions that produce the famous Pu'er (普洱) tea.

Review and practice

1 Complete the sentences with the correct words in the box.

讨厌　似乎　放弃　名不虚传
怀疑　来不及

1 早就听说这家公司生产的产品质量非常好，果然 ______。
2 离演出开始只剩十五分钟了，你现在回去换衣服肯定 ______ 了。
3 他 ______ 一点儿也不在乎别人的看法。
4 你怎么能 ______ 像她这么诚实的人呢?
5 千万别让我唱歌，我最 ______ 唱歌了。
6 这个项目我们都研究了一年多了，现在怎么能 ______ 呢?

2 Complete the passage with the correct words in the box.

四季如春　值得　宗教　享受　传说
后悔　世外桃源　印象　特点　欣赏
地道　停止

云南有一个美称，叫"彩云之南"。云南 ______ 游览的地方特别多，每个地方都有自己的 ______。昆明是个 ______ 的城市，在这里你不仅能吃到 ______ 的傣家菜，而且还能 ______ 到优美的傣族舞。丽江是一个可以让你慢下来的小城，很多人都说在这里时间是 ______ 的；品茶、散步、聊天、发呆，要 ______ 生活，这里再好不过了。还有 ______ 中的"香格里拉"——中甸，这里是真正的 ______，如画的风景、神秘的雪山、独特的藏族 ______ 和文化，一定会给你留下最深的 ______。总之，来云南看一看吧，你一定不会 ______ 的。

3 Choose the correct words to complete the sentences.

1 —这些照片都是你拍的吗？太漂亮了！你真厉害！

—______，我也就是业余水平。

a 哪里哪里　b 可以可以　c 什么什么

2 他们正在办公室里开会，______停电了。

a 果然　b 忽然　c 然后

3 这个小区的房价虽然贵了一点儿，但是环境比我______中的好多了。

a 相信　b 想象　c 体会

4 ______多么难的项目，到了她的手里都变得容易了。

a 尽管　b 既然　c 不论

5 我忘了借一本书，还得再去一______图书馆。

a 趟　b 家　c 场

4 Read the microblog entry and answer the questions.

主页 博文 关于我

我的微博

个人资料

关注(1260)

粉丝(1820)

相册(5)

不实信息曝光

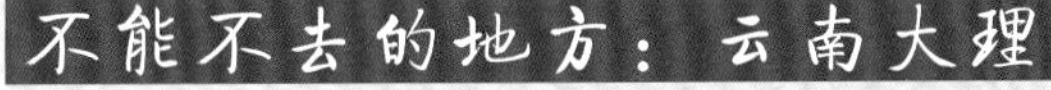

这里四季如春、风景如画。苍山的雪、洱海的月、五颜六色的山茶花、古朴优雅的大理古城，处处是绝美的风景。大理是白族的故乡，白族的歌舞、服饰、建筑、美食、传统节日，都是那么独特。如果说昆明让人觉得温暖，丽江让人觉得可爱，那么大理会让人觉得宁静而又浪漫。

1 什么季节适合去大理旅游？

2 大理有什么风景值得看？

3 白族有什么特点？

4 大理给人什么样的印象？

Now match the words with their meanings.

5 山茶花	a elegant
6 古朴	b camellia
7 优雅	c peaceful, tranquil
8 宁静	d of aged simplicity

5 Write an entry for a travel journal about the most impressive trip you have ever taken. Include:

- 你对那里的印象
- 那里的自然风景、文化特点、当地人的生活
- 你和在那里遇到的人的谈话
- 在那里难忘的事情或经历
- 你的心情和感受

Vocabulary review

Fill in the blanks.

爱好者	àihàozhě	*n.*	hobbyist, enthusiast, fan
白领	báilǐng	*n.*	white-collar worker
______	bìxū	*adv.*	must
程度	chéngdù	*n.*	degree
辞职	cízhí	*v.*	quit one's job
典型	diǎnxíng	*adj.*	typical
发呆	fādāi	*v.*	stare blankly, daydream
放弃	fàngqì	*v.*	______
风景如画	fēngjǐng-rúhuà		picturesque landscape
高原反应	gāoyuán fǎnyìng		altitude sickness
______	guǒrán	*adv.*	sure enough
后悔	hòuhuǐ	*v.*	______
______	hūrán	*adv.*	all of a sudden
怀疑	huáiyí	*v.*	______
激动	jīdòng	*v.*	excite
______	jìjié	*n.*	season
竟然	jìngrán	*adv.*	surprisingly
孔雀舞	kǒngquèwǔ	*n.*	peacock dance
来不及	láibují	*v.*	have no time
______	lǎn	*adj.*	lazy
名不虚传	míngbùxūchuán		live up to one's name
年轻人	niánqīngrén	*n.*	young people
啤酒	píjiǔ	*n.*	______
______	qí	*v.*	ride (a horse/a bike)
群	qún	*measure word*	group, flock
______	sècǎi	*n.*	colour
摄影	shèyǐng	*v./n.*	take a photograph; photography
神山	shénshān	*n.*	holy mountain
______	shēngyīn	*n.*	sound, voice

失眠	shīmián	*v.*	insomnia
十分	shífēn	*adv.*	______
实在	shízài	*adv.*	indeed, truly
世外桃源	shìwài-táoyuán	*n.*	a Shangri-La
______	sìhū	*adv.*	seemingly; as if
趟	tàng	*measure word*	(for trips)
______	tǎoyàn	*v.*	dislike, loathe
特点	tèdiǎn	*n.*	______
提到	tídào	*v.*	mention
体会	tǐhuì	*v./n.*	experience
体面	tǐmiàn	*adj.*	decent, respectable
天堂	tiāntáng	*n.*	heaven
______	tíngzhǐ	*v.*	stop
危险	wēixiǎn	*adj./n.*	______
温暖如春	wēnnuǎn-rúchūn		as warm as springtime
享受	xiǎngshòu	*v.*	enjoy
想象	xiǎngxiàng	*v.*	______
______	xiāoxi	*n.*	news
原来	yuánlái	*adv.*	as it turns out to be
______	zhǎi	*adj.*	narrow
最爱	zuì' ài	*adv.*	favourite
傣族	Dǎizú	*n.*	Dai ethnic group
葫芦丝	húlusī	*n.*	cucurbit flute
昆明	Kūnmíng	*n.*	Kunming
丽江	Lìjiāng	*n.*	Lijiang
石林	Shílín	*n.*	the Stone Forest
香格里拉	Xiānggélǐlā	*n.*	Shangri-La
雨崩村	Yǔbēng Cūn	*n.*	Yubeng Village
云南	Yúnnán	*n.*	Yunnan Province
藏族	Zàngzú	*n.*	Tibetan ethnic group
中甸	Zhōngdiàn	*n.*	Zhongdian

Review 2

Vocabulary

1 Match the words to make phrases.

1 布置	a 上司
2 解决	b 会议
3 召开	c 问题
4 把握	d 机会
5 请示	e 任务
6 享受	f 生活

2 Circle the odd words out.

1 批评 威胁 怀疑 糟糕

2 诚恳 夸奖 佩服 答谢

3 附件 请柬 提纲 讲稿

4 合作 业务 沙发 友谊

5 高材生 爱好者 年轻人 讲信用

3 Complete the sentences with the idioms in the box.

名不虚传 尽力而为 世外桃源
心想事成 手忙脚乱

1 —事情太多了，实在让我 ______。
—没关系，你只要 ______ 就行了。

2 我刚去了新西兰的皇后镇 (Queenstown)，果然 ______，真是个 ______！

3 祝你新年快乐，______！

4 Choose the correct words to complete the sentences.

1 我要好好 ______ 我的假期。
a 享受 b 欣赏 c 表扬

2 我打算从今天开始 ______ 准备下个月的考试。
a 全体 b 完全 c 全力

3 你别怪他了！他不过是个小孩子罢了，当然会 ______ 祸。
a 犯 b 闯 c 做

4 我们希望能和贵公司有进一步的 ______。
a 配合 b 会议 c 合作

5 ______ 你告诉我这个方法，解决了我失眠的问题。
a 多亏 b 幸运 c 不然

6 你这个四川人 ______ 不能吃辣的！真是太奇怪了！
a 果然 b 竟然 c 实在

7 下面我们 ______ 一下公司在过去三年中取得的成绩。
a 回顾 b 复习 c 表达

5 Match the words with their opposites.

1 夸奖	a 安全
2 讨厌	b 批评
3 危险	c 喜欢
4 谦虚	d 怀疑
5 信任	e 宽
6 窄	f 骄傲

Grammar

1 Complete the sentences with the correct words.

1 他 ______ 能过春节都不回家呢？

a 怎么　　b 要不　　c 怎么样

2 昨天的暴风雪还不 ______ 严重，我们这儿每年冬天都有好几次暴风雪。

a 是　　b 算　　c 挺

3 你们 ______ 别以为安排行程很简单！

a 可是　　b 是　　c 可

4 在客服部实习，压力 ______ 是没有别的部门大，不过工资也比较少。

a 却　　b 不　　c 倒

5 我们的新产品看起来还是不错的，但 ______ 能不能让客户满意呢？

a 究竟　　b 还是　　c 毕竟

6 不管 ______ 高原反应，他都要去爬雪山。

a 有　　b 多么　　c 有没有

7 这本书对昆明的介绍 ______ 详细不过了。

a 再　　b 还　　c 更

8 ______ 他已经道歉了，你就原谅他吧。

a 既然　　b 虽然　　c 因为

2 Complete the sentences with the words in the box.

到底	后来	然后
原来	竟然	果然

1 A: 怎么可能？我们公司的订单 ______ 被取消了！______ 是怎么回事？

B: 现在还不清楚，马克正在问。

2 A: 我昨天很晚才下班，总算把欢迎宴会的事情安排好了。

B: 昨天加班的人 ______ 是你啊。

3 A: 咱们部门的例会怎么又变了？

B: 是啊，以前月初开，______ 改成月中开，最近又变成月末开。

4 A: 你知道吗，周详已经申请去销售部了。

B: 他 ______ 不喜欢在客服部啊。

5 A: 明天的例会什么流程？

B: 各组先汇报，______ 王经理做总结。

3 Complete the conversations with the words in brackets.

1 A: 什么季节到英国旅游比较好？

B: ____________________ (不论)

2 A: 我实习结束后会留在这家公司工作。

B: 你真厉害！____________________ (要是……就好了)

3 A: 我要不要把客户的意见告诉经理呢？

B: 我看你还是不要说了，____________________ (反正)

4 A: 我从来没去过云南，你去过吗？

B: 我去过两次。

A: ____________________ (既然……那……)

5 A: 我今天吃饭的时候想跟小张聊一聊，可是他好像根本不想跟我说话。

B: 你别生气，他这个人其实挺好的，____________________ (不过……罢了)

Integrated skills

1 Listen to the speech and choose the best answers to the questions.

1 发言的主要内容是 ______。

a 实习待遇

b 实习注意事项

c 实习工作前景

2 实习生应该 ______。

a 遵守上下班时间

b 多犯错误

c 尽量独立工作

3 实习期间表现优秀的实习生，会 ______。

a 有机会转为公司正式员工

b 拿更多加班工资

c 实习愉快

2 Listen again and complete the sentences.

1 发言的人叫 ______，是 ______ 部的。

2 虽然实习生的 ______ 很强，可是态度一定要 ______。

3 一名合格的员工，不但要能独立完成任务，还要有 ______，能和同事很好地 ______。

4 实习生不要怕 ______，开会的时候要积极 ______。

3 Work in pairs. Look at the pictures and make up a coherent story.

a

b

c

d

4 Complete the passage with the correct words in the box.

负责	无论	解决	谦虚	导致
请教	道歉	忙碌	好好	高材生
陪同	闯祸	合作	请示	做不完

在实习中，我学到的第一件重要的事情是：______。实习以前，我一直是学校

里的 ______，所以有一点儿骄傲。可是实习以后才知道，经验和知识是不一样的。工作中一定要多向前辈和同事 ______，遇到问题要向上司 ______，不能自己想怎么做就怎么做。

第二，要懂得 ______ 的重要性。工作中有太多事情是需要大家一起努力才能完成的。如果大家都能把自己 ______ 的事情做好，又能 ______ 配合，那么一切都会很顺利。

第三，别怕犯错。实习既 ______ 又充实，每天都有 ______ 的事情。有些事情比较容易，比方说订酒店、订机票、______ 客户参观工厂；而有些事情就非常复杂，比如为会议做翻译、为来访的代表团准备礼物等等。______ 是容易的事情还是复杂的事情，做得不好，都可能出错，甚至 ______。犯了错误，一定要想办法马上 ______。通过真诚的 ______ 求得上司或客户的谅解，不然只会 ______ 更严重的后果。

5 Look at the questions. Choose one and write a passage expressing your opinions.

1 如果“谦虚”意味着向别人请教，那别人会不会觉得这个人能力差？

2 如果跟你一起做事情的人没有合作精神，你会不会怪他？你会怎么办？

3 如果你做错了事，道了歉，别人却不愿意原谅你，你该怎么办？

Enjoy Chinese

恋：love, long for

忘：forget

感：feel; feeling

恨：hate, regret

Ancient Chinese people believed that the heart was the organ that dominated people's minds, and people use their hearts to think, feel and love. The 心 radical also has a variant form 忄, which is called the "vertical heart radical" and used as the left part of a character. Can you find 心 and 忄 in the following characters?

爱恋　志愿
忘怀　愉快
感恩　恐怕
悔恨　思想

Can you tell the difference between the simplified and traditional characters of "love"?

UNIT 9

Qiúzhī-bùdé
求之不得！
Only too glad to!

LESSON 1

Vocabulary and listening

1 Find pairs of opposites in the sentences.

1 谦虚使人进步，骄傲使人落后。
2 失败是成功之母。
3 输赢不是关键，重要的是参与。
4 比赛的日期马上就要到了，不知道现在报名还来得及来不及？

2 Work in pairs. Talk about the feelings of participants before and after a match or competition. Use the words in the box to help you.

比赛	获奖	赢	输	紧张	放松
担心	害怕	得意		谦虚	骄傲

Now ask and answer the questions.

1 如果参加一个比赛，是不是一定要赢？
2 比赛能够帮助参赛者提高水平吗？

3 Steve is having a video chat with Wang Yu. He shows her the photos he took in Yunnan. Listen and answer the questions.

1 史蒂夫为什么又黑又瘦？
2 王玉喜欢史蒂夫拍的照片吗？为什么？
3 史蒂夫为什么犹豫是否参加摄影比赛？

4 Check the true statements.

☐ 1 由于高原反应，史蒂夫进了医院。
☐ 2 史蒂夫不光用照相机拍照。
☐ 3 王玉不希望史蒂夫参加比赛。
☐ 4 史蒂夫最后决定参加比赛了。

王玉：史蒂夫，你看起来好像黑了，也瘦了。

史蒂夫：是不是也更帅了？

王玉：哈哈，还行吧。

史蒂夫：我刚从云南回来，那边温度不高，但紫外线很强。在梅里雪山的时候，我的高原反应很厉害，差点儿进了医院，所以现在又黑又瘦的。

王玉：好在你没事，否则就太不值了。

史蒂夫：就算生病也值啊！云南太让我流连忘返了！

王玉：那快发两张得意的照片给我看看。

史蒂夫：照相机里的照片我还没来得及整理，先给你发两张手机里的吧。

王玉：你拍的雪山，有一种让人安静的力量。

史蒂夫：如果亲眼看到，你会觉得更

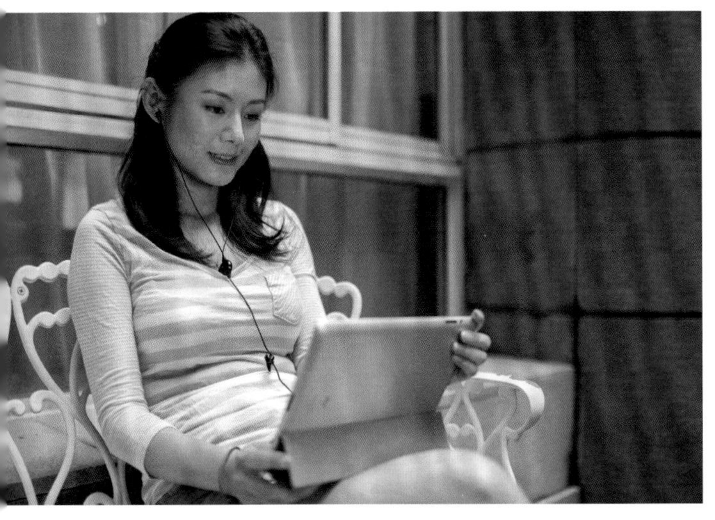

美。不过我这次拍的照片质量确实不错，不谦虚地说，快赶上专业摄影记者了。

王玉：是吗？那你可以试试给旅游杂志投稿啊。

史蒂夫：其实，我在考虑是否参加一个摄影比赛，主题就叫做"我看云南"。

王玉：多好的机会啊，你还有什么好犹豫的？

史蒂夫：截止日期快到了，我担心来不及选照片。再说，高手那么多，要得奖肯定很难。

王玉：你刚才不是还说自己够专业吗，怎么，害怕失败，不敢跟高手比了？

史蒂夫：我才不怕呢。输赢又不是关键，重在参与！

王玉：得了奖要请我吃饭！

史蒂夫：求之不得！

5 Choose all the possible answers to the questions.

1 史蒂夫为什么问"是不是也更帅了"？
- a 他觉得自己更帅了。
- b 他不确定自己是不是更帅了。
- c 他只是跟王玉开个玩笑。

2 史蒂夫对去云南有什么看法？
- a 如果会生病，云南就不值得去。
- b 即使会生病，云南也值得去。
- c 云南让他流连忘返。

3 哪句话是王玉夸奖史蒂夫的摄影水平的？
- a "你拍的雪山，有一种让人安静的力量。"
- b "我这次拍的照片质量确实不错……"
- c "……快赶上专业摄影记者了。"

生词 New words

hēi	黑	dark, tanned
wēndù	温度	temperature
zǐwàixiàn	紫外线	UV rays
chàdiǎnr	差点儿	nearly
hǎozài	好在	fortunately
fǒuzé	否则	otherwise
liúlián-wàngfǎn	流连忘返	enjoy so much as to not want to go home
déyì	得意	proud, pleased
zhàoxiàngjī	照相机	camera
láidejí	来得及	be able to make it in time
lìliàng	力量	power
qīnyǎn	亲眼	with one's own eyes
zhìliàng	质量	quality
gǎnshàng	赶上	catch up
zázhì	杂志	magazine, periodical
tóugǎo	投稿	submit for publication
yóuyù	犹豫	hesitate
jiézhǐ rìqī	截止日期	deadline
déjiǎng	得奖	win an award
hàipà	害怕	be afraid of, fear
shībài	失败	fail
gǎn	敢	dare
shū	输	lose
guānjiàn	关键	key, crux
cānyù	参与	participate in
qiúzhī-bùdé	求之不得	all that one could wish for

6 You are going to hear a conversation between two amateur photographers. Look at the statements they make and predict what they are talking about.

- "我对色彩的运用的确有我的理解。"
- "我觉得技术比器材更重要。"

Now listen and choose the correct words to complete the sentences.

1 对于女士的夸奖，男士表现得 ______。
 a 不谦虚 b 不接受 c 很得意

2 "对摄影爱好者来说，天气就像空气和水一样"，这句话的意思是 ______。
 a 天气是多变的
 b 好天气是必需的因素
 c 天气是大自然决定的

3 女士认为，要想成为摄影高手，应 ______。
 a 努力提高摄影技术水平
 b 在博客上写摄影方面的文章
 c 买很贵的高级摄影器材

7 Listen again and complete the table.

影响摄影的因素	为什么重要
1 颜色	
2	如果 ______ 不好，______
3 器材	
4	一个摄影的人，如果水平很高，不管 ______

Now work in pairs. Check your answers and talk about what you think are the most important factors for taking a photograph.

Pronunciation and speaking

1 Listen to the sentences. Notice how they imply either encouragement or confidence.

1 快发两张得意的照片给我看看。
2 不过我这批照片质量确实不错，不谦虚地说，快赶上专业摄影记者了。
3 我对色彩运用有我的理解。
4 得了奖要请我吃饭！

Now read aloud. Make sure you use the correct intonation.

2 Work in pairs. Complete the conversations with encouragement or confidence.

1 **A:** 我假期去旅游了，写了好几篇博客，还有照片。
 B: ______________________

2 **A:** 真没想到你做菜做得这么好。
 B: ______________________

3 **A:** 下个星期五我们要给客户举办一个欢迎宴会。选酒店，你负责，行吗？
 B: ______________________

4 **A:** 我们足球队马上就要去比赛了，祝我们好运吧。
 B: ______________________

3 Work in pairs. Talk about the benefits of taking part in a competition.

CHINESE TO GO

2-16

Daring responses

Wǒ cái bú pà ne 我才不怕呢。	I'm not scared at all.
Qiúzhī-bùdé 求之不得！	Only too glad to!

LESSON | 2

Reading and writing

1 Look at the meanings of the characters and complete the word map with the meanings of the words.

获 win	奖 award
参 take part in	赛 match, competition

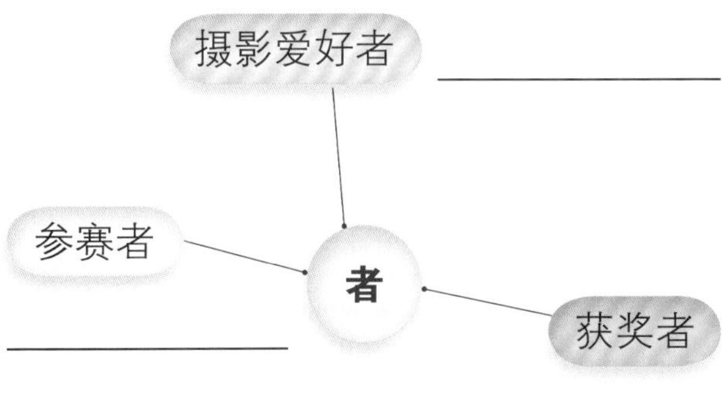

Now work in pairs. Write as many words with 者 as possible.

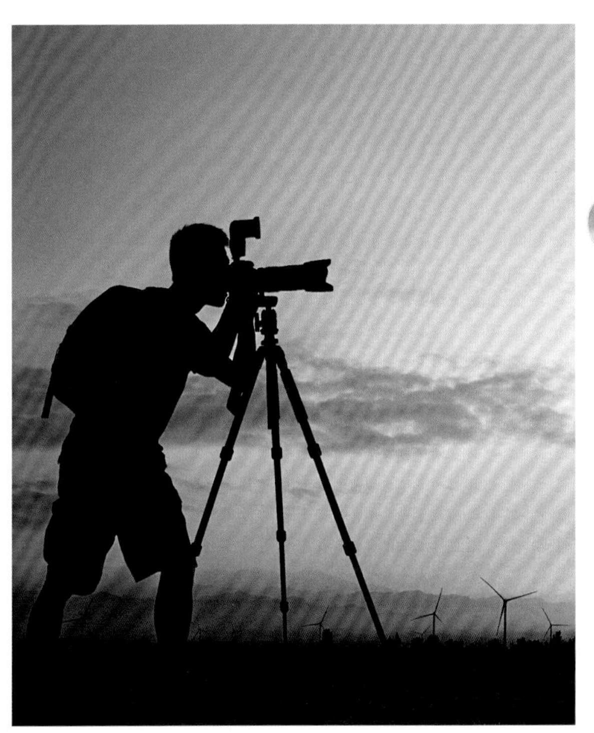

2 Match the formal expressions with their meanings.

1 须	a 是
2 为	b 没有
3 未	c 到
4 至	d 都
5 均	e 必须
6 起	f 还有
7 及	g 开始

Now make sentences with two pairs of the expressions.

所有的老师和学生都必须准时出席开学仪式。

全体师生均须准时参加开学仪式。

3 Match the words to make phrases.

1 发表	a 责任
2 展现	b 证书
3 举办	c 作品
4 颁发	d 魅力
5 承担	e 比赛

Now make sentences using three of the phrases.

4 Read the announcement about the photography competition on page 124 and write down the reasons why the competition is being held.

举办摄影比赛的目的：

1 ______

2 ______

3 ______

"我看云南"摄影比赛征稿启事

为向广大旅游摄影爱好者提供交流摄影作品的平台，通过摄影作品展现云南的魅力，推动云南省旅游业的发展，《云南旅游》杂志社和云南摄影家协会决定联合举办主题为"我看云南"的摄影比赛。

一、活动时间

1 投稿：即日起至2014年7月31日截止

2 评审：投稿截止后三周

3 结果公布：《云南旅游》2014年9月刊

二、征稿办法

1 比赛面向所有摄影爱好者。

2 作品须为2013年6月之后在云南拍摄，风格不限。

3 每人限投照片6张，每张照片须有名称和拍摄信息，包括拍摄时间、地点和照片的内容。

4 参赛者须寄送纸版照片，入选后按要求寄送电子版。照片须为原始图像，未做任何修改。

5 作品须为未发表过的原创作品。作品的一切法律责任由投稿者本人承担，参赛者须同意并遵守以上规定。

三、奖项设置

一等奖：1名，奖金5000元

二等奖：5名，奖金2000元

三等奖：10名，奖金500元

全部获奖者将获得由云南摄影家协会颁发的证书及《云南旅游》2015年全年杂志。

四、投稿地址

云南省昆明市《云南旅游》杂志社

"我看云南"大赛项目组收

邮政编码：650000

参赛者请写明姓名和联系方式。

云南摄影家协会

《云南旅游》杂志社

2014年5月15日

生词 New words

zhēnggǎo 征稿	solicit contributions	zhǐbǎn 纸版	hard copy
qǐshì 启事	notice, announcement	diànzǐbǎn 电子版	electronic version
guǎngdà 广大	numerous, enormous	yuánshǐ 原始	raw, original, primitive
zuòpǐn 作品	works	túxiàng 图像	image
píngtái 平台	platform	xiūgǎi 修改	revise; revision
zhǎnxiàn 展现	unfold, display	fābiǎo 发表	publish (original work)
mèilì 魅力	charm, charisma, glamour	yuánchuàng 原创	original, creative
tuīdòng 推动	push forward, promote	chéngdān 承担	bear, assume
lǚyóuyè 旅游业	tourism	jiǎngxiàng 奖项	prize
xiéhuì 协会	association	shèzhì 设置	set up
liánhé 联合	united, joint	jiǎngjīn 奖金	prize money, bonus
jírì 即日	this very day	huòdé 获得	win, acquire
píngshěn 评审	judge, grade, review	bānfā 颁发	award, confer, issue
gōngbù 公布	make publicly known, announce	zhèngshū 证书	certificate
kān 刊	issue (periodical)	yóuzhèng 邮政 biānmǎ 编码	postal code
miànxiàng 面向	be geared towards		
fēnggé 风格	style		

5 Choose all the correct answers to the questions.

1 这个比赛应该在什么时候投稿？
  a 七月　b 八月　c 九月

2 哪组照片不能参加比赛？
  a 2012年2月在云南拍的照片
  b 2013年11月在云南拍的照片
  c 2013年9月在内蒙古拍的照片

3 哪组照片可以参加比赛？
  a 以前参加过别的比赛，但是没得奖也没在杂志上出现过的照片。
  b 以前参加过比赛，得了奖也在杂志上出现过的照片。
  c 以前没参加过比赛，也没在杂志上出现过的照片。

4 如果照片出了法律问题，谁承担责任？
  a 参赛者本人
  b 云南摄影家协会
  c 《云南旅游》杂志社

5 二等奖会得到什么奖品？
  a 证书　b 500元奖金　c 2000元奖金
  d 5000元奖金　e 一年的《云南旅游》杂志

6 Find the sentences in the announcement with the same meanings.

1 为了让许许多多喜欢旅游摄影的人有展示、互相交流照片的机会……
2 投稿日期从现在开始到2014年7月31日。
3 照片应该是去年六月以后在云南照的，什么风格都可以。
4 参加比赛的人必须同意上面提到的规定，而且也要遵守这些规定。

7 Write an email to a photographer friend and encourage him/her to take part in a photo competition. Include:

- 你认为他/她满足参赛的条件
- 你相信他/她的摄影水平
- 参加这个比赛的好处
- 你对他/她的鼓励

Language in use

Expressing "seem to be" with 看起来

1 Look at the sentences.

Subject	看起来	Predicate
你	看起来	好像黑了，也瘦了。
那个地方的人	看起来	都很友好。
这件衣服	看起来	不如那件漂亮。
他	看起来	挺老的，其实才30多岁。
她	看起来	和你差不多高。

Now check the correct explanations.

☐ 1 看起来 is used to express "it looks like ..." or "somebody / something seems to be ...".

☐ 2 The subject should follow 看起来.

☐ 3 The predicate after 看起来 indicates what the subject appears to be like.

☐ 4 Usually the predicate contains adjectives which may appear with adverbs of degree or in different comparative structures.

☐ 5 看起来 has a connotation of objective descriptions and comparisons; therefore it does not indicate how the observer feels.

2 Work in pairs. Compare two things using 看起来.

Expressing "nearly" with 差点儿

1 Look at the sentences.

	差点儿	(就)+verb phrase
在梅里雪山的时候，我	差点儿	进了医院。
他昨天晚上睡觉的时候	差点儿	从床上掉下去。
我们	差点儿	就误会了她。
他跟我下棋的时候	差点儿	赢了我。
我们跟广州那家公司的生意	差点儿	就谈成了。

Now check the correct explanations.

☐ 1 差点儿 literally means "differing a little bit". It is an adverb and means "nearly", expressing that an event or action almost happened (but did not).

☐ 2 Since 差点儿 is used to describe something which has already occurred, 就 and 了 often appear with the affirmative forms of the verb phrases that are modified by 差点儿.

☐ 3 If the action or event is good and desired by the subject, 差点儿 implies that "it nearly happened, and it was a pity that it didn't".

☐ 4 If the action or event is bad and not desired by the subject, 差点儿 implies that "it nearly happened but luckily it didn't".

2 Choose the correct results for each of the statements.

1 我差点儿忘了做功课。
 a 我忘了做功课。 b 我没忘做功课。

2 她差点儿就喝醉了。
 a 她喝醉了。 b 她没喝醉。

3 昨天他排队排了一个多小时，差点儿就买到电影票了。
 a 他买到了电影票。 b 他没买到电影票。

Exclamations with 多……啊

1 Look at the sentences.

	多 + adj. ……（啊）	
	多好的机会啊，	别犹豫了！
所以说天气因素	多重要啊。	
	多可爱的小猫，	我们把它抱回家吧。
他每个周末都在家呆着，哪儿也不去，	多无聊！	
这里的风景	多美啊！	太值了！

Now check the correct explanations.

☐ 1 多 and 啊 are used together to intensify an adjective. This forms an exclamation and expresses a strong feeling on behalf of the speaker.

☐ 2 Adjectives or noun phrases that are modified by adjectives should be placed between 多 and 啊.

☐ 3 In this structure, 多 is optional, but 啊 is not.

☐ 4 多……啊 is usually used in oral expressions when the speaker expresses feelings or impressions about something.

2 Complete the conversations with 多……啊.

1 —请进，随便坐吧。屋子有点儿乱，不好意思啊。
—____________________

2 —____________________
—是啊，要是每天天气都能这样就好了。

3 —她的父母嫌她的男朋友年龄大，想让他们分手。
—开什么玩笑？____________

4 —你看，马克新买的自行车，才三百块，____________
—是够便宜的，我也想买一辆。

Expressing "whether or not" with 是否

1 Look at the sentences.

	是否	Verb phrase
我在考虑	是否	参加那个摄影比赛。
他们还在犹豫	是否	要跟我们公司合作。
你	是否	觉得我们都对他很不客气？
经历了这么多困难，你	是否	还相信这个世界是美好的？
我不去想我	是否	能够成功；我只努力把每一件事情做好。

Now check the correct explanations.

☐ 1 是否 means "whether or not".

☐ 2 是否 is used either in a question or in a clause that serves as the object of verbs like 考虑, 犹豫 or 想.

☐ 3 是否 is always placed before the verb phrases that it modifies.

☐ 4 是否 is interchangeable with 是不是.

☐ 5 是否 is usually used in formal written language.

2 Work in pairs. Translate the following wedding vows into formal Chinese.

（妻子、丈夫、婚姻、是否、无论……都……）

1 X, are you willing to take Y to be your husband?
2 Y, are you willing to take X to be your wife?
3 Do you promise to be true to her/him in good times and in bad, in sickness and in health, to love her/him and honour her/him all the days of your life?
4 Is this both of your understanding of marriage?

Turn to page 197 for grammar reference.

LESSON 3

Communication activity

1 Work in groups of four as editors of a photography magazine. Discuss an announcement to solicit contributions for four columns of your magazine from writers and photographers. Include:

- themes of the columns;
- deadlines for submissions;
- requirements for submissions of both photography and articles;
- compensation for accepted submissions;
- address for submissions.

2 Present your announcement to the whole class and vote for the best one.

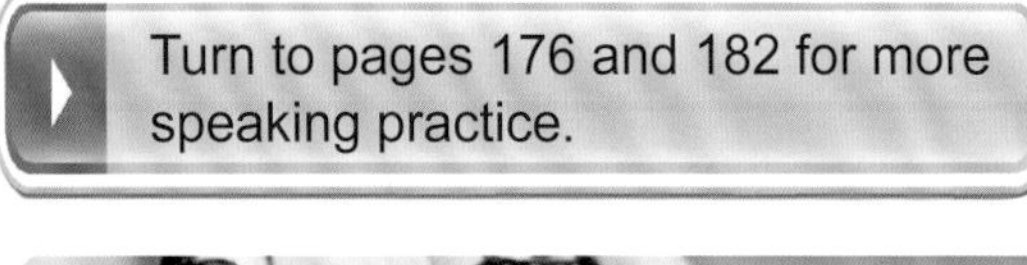
Turn to pages 176 and 182 for more speaking practice.

Review and practice

1 Complete the sentences with the correct words in the box.

得意　亲眼　赶上　犹豫　充分　公布

1 我还在 ______ 是选历史专业，还是法律专业。
2 今年获得奖学金的学生名单将在明天 ______。
3 我哥哥的学习、运动、工作，样样都特别厉害，我是不可能 ______ 他了。
4 他刚才在路上给几个中国人指路，他们说他中文好，他现在可 ______ 了。
5 他新建的房子特别棒，温度、光线、电器都可以用声音控制。你一定要 ______ 看一看。
6 客户可以在 ______ 了解产品信息以后再决定买不买。

Cultural corner

Four-character idioms in Chinese

Four-character idioms abound in Chinese, and account for more than 95% of all Chinese idioms. Though many are quite ancient, they remain frequent in modern Chinese, where they can emphasize a point, give a vivid description, or lend a more literary or formal touch. The sources of such idioms include ancient scripts (see 名不虚传), historical events (see 后顾之忧), parables (see 南辕北辙), metaphors (see 风景如画) and folk wisdom. A four-character idiom can be a noun phrase, a verb phrase, or an adjective phrase, but it is completely fixed in its structure, and changes cannot be made to any part of it. Because four-character idioms are fixed in structure, rich in meaning, and loaded with historical references—and because there are so many of them—they are very hard for learners of Chinese to become proficient in.

2 Choose the correct words to complete the sentences.

1 我觉得什么钱都可以省，只有吃饭的钱 ______ 不能省。
   a 果然　b 绝对　c 竟然

2 他的手机和小王的一样，他 ______ 就把小王的手机拿走了。
   a 差不多　b 差点儿　c 几乎

3 —听说你的车被撞了。你没事吧？
   —没事，______ 撞我的那辆车车速不快，我没受什么伤，不过我的车得修一修。
   a 好像　b 好在　c 正好

4 周末是我好朋友的婚礼，可是我得加班，不能 ______ 她的婚礼。
   a 参加　b 参与　c 参观

5 —明天晚上我们组的人要一起去唱卡拉OK。你有没有兴趣一起去啊？
   —______！
   a 尽力而为　b 心想事成　c 求之不得

3 Complete the passage with the correct words in the box.

写明	害怕	关键	寄送	通过
电子版	证书	发表	风格	奖金
面向	展示	表现		

摄影比赛

我参加过各种各样的摄影比赛。这些比赛一般都会 ______ 所有的摄影爱好者。参赛者要向比赛提交多张照片，还要 ______ 每张照片的拍摄信息，包括拍摄时间、地点和照片要 ______ 的主题等等。虽然很多比赛 ______ 不限，但是参赛者必须使用未 ______ 过的原创作品。随着科技的发展，越来越多的比赛已经不再要求参赛者 ______ 纸质照片了，而只需要 ______ 照片。很多比赛奖品丰厚，除了获奖 ______ 以外，还会有 ______ 和其他奖品。有的人可能 ______ 失败，不敢参加比赛。其实我觉得比赛输赢并不是 ______，重在参与。这些比赛不但向广大摄影爱好者提供了 ______ 作品的平台，而且也让大家 ______ 比赛提高了摄影水平。

Now check the true statements.

☐ 1 不是所有的摄影比赛都允许任何摄影爱好者参加。
☐ 2 这些比赛对照片是否为原创没有要求。
☐ 3 很多比赛都既要求纸质照片也要求电子版照片。
☐ 4 比赛并不能帮助摄影爱好者提高摄影水平。

4 Write an announcement about a Chinese speech contest next year. Include the following:

中文演讲比赛通知

- 比赛的主题
- 目的及组织者
- 比赛时间
- 比赛办法
- 奖项设置
- 组织者的联系方式

Vocabulary review

Fill in the blanks.

颁发	bānfā	*v.*	award, confer, issue
参与	cānyù	*v.*	participate in
差点儿	chàdiǎnr	*adv.*	nearly
承担	chéngdān	*v.*	bear, assume
得奖	déjiǎng	*v.*	______
得意	déyì	*adj.*	proud, pleased
电子版	diànzǐbǎn	*n.*	electronic version
______	fābiǎo	*v.*	publish (original work)
风格	fēnggé	*n.*	______
______	fǒuzé	*conj.*	otherwise
______	gǎn	*v.*	dare
赶上	gǎnshàng	*v.*	catch up
公布	gōngbù	*v.*	make publicly known, announce
关键	guānjiàn	*adj.*	key, crux
广大	guǎngdà	*adj.*	numerous, enormous
______	hàipà	*v.*	be afraid of, fear
好在	hǎozài	*adv.*	fortunately
黑	hēi	*adj.*	______
获得	huòdé	*v.*	win, acquire
即日	jírì	*n.*	this very day
奖金	jiǎngjīn	*n.*	______
奖项	jiǎngxiàng	*n.*	prize
截止日期	jiézhǐ rìqī		deadline
刊	kān	*n.*	issue (periodical)
来得及	láidejí	*v.*	be able to make it in time
______	lìliàng	*n.*	power
联合	liánhé	*adj.*	united, joint
流连忘返	liúlián-wàngfǎn		enjoy so much as to not want to go home
旅游业	lǚyóuyè	*n.*	tourism
魅力	mèilì	*n.*	charm, charisma, glamour
面向	miànxiàng	*v.*	be geared towards
平台	píngtái	*n.*	platform
评审	píngshěn	*v.*	judge, grade, review
启事	qǐshì	*n.*	notice, announcement
亲眼	qīnyǎn	*adv.*	______
求之不得	qiúzhī-bùdé		all that one could wish for
设置	shèzhì	*v.*	set up
______	shībài	*v.*	fail
输	shū	*v.*	______
投稿	tóugǎo	*v.*	submit for publication
图像	túxiàng	*n.*	image
推动	tuīdòng	*v.*	push forward, promote
______	wēndù	*n.*	temperature
协会	xiéhuì	*n.*	association
修改	xiūgǎi	*v./n.*	______
犹豫	yóuyù	*v.*	hesitate
邮政编码	yóuzhèng biānmǎ		postal code
原创	yuánchuàng	*v.*	original, creative
原始	yuánshǐ	*adj.*	raw, original, primitive
杂志	zázhì	*n.*	______
展现	zhǎnxiàn	*v.*	unfold, display
照相机	zhàoxiàngjī	*n.*	camera
征稿	zhēnggǎo	*v.*	solicit contributions
证书	zhèngshū	*n.*	certificate
纸版	zhǐbǎn	*n.*	hard copy
______	zhìliàng	*n.*	quality
紫外线	zǐwàixiàn	*n.*	UV rays
作品	zuòpǐn	*n.*	______

UNIT 10

Zhège tímù shì bú shì tài dà le
这个题目是不是太大了？

Isn't this topic too broad?

LESSON 1

Vocabulary and listening

1 Work in pairs. Talk about the topics below and order them in terms of difficulty for use in a speech.

a 为什么学中文
b 科技发展与现代生活
c 网络对生活的影响
d 金钱可以带来幸福吗

2 Look at the meanings of the words and complete the sentences.

1	看来看去: look back and forth 想来想去: think about something over and over 走来走去: walk to and from	The meaning of ……来……去 is ________.
2	说出来: speak (it) out 走出来: walk out 拿出来: take (it) out	The meaning of ……出来 is ________.
3	说下去: go on speaking 做下去: continue to work on (it) 听下去: keep on listening	The meaning of ……下去 is ________.

3 Yeong-min and Xiaowen are planning the upcoming contests for the campers. Listen to their conversation and answer the questions.

1 永民和小文在讨论什么事情？
2 小文想出了几个题目？永民觉得这些题目怎么样？
3 永民为什么觉得“金钱可以带来幸福吗”这个题目好？
4 永民觉得小文的性格怎么样？

永民：这里挺凉快的，咱们坐这儿吧。

小文：好的。永民，演讲和辩论赛的题目，我想来想去才想出来三个。第一个是“我为什么学中文”，这对夏令营的同学来说应该不算太难，他们肯定有话可说。

永民：但是有话可说并不能保证他们一定感兴趣。咱们的题目得让参赛的同学愿意说、观众也愿意听才行。你还想出了什么题目？

小文：第二个题目是“科技发展与现代生活”。你觉得怎么样？

永民：这个题目是不是太大了？即使同学们有想法，也不见得能用中文说清楚。稍微具体一些比较好吧。

小文：那第三个题目挺具体的：“网络对生活的影响”。我记得开营那天，有几个同学知道没什么机会上网，好像很失望。这个题目还不错吧？

永民：嗯，的确比前两个好多了，不过……

小文：哎呀，这也不行，那也不行，这么讨论下去三天也弄不出个结果！

永民：小文，你先别急，听我说完。我觉得这个作演讲比赛的题目很不错，但作为辩论赛的题目还不够有争议性。

小文：这倒是没错。有了！这个怎么样："金钱可以带来幸福吗？"

永民：你真聪明！这个问题什么样的回答都有可能，也没有固定的结论，不管什么立场都有话可说，我看行！

小文：真的？对不起啊永民，我的脾气挺坏的……

永民：我跟你的看法相反，我觉得你的性格直来直去，有什么说什么，挺可爱的！

4 **Match the topics with Yeong-min's comments.**

1 "我为什么学中文"

2 "科技发展与现代生活"

3 "网络对生活的影响"

a 同学们有话可说

b 同学们可能不感兴趣

c 观众不一定愿意听

d 题目太大了

e 同学们很难用中文说清楚

f 不够有争议性

生词 New words

liángkuai 凉快	nice and cool	shīwàng 失望	disappointed
yǎnjiǎng 演讲	speech	nòng 弄	manage to get
biànlùn 辩论	debate	zhēngyìxìng 争议性	argumentativeness
……lái 来 ……qù 去	(doing something) over and over	jīnqián 金钱	money
		huídá 回答	answer
bǎozhèng 保证	guarantee	gùdìng 固定	fixed
jíshǐ 即使	even if	jiélùn 结论	conclusion
xiǎngfǎ 想法	ideas, thoughts	lìchǎng 立场	standing, position
bújiàndé 不见得	not necessarily	huài 坏	bad
shāowēi 稍微	slightly	xiāngfǎn 相反	opposite

5 Work in pairs. List the aspects that Yeong-min thinks should be considered when choosing topics for the debate.

6 Look at the table and predict what you are going to hear.

Now listen and complete the table.

	辩题：________	
	正方 the Affirmative	反方 the Negative
1	金钱可以买到 ________	
2		表达感情 ________
3	金钱越多，经历越多，快乐也越多。	
4		没有钱也可以帮助别人。

7 Listen again and choose the correct answers to the questions.

1 金钱买不到什么？
   a 亲情　b 友情　c 爱情

2 哪件事情不花钱也可以做到？
   a 去电影院看电影
   b 去很远的地方旅行
   c 看一本从图书馆借的书

3 什么事情可能不会让人感到快乐？
   a 满足自己的需要
   b 有新鲜的、特别的经历
   c 帮助别人

4 正方觉得反方实际上讨论的是哪个问题？
   a 没有金钱也可以快乐
   b 金钱不能带来快乐
   c 金钱可以带来快乐

Now listen again and check.

Pronunciation and speaking

2-20

1 Listen to the sentences expressing disagreement or objection.

1 但是有话可说并不能保证他们一定感兴趣。
2 这个题目是不是太大了？即使同学们有想法，也不见得能用中文说清楚。
3 这个的确比前两个好多了，不过作为辩论赛的题目还不够有争议性。
4 我跟你的看法相反。
5 你说的有一定道理，可是帮助别人有很多种方法，不一定都需要钱。

Now listen again and repeat.

2 Make appropriate responses to the following statements. Use the underlined words from Activity 1.

1 照顾小孩子，最重要的是让他们吃得健康，身体好。
2 他已经学了三年英文了，去英国生活肯定没问题。
3 我觉得在现代社会中男人比女人更辛苦。

3 Write four main points to support your response to one of the statements in Activity 2.

Now work in pairs and exchange your ideas.

CHINESE TO GO

2-21

Responses to frustrations

Zhè yě bù xíng　nà yě bù xíng
这也不行，那也不行！
Nothing works!

Yǒu le　Zhège zěnmeyàng
有了！这个怎么样？
I've got a new idea! How about this one?

Wǒ kàn xíng
我看行！
I like this one!

LESSON 2

Reading and writing

1 Work in pairs. Talk about your own experience of social networking. Use the words to help you.

登录	社交网站	更新状态
消息	陌生人	评价

2 Match the words with their opposites.

1 亲近	a 熟悉
2 陌生	b 有趣
3 无聊	c 疏远
4 结束	d 开始
5 具体	e 个人
6 集体	f 大概

Now talk about social networking using the words.

—我觉得社交网络会让人们变得更亲近。
—我不这么想，我认为它让人们变得疏远。

3 Look at the words and the sentences.

安静 → 安安静静地

图书馆里非常安静。

他坐在那里安安静静地看书。

Now make two sentences using each of the words in the box.

仔细　高兴　开心　舒服

4 Read the essay from the Summer Camp on page 136 and answer the questions.

1 为什么说"我"的生活离不开网络?
2 没有网络的夏天，"我"的生活发生了哪三个变化?
3 夏天结束的时候，"我"对网络的看法发生了什么变化?

暑期项目

输入关键字，如：获奖、夏令营

夏令营首页 | 活动风采 | 论坛 | 辩论赛 | 演讲赛 | 优秀作文

当前位置：| 第四届国际中学生夏令营优秀作文>网络和我

没有网络的夏天

过去我一直认为，互联网是我最好的朋友，有了网络我可以做任何事情。比方说，我几乎天天在网上看体育节目；每隔一段时间就登录社交网站更新自己的状态，顺便了解朋友们的最新消息；去饭馆吃饭以前先看看网上的评价；要去陌生的地方，会事先在网上查好地图；出远门之前，会在网上看天气、买机票、订酒店等等。

这次来北京参加夏令营，我住的地方不方便上网。我本来以为这个夏天一定会过得很无聊。然而夏令营结束的时候，我发现，没有网络虽然有一点儿不方便，可是我的生活也发生了很多积极的变化。

首先，我参加了很多集体活动，亲近大自然，跟同学和老师之间的交流也多了很多。这不但让我们建立了很深的感情，也让我的中文有了很大的进步。其次，由于发电子邮件和登录社交网站都不方便，所以我跟在美国的朋友们的联系方式主要是打电话，我还给他们寄了有中国特色的明信片。这让他们特别开心，因为他们能看到我亲笔书写的信息和祝愿。另外，由于不能上网听音乐、看视频，我反而多了很多时间可以安安静静地专心看书了。

这个夏天的经历使我明白，网络在给我们的生活带来很多方便的同时，也使我们与真实的世界疏远了很多。现在，虽然我的生活还是离不开网络，但是我不会把时间都浪费在网上。我不再让网络支配我的时间，而是要让它更好地为我服务。

在线用户

熊猫先生
+关注TA

小Q
+关注TA

人在中国
+关注TA

评论

一 祝贺你走出网络世界，走进现实生活！

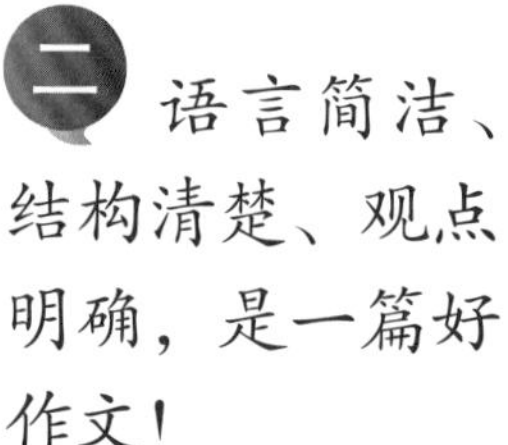
二 语言简洁、结构清楚、观点明确，是一篇好作文！

三 不再让网络限制生活，而是让它更好地为我们服务，这个结论太好了！

生词 New words

jiémù	节目	programme	qīnjìn	亲近	get close to
gé	隔	every other; separate	jiànlì	建立	establish
dēnglù	登录	log in	shēn	深	deep
shèjiāo	社交	socialize	gǎnqíng	感情	feelings
gēngxīn	更新	update	shìpín	视频	video clips
zhuàngtài	状态	status	fǎn' ér	反而	on the contrary
shùnbiàn	顺便	while you are at it, conveniently	zhuānxīn	专心	focused
píngjià	评价	review	shǐ	使	make
mòshēng	陌生	strange, unfamiliar	tóngshí	同时	at the same time
chūyuǎnmén	出远门	go far	shūyuǎn	疏远	alienate, become distant
yǐwéi	以为	assumed (incorrectly)	lí bù kāi	离不开	cannot do without
guò	过	spend	làngfèi	浪费	waste
wúliáo	无聊	boring	zhīpèi	支配	arrange, allocate
rán' ér	然而	however	fúwù	服务	serve; service
jítǐ	集体	group			

5 **Match the activities with when or how often they take place.**

1 看天气、买机票、订酒店	a 几乎天天在网上
2 看看网上的评价	b 每隔一段时间
3 看体育节目	c 去饭馆吃饭以前
4 登录社交网站	d 去陌生的地方之前
5 查好地图	e 出远门以前

6 **Choose all the correct answers to the questions.**

1 没有了网络，"我"觉得怎么样？
- a 很无聊
- b 有一点儿不方便
- c 生活变得更积极了

2 参加集体活动对"我"有什么好处？
- a 跟别人的交流变多了
- b 想念网络
- c 有了更多亲近大自然的机会

3 夏令营期间，"我"跟在美国的朋友们联系的时候，不用什么方式？
- a 打电话
- b 发电子邮件
- c 用社交网站

4 在夏令营期间，"我"把更多时间花在什么事情上？
- a 听音乐　b 看视频　c 看书

7 **Complete the passage.**

以前，我认为 ____________，有了网络 ____________。现在我明白了网络在 __________ 的同时，也使 ____________。以后，虽然我的生活还是 __________，但是我不会 ____________。

8 **Write a passage on the influence of the Internet on your life. Use examples to support your arguments. Include the following aspects:**

- 网络的好处
- 网络的坏处
- 网络生活和现实生活
- 离开网络，我的生活会怎样

Language in use

Continual repetition of an action with Verb 来 verb 去

1 Look at the sentences.

Subject	Verb 来 verb 去	Verb + complement + (object)
我	看来看去	也看不明白她写的是什么意思。
我	想来想去	才想出来三个题目。
他	找来找去	终于找到了那本书。
他	说来说去	也说不清楚去博物馆应该怎么走。
他们	商量来商量去，	终于商量出来一个办法。

Now check the correct explanations.

☐ 1 Verb 来 verb 去 is used to express continual repetition of an action.

☐ 2 来 and 去 have lost their meanings as indicators of direction, and instead indicate the performance of a certain action over and over again.

☐ 3 Very often a verb-complement structure follows Verb 来 verb 去 in order to indicate the result of the repeated action.

☐ 4 The complement can be either a resultative complement, or the negative form of a potential complement.

☐ 5 If there is an object of the verb, it should be inserted between the verb and its complement.

2 Work in pairs. Talk about the following experiences using ……来……去.

1 你碰到一个熟人，可是你忘了他/她的名字，你后来想起来他/她的名字了吗？

2 在你看过的书里，哪本书最难懂？

3 你给别人解释一件事情的时候，他们总是能明白你的意思吗？

Indicating a continuing action with the complement 下去

1 Look at the sentences.

	Verb(不)下去	
我们这么	讨论下去，	三天也讨论不出个结果。
这儿我一个人都不认识，要是继续	住下去，	我肯定会无聊死的。
不管多么困难，我们都要	坚持下去。	
这个演讲太无聊了，我	听不下去	了。
她说着说着哭起来，	说不下去	了。

Now check the correct explanations.

☐ 1 下去 literally means "going down". It can be used as a directional complement. It also has a more abstract meaning which indicates a continuing action.

☐ 2 As a complement, 下去 follows the action verb.

☐ 3 The negative form is 不 verb 下去, which means that the subject is not able to continue the action.

☐ 4 讨论下去 means "continue the discussion" while 讨论不下去 means "cannot continue the discussion".

2 Work in pairs. Ask and answer the questions.

1 你觉得跟谁讨论问题会讨论不下去？为什么？

2 你愿意在你现在的地方生活下去吗？

3 你认为最难坚持下去的三件事情是什么？

4 哪部电影或电视节目，你看了几分钟就看不下去了？

Talking about disposal of time/money/energy with 把

1 Look at the sentences.

Subject	把	Time/ money/ energy	Verb 在……上
我不会	把	时间	都浪费在网上。
他	把	时间	都花在打游戏上了。
你不能	把	钱	浪费在没有用的东西上。
父母希望	把	钱	用在孩子的教育上。
她	把	精力	都放在找工作上了。

Now check the correct explanations.

☐ 1 把……verb 在……上 is used to express how one disposes of one's time, money or energy.

☐ 2 The verb can only be 花, 用, or 浪费 in this structure.

☐ 3 The phrases that are inserted between 在……上 can be either nouns or verbs.

2 **Work in pairs and complete the conversation.**

A: 昨天我花了500块钱买游戏机，我的父母很不高兴。

B: 为什么？

A: 因为他们觉得 ______________ 很不值得。

B: 我同意你父母的看法。如果我是他们，我也会跟你说不要 ______________。

A: 可是我真的非常喜欢那个游戏机。

B: 我觉得你应该______________，或者______________。

Expressing "even if" with 即使……也……

1 Look at the sentences.

(即使) clause 1	(也) clause 2
即使他们有想法，	也不见得能用中文说清楚。
即使没时间参加她的生日聚会，	你也该给她发条短信祝她生日快乐。
即使明天下大雨，	我也要去看那个演出。
即使输掉了一切，	她也会微笑着面对。

Now check the correct explanations.

☐ 1 The conjunctive structure 即使……也…… means "even if …, still …". It is used to express that even if the condition in the first clause were realized, the situation in the second clause would not change.

☐ 2 即使 is placed at the beginning of the first clause.

☐ 3 If there is a subject in the second clause, it should be placed after 也.

☐ 4 即使……也…… has the same meaning and function as 就算……也……, but it is more formal than the latter.

☐ 5 即使 is different from 虽然 because 虽然 introduces a fact while 即使 introduces a hypothetical condition.

2 **Work in pairs. Ask each other how much you want your dream job.**

A: 你最想做的工作是什么？

B: 我最想______________。

A: 如果这个工作每天都得加班，你还做吗？

B: 即使______________，我也会做。

A: 如果______________，你还做吗？

B: 即使______________，我也会做。

A: 看来你真的喜欢这个工作。祝你美梦成真！

Turn to page 199 for grammar reference.

LESSON 3

Communication Activity

Work in groups of three. Brainstorm ideas for a business plan competition for students.

- **Student A:** You are creative. You come up with some ideas very quickly and discuss them with Students B and C. You show your impatience at times during the discussion.
- **Student B:** You are cautious and foresee risks and want to avoid pitfalls. You show your cautiousness at times in your discussion with Students A and B.
- **Student C:** You are a peacemaker. You weigh pros and cons and help Students A and B to reach an agreement.

Now present the process of your discussion and final plan to the class and vote for the best one.

Turn to pages 176 and 182 for more speaking practice.

Review and practice

1 Complete the sentences with the correct words in the box.

稍微	争议性	评价
积极	亲近	专心

1 她是这个时代最有 ______ 的人物，有人说她是艺术家，有人说她是个疯子。

2 我向总经理汇报了我对新项目的想法，可是他的反应好像不太 ______ 。

3 你别打电话了，开车的时候就要 ______ 开车，一边开车一边打电话多危险啊！

4 上个学期我的课特别多，每天都忙得不得了，这个学期 ______ 好一点儿了。

5 去动物园不但可以 ______ 动物，还可以学到很多知识。

6 人们对新经济政策 ______ 很差。

Cultural corner

The Four Great Inventions

Known as "The Four Great Inventions", the compass, gunpowder, papermaking and printing only became known in Europe hundreds of years after they were first invented in China. These inventions changed not only China, but eventually the whole world. Paper provided a convenient and cheap material for writing and recording human knowledge; the invention of printing spread knowledge faster and easier; the emergence of the compass led to a boom in maritime exploration; and the invention of gunpowder brought modern war. The Four Great Inventions represent the scientific and technological advantage that the Chinese enjoyed over other civilizations for many centuries. However, while Europe was going through a scientific revolution in the 16th and 17th centuries, the development of science and technology in China had already stagnated, and China eventually fell behind.

2 **Complete the sentences with the correct words.**

1 我觉得她很眼熟，可是想来想去也 ______ 在哪儿见过她。

a 想不出来　b 想不起来　c 想不下去

2 我一定要去爬梅里雪山，______ 高原反应可能会让我住院，我也不能错过这次机会。

a 既然　b 虽然　c 即使

3 在比赛中那些最想赢的人 ______ 很容易输。

a 反正　b 反而　c 然而

4 要是每天都能有一段时间安安静静 ______ 看看书就好了。

a 地　b 的　c 得

5 这次的旅行 ______ 让我体会到了大自然的魅力。

a 经验　b 经历　c 经过

3 **Put the following sentences into the correct order.**

手机病

____ a 什么是手机病？这是一种只有现代人才会得的病。

____ b 你可能有这样的经历，跟朋友一起吃饭的时候，大家不是在热闹地聊天儿，而是都低着头忙着看自己的手机。

____ c 你用手机查邮件、看电子书、听音乐，甚至拍下每顿饭的照片再上传到网上。

____ d 手机在为你服务的同时，也限制了你的生活。没错，你已经得了很严重的"手机病"。

____ e 得了这种病的人一离开手机就会觉得很紧张，他们必须一直把手机拿在手里或者放在身边，并且每隔几分钟都要看一看是不是有电话、有短信或者有别的信息需要查看。

____ f 你的室友就住在你的隔壁房间，可是你们并不面对面地交流，而是用发短信的方式告诉对方这个星期该你打扫卫生了。

____ g 要是有一天你的手机不小心丢了，你会非常难过，因为你的生活真的不能没有手机。

Now answer the following questions.

1 什么是"手机病"？得了这种病的人有什么表现？

2 哪些例子能说明现代人得了"手机病"？

3 请根据这些例子检查一下，你自己是不是也得了"手机病"？你的"手机病"严重吗？

4 你觉得手机限制了你的生活还是让你的生活更方便了？

4 **Write down your argument with supporting examples for the topic below.**

题目：金钱可以带来快乐吗

- 我的看法 ______________________
- 我的例子（正，反）

1 ______________________

2 ______________________

3 ______________________

Now write a complete passage to demonstrate your points.

Vocabulary review

Fill in the blanks.

保证	bǎozhèng	*v.*	________
辩论	biànlùn	*v.*	debate
不见得	bújiàndé	*adv.*	not necessarily
出远门	chūyuǎnmén		go far
登录	dēnglù	*v.*	________
反而	fǎn' ér	*adv.*	on the contrary
____	fúwù	*v./n.*	serve; service
感情	gǎnqíng	*n.*	________
隔	gé	*v.*	every other; separate
更新	gēngxīn	*v.*	update
固定	gùdìng	*adj.*	fixed
____	guò	*v.*	spend
坏	huài	*adj.*	________
____	huídá	*v./n.*	answer
____	jíshǐ	*conj.*	even if
集体	jítǐ	*n.*	group
建立	jiànlì	*v.*	establish
节目	jiémù	*n.*	programme
结论	jiélùn	*n.*	________
____	jīnqián	*n.*	money
……来……去	...lái...qù		(doing something) over and over
浪费	làngfèi	*v.*	________
离不开	lí bù kāi		cannot do without
立场	lìchǎng	*n.*	standing, position
凉快	liángkuai	*adj.*	________
____	mòshēng	*adj.*	strange, unfamiliar
弄	nòng	*v.*	________
评价	píngjià	*v./n.*	review
亲近	qīnjìn	*v.*	get close to
然而	rán' ér	*conj.*	however
稍微	shāowēi	*adv.*	slightly
社交	shèjiāo	*v.*	socialize
____	shēn	*adj.*	deep
失望	shīwàng	*adj.*	disappointed
使	shǐ	*v.*	________
视频	shìpín	*n.*	video clips
疏远	shūyuǎn	*v.*	alienate; become distant
顺便	shùnbiàn	*adv.*	while you are at it, conveniently
____	tóngshí	*conj.*	at the same time
无聊	wúliáo	*adj.*	boring
相反	xiāngfǎn	*adj.*	________
想法	xiǎngfǎ	*n.*	ideas, thoughts
演讲	yǎnjiǎng	*n.*	speech
____	yǐwéi	*v.*	assumed (incorrectly)
争议性	zhēngyìxìng	*n.*	argumentativeness
支配	zhīpèi	*v.*	arrange, allocate
专心	zhuānxīn	*adj.*	________
状态	zhuàngtài	*n.*	status

UNIT 11

Huíjiā de gǎnjué zhēn hǎo

回家的感觉真好！

It feels so good to be back home!

LESSON 1

Vocabulary and listening

1 **Work in pairs. Check what you are most likely to talk about with a friend whom you have not seen for a long time. Add more to the list.**

- ☐ 1 自己最近的情况
- ☐ 2 对方最近的情况
- ☐ 3 家人的情况
- ☐ 4 两人共同的朋友

2 **Steve is meeting up with Wang Yu, who has just come back to Beijing. Listen to their conversation and answer the questions.**

1 王玉对回国的感觉怎么样？

2 史蒂夫为什么不能把照片放在自己的博客上？

3 史蒂夫为什么说"我欠你一顿饭"？

史蒂夫：王玉，没想到你这个时候回国啊，挺突然的。

王玉：放假了，周围的同学都走了，我一个人呆着特别无聊。回家的感觉真好！每天想吃什么就吃什么，想睡到什么时候就睡到什么时候。

史蒂夫：这半年你一个人在异国他乡，挺不容易的吧？

王玉：刚去的时候不太适应，流了不少眼泪。说真的，生活上，学习上，苦点儿累点儿都能应付；最难克服的是那种孤单、寂寞的感觉。由于时差的关系，也不能随时跟家人通电话。高兴的事情没人分享，难过的时候常常要一个人默默忍受。

史蒂夫：其实你可以随时给我打电话。虽然我帮不上你什么忙，但至

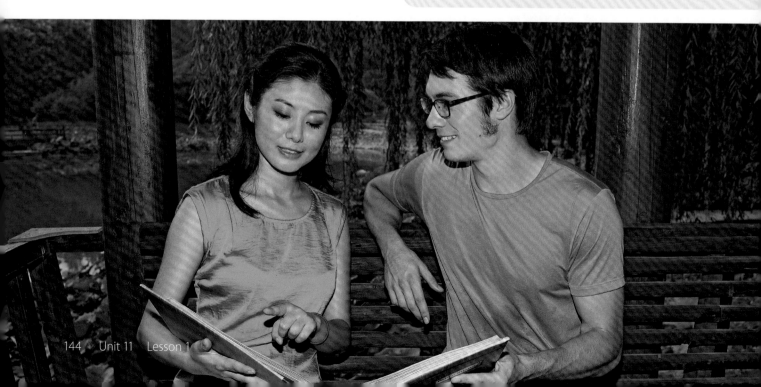

少可以做一个忠实的听众。

王玉：我知道。不过最难熬的那段时间已经过去了。别光说我了，你怎么样？摄影比赛的结果出来了吗？

史蒂夫：哈哈，我有个好消息要告诉你。我得了二等奖，是唯一获奖的外国人。

王玉：太棒了，祝贺你！快让我看看你的作品！……照片真好看，怎么没放到你的博客里呢？

史蒂夫：不是我不想放。这批照片的版权已经被一家图片公司买下来，不属于我了。我们说好了的，我欠你一顿饭，正好也给你接风。说吧，想吃什么？

王玉：我刚好也饿了，现在特别馋火锅，咱们去吃火锅吧！顺便也庆祝你得奖！

生词 New words

tūrán 突然	all of a sudden	tīngzhòng 听众	listener
yìguó-tāxiāng 异国他乡	foreign land	nán'áo 难熬	hard to endure
liú yǎnlèi 流眼泪	shed tears	wéiyī 唯一	the one and only
kǔ 苦	bitter, difficult	shǔyú 属于	belong
yìngfù 应付	deal with	qiàn 欠	owe
gūdān 孤单	lonely	dùn 顿	(for meals)
shíchā 时差	time difference	jiēfēng 接风	give a reception in a guest's honour
fēnxiǎng 分享	share (good things)	gānghǎo 刚好	it so happened that
mòmò 默默	silently	è 饿	hungry
rěnshòu 忍受	tolerate	chán 馋	covet; covetous
bāng bú shàng 帮不上	cannot help	huǒguō 火锅	hot pot
zhōngshí 忠实	loyal		

3 Check the true statements.

☐ 1 史蒂夫觉得王玉这个时候回国很突然。

☐ 2 对王玉来说，孤单比学习上的辛苦更难克服。

☐ 3 王玉再回美国的时候就不会觉得日子太难熬了。

☐ 4 这次摄影大赛，除了史蒂夫以外，没有别的外国人获奖。

☐ 5 王玉想吃火锅。

4 Choose the correct answers to the questions. There may be more than one possible answer.

1 王玉为什么回国？
- a 她很想家。
- b 她想回来看史蒂夫的摄影作品。
- c 周围的同学都走了，她一个人很无聊。

2 在异国他乡，王玉是怎样应付孤单的？
- a 她常常跟家里通电话。
- b 她一个人默默忍受。
- c 她跟身边亲近的朋友交流。

3 对于王玉的孤单，史蒂夫表示他可以怎么帮助她？
- a 他随时给她打电话、跟她聊天儿。
- b 他随时接听她的电话、听她讲她的事情。
- c 他其实一点儿忙也帮不上。

5 Check how Wang Yu feels about her life in the US.

- ☐ 1 总是特别无聊
- ☐ 2 感觉真好
- ☐ 3 不太适应
- ☐ 4 想吃什么就吃什么
- ☐ 5 高兴的事情没人分享
- ☐ 6 很孤单
- ☐ 7 想睡到什么时候就睡到什么时候
- ☐ 8 难过的时候只能默默忍受

2-24

6 You are going to hear an interview. Look at the questions and predict what it is about.

- ☐ 1 如何决定参加这次比赛？
- ☐ 2 如何看到比赛征稿启事？
- ☐ 3 怎样拍出照片？
- ☐ 4 如何选出照片？
- ☐ 5 比赛前的心情如何？
- ☐ 6 获奖后的心情如何？

Now listen and check the three questions asked.

2-24

7 Listen again and check the correct statements.

- ☐ 1 记者一眼就认出了史蒂夫，因为他是一个外国人。
- ☐ 2 史蒂夫觉得自己的水平还差得远，所以一直在犹豫是否参赛。
- ☐ 3 史蒂夫的摄影作品主题鲜明是他获奖的重要原因。
- ☐ 4 史蒂夫觉得每一张照片都很特别、都值得选入。
- ☐ 5 史蒂夫想用他的镜头和照片表现出云南人的生活、文化和故事。
- ☐ 6 史蒂夫接到电话通知的时候，他的耳朵正好出了点儿问题，所以他不相信自己听到的。

Pronunciation and speaking

2-25

1 Listen to the greetings between friends.

1 这半年你一个人在异国他乡，挺不容易的吧？

2 其实你可以随时给我打电话，虽然我帮不上你什么忙，但至少可以做一个忠实的听众。

3 我请你吃饭，为你接风！说吧，想吃什么？

4 别光说我了，你怎么样？

Now read aloud.

2 Complete the conversation with the sentences in Activity 1.

A: 真高兴你回来了。________

B: 是啊，所有的事情都得自己做决定，有的时候真不知道该怎么办。

A: ________

B: 谢谢你。别光说我了，你怎么样？

A: 我挺好的，不算太忙。一会儿一起吃饭吧，________

B: 你决定吧，吃什么都好。

3 Work in pairs. Talk about the biggest change in your life, including the following:

- 你当时的感觉
- 跟谁分享了这件事情
- 用了多长时间适应这个变化

CHINESE TO GO

2-26

Showing frankness

Shuō shízài de 说 实在 的，……	To be honest with you, …
Wǒmen shuōhǎo le de 我们 说好 了 的。	We made a deal.

LESSON 2

Reading and writing

1 Work in pairs. Choose the three most important things in an award winner's profile and explain why.

1 身高、长相
2 生活环境
3 以前的经历
4 参加比赛的原因
5 参加比赛的经历
6 对自己影响最大的人
7 获奖以后的心情
8 未来的打算

2 Look at the explanations for these three measure words.

次 → emphasizes the frequency of the action

遍 → emphasizes the course and thoroughness of the action

趟 → measures trips to somewhere

Now complete the sentences with the correct measure words.

1 这个电影我看了三 ______。
2 他一个月去三 ______ 中国城。
3 你打算什么时候回一 ______ 国？
4 那个地方我跟你提过一 ______。
5 你的解释我没有听清楚，麻烦你再说一 ______。
6 他学开车很快，学了三 ______ 就会了。

2-27

3 Work in pairs. Compare the verbs and the verb phrases with resultative complements.

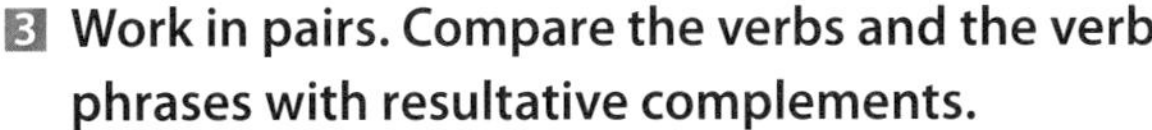

认: identify	认出: recognize
爱: love	爱上: fall in love with
留: leave	留下: mark
提: bring up	提到: mention

Now write down more verb phrases with resultative complements.

4 Look at the example sentences and make two sentences with each of the given words.

我的好朋友鼓励我参加这次演讲比赛。

受到老师的鼓励以后，我的中文越学越好。

跟总统握手让我很兴奋！

他的握手很有力。

我在附近的一个公司兼职。

在中国旅游的时候，他还兼职做英文老师。

代表团主要考察了我们公司今年的销售状况。

他们对当地的气候和环境做了认真的考察。

这份会议记录非常详细。

父母常常用照片记录孩子的成长。

5 Read the report about Steve and check the main points included.

☐ 1 外貌
☐ 2 在中国的经历
☐ 3 参加摄影比赛的经历
☐ 4 戴维斯对史蒂夫的影响
☐ 5 学习摄影的经历
☐ 6 学中文的经历
☐ 7 来中国以前的经历

足迹

□ 特约记者/小爱

在北京民族大学附近的傣家饭馆，我一眼就认出了我的采访对象史蒂夫，一个来自英国伦敦的小伙子，也是《我看云南》摄影大赛中唯一获奖的外籍人士。他戴着一副近视眼镜，镜片后面的蓝眼睛亮亮的，总是带着笑意；史蒂夫的握手真诚而有力，他的中文也很好，语速不紧不慢。

两年前史蒂夫大学毕业后，决定留在北京生活。这期间除了继续学汉语以外，他还为一家英国杂志兼职做记者。史蒂夫最喜欢做的事情就是带着心爱的相机去中国各地旅游。长江、长城、嵩山少林寺、内蒙古大草原……他一路走，一路拍。用他自己的话说，他是以拍照的方式记录自己的足迹。

史蒂夫告诉我，他本来对参加《我看云南》的比赛并不是很有信心，之所以决定参加，是因为受到中国朋友的鼓励。对于获奖，史蒂夫感到特别高兴。他喜欢中国，更喜欢中国人。史蒂夫获奖的照片，就是以云南各地的不同人物为主题。这次云南之行，还让他认识了很多像他一样爱上云南的朋友。

在采访中，史蒂夫特别提到一位英国人，戴维斯（H.R. Davis）。一百多年前，这名英国学者先后花了六年的时间，四次探访云南，用文字和照片对云南各地的气候、物产、人文、地理做了详细的考察，留下了珍贵的记录。“有机会我真的很希望能在云南生活一段时间，而不只是作为一个过客，看看风景、拍拍照就离开了。”史蒂夫说他有一个愿望，就是沿着戴维斯的足迹，重走一遍云南。

生词 New words

zújì	足迹	footprint	Cháng Jiāng	长江	The Yangtze River
tèyuē jìzhě	特约记者	special reporter	Chángchéng	长城	The Great Wall
yìyǎn	一眼	at a glance	duìyú	对于	as for
rènchū	认出	recognize	Dàiwéisī	戴维斯	Davis
xiǎohuǒzi	小伙子	young guy	tànfǎng	探访	visit, investigate
wàijí	外籍	foreign nationality	wùchǎn	物产	produce
rénshì	人士	person, people (formal)	rénwén	人文	humanities, culture
dài	戴	wear	dìlǐ	地理	geography
jìnshì	近视	nearsighted	zhēnguì	珍贵	valuable
jìngpiàn	镜片	lens	guòkè	过客	passer-by
liàng	亮	bright, shining	yuànwàng	愿望	wish
wòshǒu	握手	handshake	yánzhe	沿着	along, following
zhēnchéng	真诚	sincere	chóng	重	again, afresh
yǒulì	有力	with force	biàn	遍	(for number of times)
jiānzhí	兼职	part-time			

6 **Write down the words and phrases used to describe the journalist's first impression of Steve.**

1 样子 ....

2 握手 ....

3 眼睛 ....

4 语言 ....

7 **Choose all the possible answers to the questions.**

1 记者觉得史蒂夫是什么样的人？
  a 严肃 b 热情 c 真诚
2 史蒂夫大学毕业以后做了什么？
  a 留在北京继续学汉语
  b 为一家杂志社兼职做记者
  c 在中国各地旅游、拍照
3 史蒂夫获奖照片的主题是什么？
  a 云南各地的风景
  b 云南各地的人物
  c 爱上云南的人们
4 对史蒂夫来说，拍照意味着什么？
  a 只不过是他的业余爱好而已
  b 用拍照的方式记录自己在中国的旅程
  c 拍下人物或风景留作纪念
5 将来史蒂夫可能会做什么事情？
  a 去云南生活一段时间
  b 去了解云南
  c 沿着戴维斯走过的路再走一遍云南

8 **Complete the table about H. R. Davis.**

戴维斯	
国籍	
时代	
经历	1
	2
	3
对史蒂夫的影响	

9 **Write a short biography of an important historical figure. Include:**

- 生活经历
- 成就 (achievements)
- 趣事
- 他/她的影响

Language in use

Expressing "as one pleases" with 想……就……

1 Look at the sentences.

Subject 1	想+ verb + question word	Subject 2	就+ verb + question word
我每天	想吃什么		就吃什么。
我	想睡到什么时候		就睡到什么时候。
孩子	想去哪儿，	父母	就去哪儿。
周末你	想玩到几点		就玩到几点。
你的生日晚会	想请谁，	我们	就请谁。

Now check the correct explanations.

☐ 1 想……就…… is used to express that someone can do something as he/she pleases.

☐ 2 The "verb + question word" following 想 and 就 must be the same.

☐ 3 The question word after "就+verb" is optional.

☐ 4 The question word in this structure is used as an indefinite reference.

☐ 5 The subjects preceding 想 and 就 cannot be the same.

2 Work in pairs. Ask and answer questions with 想……就…….

1 —我们晚上看什么电影？
—____________________

2 —周末去博物馆，咱们几点出发？
—____________________

3 —我从中国带回来的纪念品，应该送给谁呢？
—____________________

4 —咱们一会儿去哪家饭馆吃饭？
—____________________

Emphasizing a particular manner of carrying out an action using Verb 1着+ verb 2

1 Look at the sentences.

Subject	Verb 1 着(object 1)	Verb 2 (object 2)	
他喜欢	带着心爱的相机	去中国各地旅游。	
他总是	笑着	跟人说话。	
老师	抱着很多书	走进来。	
你别	站着	说话，	快坐下吧。
很多孩子每天都得	背着很重的书包	去上学。	

Now check the correct explanations.

☐ 1 Verb 1着 + verb 2 is used to express "to conduct an action in a particular manner or state".

☐ 2 Verb 1着 (object) is not the main action, but is used to indicate a particular manner or state.

☐ 3 Verb 2 (object) is the main action, which is conducted in the particular manner expressed in verb 1着 (object).

☐ 4 Both verb 1 and verb 2 are main actions.

2 Describe what people are doing in the pictures using verb 1 着 + verb 2.

a
b

Emphasizing the reason for a result with 之所以……是因为……

1 Look at the sentences.

Subject	之所以……	是因为……
史蒂夫	之所以最后决定参加比赛，	是因为受到一位中国朋友的鼓励。
写作	之所以重要，	是因为它可以锻炼人的思维。
这部小说	之所以能成功，	是因为它真实地反映了这个时代下人们的生活。
她	之所以爱上他，	是因为多年前她曾经读过他写的诗。
他	之所以放弃这次机会，	是因为他不想离家太远。

Now check the correct explanations.

☐ 1 之所以……是因为…… is used to show result and reason.

☐ 2 是因为…… indicates the reason, and 之所以…… introduces the result.

☐ 3 Compared with 因为……所以……, 之所以……是因为…… is an informal expression and often appears in colloquial speech.

☐ 4 The subject should go after 之所以.

2 Rewrite the following sentences using 之所以……是因为…….

1 因为他们热情地帮助了我们，所以我们非常感谢他们。

2 他不喜欢那家公司的办事方式，所以他离开了那家公司。

3 他的父母认为研究艺术没有前途，所以反对他选择艺术史作为专业。

4 由于弄错了数据，结果这个项目的研究报告完全不可信。

Expressing "to regard A as B" using 以……为……

1 Look at the sentences.

Subject	以 A	为 B
史蒂夫的照片	以云南各地的不同人物	为主题。
法律就应该	以事实	为根据。
服务当然要	以用户	为中心。
我们	以北京时间	为标准。
英国	以英里、码、英尺、英寸	为长度单位。

Now check the correct explanations.

☐ 1 以……为…… is used to express "to regard A as B". For example, "以北京时间为标准" means "to regard Beijing time as the reference".

☐ 2 以……为…… is an informal expression. Its formal counterpart is "把 A 当作 B".

☐ 3 以……为…… means "assumed wrongly".

2 Work in pairs and talk about the meanings of the following Chinese sayings.

1 民以食为天。

2 与人相处应以和为贵。

3 以史为镜，可以知兴替。

4 物以稀为贵。

3 Work in pairs. Ask and answer the questions.

1 一个公司的发展应该以什么为中心？

2 如果你可以主办一次摄影展览，你会以什么为主题？

3 在你的国家，是以什么为标准长度单位？以什么为标准重量单位？

4 在你的国家，官方语言是以什么语音为标准音？

Turn to page 200 for grammar reference.

LESSON 3

Communication activity

1 Work in groups of three.

Student A: You are a journalist from a Chinese TV station. Prepare a list of questions to ask the participants. They may have won or lost.

Student B: You won the first prize in the competition. Answer Student A's questions.

Student C: You participated in the competition but did not win anything. Answer Student A's questions.

2 Act out the interview in front of the whole class and vote for the best.

Turn to pages 177 and 183 for more speaking practice.

Review and practice

1 Complete the sentences with the correct words from the box.

随时　属于　受到　鼓励　不紧不慢

1 他的脾气就是这样 ______，我们都在为毕业论文着急，他却说要慢慢做。

2 要不是林教授一直 ______ 我继续这项研究，我肯定早就放弃了。

3 这是我的手机号，有事 ______ 跟我联系，别怕麻烦我。

4 她父母是医生，哥哥和姐姐也是医生，______ 家人的影响，她也决定学医。

5 王心起初并不喜欢这座城市，但是通过努力，她很快融入了周围的人们，找到了 ______ 自己的位置。

Cultural corner

The modern "Marco Polo"

Marco Polo, the famous Italian explorer and merchant who travelled to China during the Yuan Dynasty (1206–1368), is so well known to the Chinese that his name has long been synonymous with any European in China. Early travellers to China were mostly missionaries, explorers, merchants and scholars. Modern-day "Marco Polos" came to China after it re-opened its doors to the world in 1979. Initially, there were very few people from overseas in China, so they were generally welcomed by the Chinese and were given favourable treatment. Over the past several decades, as China has become a major economic force in the world, more and more immigrants have been attracted to China to study, to work, and to do business. Now the presence of people from overseas is becoming common in major Chinese cities, and more and more expatriates have started to live like the local Chinese.

2 Complete the sentences with the correct words.

1 你有什么困难，就说出来，就算我 _______ 什么忙，也可以帮你出出主意。
a 帮不上 b 帮不下 c 帮不出

2 他是这所学校 _______ 参加过国际马拉松比赛的学生。
a 只有 b 只 c 唯一

3 这 _______ 产品的质量似乎没有之前的好。
a 段 b 批 c 遍

4 她很喜欢这个电视节目，每个星期都要看，绝对是最 _______ 观众。
a 忠实 b 诚实 c 真诚

5 开会的时候，经理特别 _______ 两年前的一份订单。
a 提出 b 提到 c 提高

3 Complete the passage with the correct words from the box.

带着	作为	探访	之所以
先后	是否	是因为	详细

听说过戴维斯的人可能很多。他本来是一个英国军官。他 _______ 去了中国云南， _______ 1894年英国政府派他带队去考察修建一条从缅甸通往云南的铁路 _______ 可行，当时他才29岁。当时中国的政府是清朝政府。他 _______ 清朝政府给他的护照， _______ 花了六年时间，四次徒步 _______ 云南。他几乎走遍了云南所有重要的地区，甚至是一些非常偏远的地区，对那些地方的气候、物产、人文、地理都做了 _______ 的考察和记录，而这些内容后来都被收录在他在1909年出版的游记中。除了文字以外，他的书中还附有大量珍贵的照片。虽然他的书并不是学术研究著作，但是 _______ 第一个详细记录云南风土人情的西方人，他为我们讲述了他所看到的那个时代的云南故事。

Now choose the correct answers to the questions.

1 戴维斯最后离开云南大概是在哪一年？
a 1894年 b 1890年 c 1909年

2 戴维斯为什么会去云南考察？
a 英国政府派他去的。
b 他对云南的风土人情很感兴趣。
c 他是一个研究人文地理的学者。

3 他在云南时使用的护照是谁给他的？
a 英国政府 b 清朝政府 c 缅甸政府

4 为什么戴维斯的书很重要？
a 他的书是第一本关于云南的学术研究著作。
b 他的书是第一本详细的云南游记，甚至介绍了很多偏远的地区。
c 他的书是西方人详细记录云南的最早的珍贵资料。

4 Interview a person who lives overseas. Ask about:

- 他/她的身份
- 他/她给你的印象
- 他/她在这个地区生活了多长时间，生活得怎么样
- 他/她的特别经历
- 他/她的愿望

Now write a passage about his/her life.

Vocabulary review

Fill in the blanks.

帮不上	bāng bú shàng		cannot help
____	biàn	*measure word*	(for number of times)
馋	chán	*v./adj.*	covet; covetous
长城	Chángchéng	*n.*	____
长江	Cháng Jiāng	*n.*	____
____	chóng	*adv.*	again, afresh
戴	dài	*v.*	wear
地理	dìlǐ	*n.*	geography
对于	duìyú	*prep.*	____
____	dùn	*measure word*	(for meals)
饿	è	*adj.*	hungry
____	fēnxiǎng	*v.*	share (good things)
刚好	gānghǎo	*adv.*	it so happened that
孤单	gūdān	*adj.*	____
过客	guòkè	*n.*	passer-by
火锅	huǒguō	*n.*	hot pot
兼职	jiānzhí	*v./n.*	part-time
接风	jiēfēng	*v.*	give a reception in a guest's honour
近视	jìnshì	*adj.*	____
镜片	jìngpiàn	*n.*	lens
____	kǔ	*adj.*	bitter, difficult
____	liàng	*adj.*	bright, shining
流眼泪	liú yǎnlèi		shed tears
默默	mòmò	*adv.*	silently
难熬	nán' áo	*adj.*	hard to endure
欠	qiàn	*v.*	owe

人士	rénshì	*n.*	person, people (formal)
人文	rénwén	*n.*	humanities, culture
忍受	rěnshòu	*v.*	____
____	rènchū	*v.*	recognize
时差	shíchā	*n.*	time difference
属于	shǔyú	*v.*	belong
探访	tànfǎng	*v.*	visit, investigate
特约记者	tèyuē jìzhě		special reporter
听众	tīngzhòng	*n.*	____
突然	tūrán	*adj.*	all of a sudden
外籍	wàijí	*n.*	foreign nationality
____	wéiyī	*adj.*	the one and only
握手	wòshǒu	*v.*	handshake
物产	wùchǎn	*n.*	produce
小伙子	xiǎohuǒzi	*n.*	young guy
沿着	yánzhe	*prep.*	along, following
一眼	yìyǎn		at a glance
异国他乡	yìguó–tāxiāng		foreign land
应付	yìngfù	*v.*	deal with
有力	yǒulì	*adj.*	____
愿望	yuànwàng	*n.*	wish
珍贵	zhēnguì	*adj.*	valuable
____	zhēnchéng	*adj.*	sincere
忠实	zhōngshí	*adj.*	____
足迹	zújì	*n.*	footprint
戴维斯	Dàiwéisī		Davis

UNIT 12

Yǒu fùchū, cái yǒu shōuhuò

有付出，才有收获。

No pain, no gain.

LESSON | 1

Vocabulary and listening

1 Work in pairs. Talk about who you like best in *Discover China* and why. Use the words in the box to help you.

勇敢	粗心	马虎	成熟
漂亮	帅	可爱	热情

我觉得 _____ 很 _____，比方说 _____。

2 Work in pairs. Ask and answer the questions.

1 老朋友聚会有哪些常聊的话题？
2 聚会总是会让人愉快吗？

2-28

3 The four friends are reunited in the summer. Listen to their conversation and answer the questions.

1 哪四个人参加了聚会？
2 在过去的一年中，大家都去了哪些地方，做了些什么事？
3 永民宣布了一个什么好消息？
4 你认为谁的收获最大？为什么？

永民：咱们上次聚在一起是去年夏天吧？转眼就一年了！

王玉：是啊。大家看起来好像都成熟了不少。

史蒂夫：我想大家这一年都有些经历吧，不如都讲讲？

马克：我先来！其实你们都知道了，我去了深圳实习。虽然偶尔也觉得很辛苦，可是学到了不少东西，还改掉了马虎、粗心的毛病。经理还说欢迎我毕业后去正式工作呢。

史蒂夫：马克，你真行！

马克：别光表扬我了，你才了不起呢，旅游的时候随便拍几张照片都能获奖！

王玉：马克，你这么说我反对。史蒂夫可不是随便拍的，他一直都在努力提高摄影水平。有付出，才有收获。

史蒂夫：谢谢你，王玉。你也很不容易，孤身一人在美国，什么都要自己来。

王玉：在美国的时候我常常梦见你们，醒了就觉得很失落。可现在我们不是又聚在一起了！永民，你怎么样？

永民：说来惭愧，我只是去了学校的夏令营帮忙。不过我有个好消息：和我一起在夏令营工作的小文现在是我的女朋友了！

马克：你太让我们吃惊啦，永民！快说说，你是怎么追女孩儿的，不许保密！

永民：男人嘛，勇敢一点儿就行了！

史蒂夫：你真行，永民！今天怎么没把小文带来啊？

永民：她有点儿不好意思，下次吧。

王玉：看来大家的收获都不小！

马克：我看还是永民的收获最大！

4 Check the true statements.

- ☐ 1 大家成熟了是因为又长了一岁。
- ☐ 2 大家聊起了各自的经历。
- ☐ 3 马克觉得他的实习很轻松。
- ☐ 4 大家没想到永民已经有女朋友了。
- ☐ 5 小文不知道他们要聚会，所以这次没来。

5 Choose the correct answers to the questions. There may be more than one possible answer.

1 马克去深圳实习的收获是什么？
  - a 他学到了不少东西。
  - b 他改掉了马虎、粗心的毛病。
  - c 他得到了一份正式工作的邀请。

2 王玉认为史蒂夫为什么会获奖？
  - a 他随便拍了几张照片就获奖了。
  - b 他一直在努力提高摄影水平。
  - c 他去旅游了。

3 王玉在美国的生活是什么样的？
  - a 她每天都很失落。
  - b 她非常想念她的朋友们。
  - c 她孤身一人，很不容易。

4 永民是怎么追小文的？
  - a 他勇敢地保护了小文。
  - b 他把自己的秘密告诉了小文。
  - c 他勇敢地向小文表达自己的感情。

生词 New words

jù	聚	gather, meet
zhuǎnyǎn	转眼	in a flash
chéngshú	成熟	mature
ǒu' ěr	偶尔	occasionally
gǎidiào	改掉	give up, drop
mǎhu	马虎	careless, perfunctory
cūxīn	粗心	careless, thoughtless
máobìng	毛病	defect
biǎoyáng	表扬	praise, commend
fǎnduì	反对	object, oppose
nǔlì	努力	trying hard; make a great effort
fùchū	付出	pay, put in a lot of hard work
gūshēn-yìrén	孤身一人	all on one's own
mèng	梦	dream
xǐng	醒	wake up
shīluò	失落	feeling lost
cánkuì	惭愧	ashamed, abashed
chījīng	吃惊	be startled, be shocked, be taken aback
bùxǔ	不许	not allow, must not, prohibit
bǎomì	保密	keep secret
yǒnggǎn	勇敢	brave

6 Listen again and complete the table.

人物	事情	收获
	参加摄影比赛 去云南旅游	
		有了一个女朋友

7 You are going to hear three schoolmates at their reunion. Predict what they will talk about.

Now listen and check the correct statements.

☐ 1 他们每年聚一次。
☐ 2 阿风大学毕业后没有换过公司。
☐ 3 小爱主要写人物采访报道。
☐ 4 小爱在大学时就是校报的记者。
☐ 5 陈博发现自己不喜欢做饭。
☐ 6 陈博之所以被叫做"陈博"，是因为他以前的愿望是读博士。

8 Listen again and complete the table.

	大学时的梦想 / 做过的事情	现在的梦想 / 在做的事情
阿风		
小爱		
陈博		

Now work in pairs and check your answers.

Pronunciation and speaking

1 Listen to the sentences used for exchanging praise or feelings.

1 别光表扬我了，你才了不起呢！
2 谢谢你。你也很不容易。
3 你太让我们吃惊啦！我看你的收获最大！
4 我有个好消息……

2 Complete the conversations in an appropriate way.

1 A: 你太厉害了！这么多人参加的比赛，你都能获奖！我真佩服你。
B: ______________________

2 A: 我听说你这个学期选了五门课，这些科目都特别难，你太辛苦了。
B: ______________________

3 A: 我要宣布一个好消息：我已经被去年实习过的公司正式录用了！
B: ______________________

4 A: 你是我见过的最努力的人。你不管做什么事情，都特别认真。
B: ______________________

Now work in pairs. Act out the conversation using the correct intonations.

3 Work in pairs. Talk about two or three improvements that you have made in learning Chinese and praise each other.

CHINESE TO GO

2-31

Chit-chat

Wǒ xiān lái
我先来！ I'll go first.

Kuài shuōshuo
快说说，…… Quickly, tell me...

Bùxǔ bǎomì
不许保密！ Don't keep it to yourself!

Nánrén ma yǒnggǎn yìdiǎnr jiù xíng le
男人嘛，勇敢一点儿就行了！
Man, just be brave!

LESSON 2

Reading and writing

1 **Work in pairs. Talk about a reunion with your former schoolmates and how you felt.**

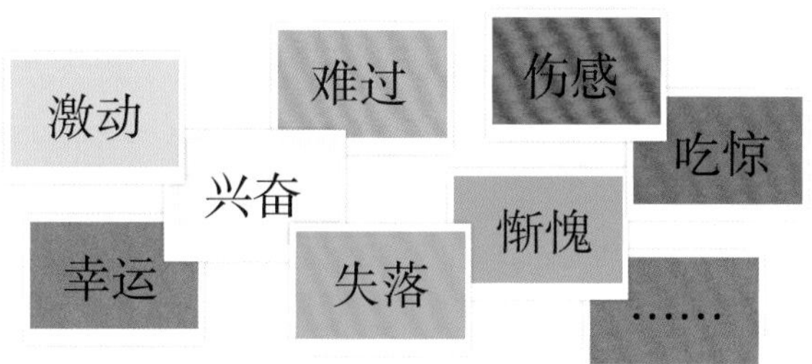

2 **Describe your best friend. Use three words from the box and give some examples.**

开放　乐观　积极　努力
勇敢　粗心　成熟　活泼

3 **Match the words to make phrases.**

1 突破	a 意见
2 坚持	b 眼界
3 走遍	c 世界
4 开阔	d 自己

Now work in pairs. Make sentences with the phrases you have made.

4 **Look at the characters on the left and write down the meanings of the words on the right.**

聚: meet, assemble, gather	聚会: 聚在一起: 聚餐: 每两年聚一次:
离: part, separate, leave	离开: 离去: 离别: 距离: 分离:

2-32

5 **Read Wang Yu's blog post on page 160 about the reunion. Check the main ideas.**

☐ 1 聚会那天的天气
☐ 2 聚会的地点
☐ 3 聚会的时候吃了什么
☐ 4 重逢时的心情
☐ 5 朋友们的最新情况
☐ 6 朋友们给自己的激励
☐ 7 自己今后的打算

新浪微博 weibo.com 首页 热门 应用 游戏 大家正在热搜： 王玉

王玉 LV1

16 关注 69 粉丝 14 微博

玩转微博
首页
消息
收藏
发给我的
好友圈
分组
特别关注
同事
同学
好友
展开

八月的重逢

这个夏天北京很闷热，已经是八月下旬了，温度还迟迟降不下来。今天早上下了一场雨，总算凉快了一点儿，有了秋天的意思。

今天去参加朋友聚会以前，我的心情很复杂。能跟老朋友见面让我很激动，可是一想到很快就要回美国，不知道下次什么时候才能再聚，心里又有点儿难过。聚会的时候，有朋友提议大家每两年聚一次，可以在地球上的任何地方，这让我的心情一下子变好了。是啊，离别是为了下一次的重逢，我又何必这么伤感呢！

在美国求学并不容易，这半年来流过的汗水和泪水都不少。可每当我想到这几个朋友，就有了勇气和力量。几年前他们刚到中国的时候，也都是孤身一人，语言不通、饮食习惯不同，还要面对各种各样的文化冲击，但他们都适应得很快也很好。M打算毕业后在中国长期工作；S参加一个中国杂志的摄影比赛获了奖；Y还找了一个中国女朋友。他们的中文也都突飞猛进！

他们最值得我学习的地方，就是一直保持乐观、开放的态度，乐于接受新事物。比方说，他们都热爱旅游。在中国短短的两三年时间，去过的地方比我还多。别说深圳、西安这样的大城市，就是内蒙古和云南这样的偏远地区也有他们的足迹。他们还打算走遍全中国呢！

我很幸运自己有这样的朋友，可以激励我不断地突破自己。我也要更积极、乐观地面对自己生活中的困难和问题。即使我不能走遍世界，也要尽可能地多看一看、走一走，开阔自己的眼界。

推广 | 👍 | 转发 | 收藏 | 评论

大家又聚在一起了，真好！我想死你们了，下次聚会我一定要参加！

评论

阿曼达，我们也都很想你！说不定下次聚会我们就去巴西找你了！☺

回复

生词 New words

chóngféng 重逢	reunite	miànduì 面对	face
mēnrè 闷热	muggy, sultry	chōngjī 冲击	impact
xiàxún 下旬	last ten days of the month	chángqī 长期	long term
chíchí 迟迟	very late	tūfēi-měngjìn 突飞猛进	a spurt of progress
jiàng 降	lower, decrease, fall	lèyú 乐于	be happy to
chǎng 场	(for rain/snow)	shìwù 事物	things, matters
jùhuì 聚会	get-together, gathering	zǒubiàn 走遍	travel all over
dìqiú 地球	the earth, the globe	jīlì 激励	inspire, encourage
yíxiàzi 一下子	at once, instantly	búduàn 不断	nonstop, incessantly
líbié 离别	part, separate, say goodbye	tūpò 突破	break through
hébì 何必	why do you need to…	jǐnkěnéng 尽可能	to the best of one's ability
shānggǎn 伤感	melancholy	kāikuò 开阔	broaden, open
hànshuǐ 汗水	sweat	yǎnjiè 眼界	horizon
yǒngqì 勇气	courage	shuōbudìng 说不定	perhaps
bùtōng 不通	blockage, barrier		

6 Match the adverbs with their meanings.

1 一下子	a to the best of one's ability
2 迟迟	b perhaps, possibly
3 不断	c nonstop
4 尽可能	d long-term
5 说不定	e at once
6 长期	f late

7 Choose all the possible answers to the questions.

1 王玉和朋友们下次聚会可能会在哪里?
a 巴西 b 美国 c 哪里都可能

2 王玉的朋友们去过哪些地方旅游?
a 一些大城市
b 一些偏远地区
c 走遍了全中国

3 朋友们给王玉的启发是什么?
a 要热爱旅游
b 乐于接受新事物
c 保持乐观、开放的态度

4 王玉打算做什么?
a 走遍全中国
b 走遍全世界
c 尽量开阔眼界

8 Check the difficulties that Wang Yu faces in the US.

- ☐ 1 孤身一人
- ☐ 2 天气很难适应
- ☐ 3 毕业以后很难找工作
- ☐ 4 语言不通
- ☐ 5 饮食习惯不同
- ☐ 6 要面对各种文化冲击
- ☐ 7 出去旅游的机会不多

9 Write a blog post summarizing your experiences or main achievements last year. Include:

- 这个经历或者收获具有的特殊意义
- 它对你的启发和影响
- 你对来年或将来的期望

Language in use

Expressing an emphatic tone using 才……呢

1 Look at the conversations.

	Subject + 才……呢
A: 马克，你真棒！	B: 你才了不起呢！
A: 今天的球赛怎么样？	B: 昨天的球赛才有意思呢！你没看太可惜了。
A: 西安的天气真好。	B: 这也叫好？昆明的天气才好呢！
A: 去他家看他，不带礼物好吗？	B: 没关系，他才不在乎呢。
A: 你真不给她打电话解释一下吗？	B: 我才没时间理她呢。

Now check the correct explanations.

☐ 1 才……呢 is used when the speaker wants to emphasize a fact or situation in response to a question or statement.

☐ 2 才 as an adverb should go after the subject.

☐ 3 才……呢 can only be used to emphasize the positive form of an adjective or verb.

2 Work in pairs and complete the conversations using 才……呢.

1 A: 你的中文说得真流利。
B: ____________________

2 A: 最新的007电影大家都说不好看，你觉得呢？
B: 最新的这部还算不错，__________

3 A: 王玉的生日聚会你不去，没关系吗？
B: ____________________

4 A: 你就帮我这一次吧，最后一次，还不行吗？
B: 又是"最后一次"？__________

Expressing unnecessariness using 何必……呢

1 Look at the sentences.

Clause 1	何必……呢
离别是为了下一次的重逢，	我又何必这么伤感呢？
你跟他是这么多年的朋友，	何必为了一点儿小事情吵架呢？
既然你不相信我说的话，	何必还来问我呢？
你家楼下的小商店不就是卖水果的吗？	何必跑去远处的超市呢？
反正我也没时间见他，	何必让他白来一趟呢？

Now check the correct explanations.

☐ 1 何必……呢 is used in a rhetorical question to express that "there is no need to do something" or "it's not necessary to do something".

☐ 2 The clause preceding 何必……呢 introduces a reason or premise which explains why there is no need to do the thing.

☐ 3 If there is a subject in the second clause, the subject should follow 何必.

☐ 4 呢 can never be dropped.

2 Work in pairs. Talk about how you feel about the following using 何必……呢.

1 衣服的款式、质量、牌子、价格

2 餐馆的味道、服务、环境、价格

—去餐馆吃饭，你觉得环境重要吗？

—我觉得只要饭菜的味道好就行了，何必在乎环境呢？

Expressing "let alone" with 别说A，就是B，也/都……

1 Look at the sentences.

	别说A	就是B	也/都 + comment
	别说深圳、西安这样的大城市，	就是内蒙古和云南这样的偏远地区，	也已经有他们的足迹了。
毕业以后，	别说每年聚一次，	就是五年一聚，	都不容易。
他的成绩这么好，	别说上普通大学了，	就是上最好的大学，	也肯定没有问题。
	别说去外国，	就是北京、上海，	我奶奶都没去过。
这么难看的衣服，	别说一百块钱，	就是十块钱，	我也不买。

Now check the correct explanations.

- ☐ 1 别说 means "let alone", "not to mention".
- ☐ 2 Topics A and B are related, but A is a more extensive case than B in terms of the comment following 也/都.
- ☐ 3 If the comment can be applied to topic B, then the comment can also be applied to A.
- ☐ 4 If there is a subject, it should be placed after 也 or 都 in the comment clause.

2 Work in pairs and complete the conversations.

1 A: 这个世界上还有很多地方非常落后。
B: 是啊，______________________

2 A: 你听得懂中文新闻吗？
B: 我的中文水平，______________

3 A: 你喝过普洱茶吗？
B: 普洱是一种茶吗？____________

Indicating "constantly" or "non-stop" with 一直 or 不断

1 Look at the sentences.

Subject	一直/不断(地)	Verb phrase
他	一直	都在努力提高摄影水平。
他们	一直	保持乐观、开放的态度。
他们激励我	不断地	突破自己。
这个地区的人口近年来	一直在不断地	增加，带来很多环境问题。

Now check the correct explanations.

- ☐ 1 Both 一直 and 不断 are adverbs used to indicate that the action is continuous. But they do not always apply to the same context.
- ☐ 2 一直 means "all along" or "all the time", expressing the continuation of an action or an unchangeable circumstance within a certain period of time. The verbs or adjectives modified are usually durative. It can also be used together with structures indicating ongoing actions such as V 着 or 在 V.
- ☐ 3 不断 literally means "non-stop" or "unceasingly". The verbs modified usually express a single occurrence, so 不断 is used to express that the action is repeated over and over again.
- ☐ 4 一直 and 不断 cannot be used together.

2 Complete the sentences with 一直 or 不断 (地).

1 我 _____ 想知道古时候的厕所是什么样的。
2 他 _____ 给一些报纸打电话，希望他们能报道他的故事。
3 从七月到现在气温 _____ 都是三十五六度。
4 在研究中，我 _____ 发现新问题。
5 我今年 _____ 忙得不得了。

Turn to page 202 for grammar reference.

LESSON 3

Communication activity

1 Work in pairs. Tell each other about a friend who has inspired you most in the past year. Ask and answer questions for more details. Include:

- basic information about the friend;
- his/her story or experience;
- why he/she is so inspiring to you.

Now discuss and decide whose story you would like to tell the whole class.

2 Tell the story to the class and vote for the best.

Turn to pages 177 and 183 for more speaking practice.

Review and practice

1 Choose the correct words to complete the sentences.

1 你觉不觉得我这一年 _____ 更成熟了？
a 变 b 变得 c 变成

2 既然他不喜欢你， 你又 _____ 把时间浪费在他身上？
a 不必 b 必要 c 何必

3 —你做的蛋糕真好吃！
—我也就是比业余水平高一点点，人家蛋糕店里卖的 _____ 好吃呢。
a 才 b 就 c 还

4 小王，你女朋友今天 _____ 没跟你一起来？
a 怎么 b 什么 c 怎样

5 没想到快到十月了， 温度还这么高，老是 _______。
a 不能降 b 不降下来 c 降不下来

2 Complete the sentences with the correct words from the box.

偶尔	改掉	坚持
面对	提议	尽可能

Cultural corner

Chinese symbols of good fortune

There are many symbols in Chinese culture that are associated with good fortune, which are widely used in design and displayed during holidays and on special occasions:

- The colour red symbolizes prosperity. Red envelopes (红包) containing money are given out as gifts, and red is the traditional colour of Chinese weddings.
- The pronunciation of the number eight (八) sounds very similar to the word meaning "becoming rich (发财)". Many Chinese like their phone number or address to contain 8 as many times as possible.
- Double Happiness (囍) is a famous ornamental design used in Chinese weddings. It is almost always red.
- The Chinese character for good fortune (福) is used as another ornamental symbol during Chinese New Year.
- The bat (蝙蝠) and the magpie (喜鹊) are auspicious animals because of their phonetic association with the character 福 and the character 喜. The animals are widely used as decorative symbols in charms and textiles.

1 有人 _____ 下次的聚会我们应该一起去黄山旅游。
2 晚睡、久坐、暴饮暴食 (overeating)，这些都是需要 _____ 的坏习惯。
3 在现代社会中，很多人每天都 _____ 着巨大的学习压力或工作压力。
4 你放心，我会 _____ 在最短的时间内把这件事情做完。
5 伦敦的地铁一般来说都是很可靠的，不过 _____ 也会出问题。
6 锻炼身体不是一天两天的事情，一定要每天都 _____ 才能看到效果。

3 **Put the sentences into the correct order.**

泰瑞·福克斯

a 1980年4月12日，泰瑞出发了。他每天大约跑28英里，一共跑了143天，共3339英里，最后他一共募到了2400万加元。

b 一直到现在，每年9月的第二个周末，全世界很多国家的人都会聚在一起参加“希望马拉松”，继续为癌症研究筹款。

c 然而事实并不是这样。手术以后，他装上了假肢、穿上了跑鞋。他打算从加拿大的最东边跑到最西边，为癌症研究筹款。他的这项计划叫做“希望马拉松”。

d 他是加拿大人。他本来只是一个很普通的青年，热爱生活、热爱运动。

e 你也许从来没听过泰瑞·福克斯这个名字，可是他却是对我影响最大的人。

f 故事说到这里，很多人会猜，他可能从此以后就生活在痛苦中了。

g 尽管他没能跑到加拿大的最西边就倒下了，癌症夺去了他的生命，可是他的精神和勇气却感动了许许多多的人。

h 不幸的是，十八岁的时候，他被查出得了骨癌，之后他失去了他的右腿。

1 _____ 2 _____ 3 _____ 4 _____
5 _____ 6 _____ 7 _____ 8 _____

Now match the words with their meanings.

9 癌 ái 症	i bone cancer
10 骨癌	j cancer
11 募 mù 款	k marathon
12 马拉松	l raise money
13 夺 duó 去	m courage
14 勇气	n take away

4 **Read the story in Activity 3 again and choose all the correct answers to the questions.**

1 泰瑞·福克斯是哪一年开始募款长跑的？
a 1979年 b 1980年 c 1981年

2 泰瑞在知道自己得了骨癌并失去一条腿以后做了什么事情？
a 每天都生活在痛苦中
b 装上了假肢
c 跑“希望马拉松”

3 他跑了多远？
a 28英里 b 3339英里
c 从最东边跑到了最西边

4 泰瑞对人们有什么样的影响？
a 很多人为癌症研究捐款。
b 很多人每年都参加 “希望马拉松”。
c 很多人继续为癌症研究募款。

5 **Write a journal report introducing someone who has influenced you or inspired you. Include:**

- 为什么对你影响很大
- 他/她的经历对你有什么启发
- 你在哪些时候想到了他/她
- 没有他/她，你的生活会不一样吗

Vocabulary review

Fill in the blanks.

保密	bǎomì	*v.*	keep secret
______	biǎoyáng	*v.*	praise, commend
不断	búduàn	*adv.*	______
不通	bùtōng	*v.*	blockage, barrier
______	bùxǔ	*v.*	not allow, must not, prohibit
惭愧	cánkuì	*adj.*	ashamed, abashed
长期	chángqī	*n.*	______
场	chǎng	*measure word*	(for rain/snow)
成熟	chéngshú	*v./adj.*	mature
______	chījīng	*v.*	be startled, be shocked, be taken aback
迟迟	chíchí	*adv.*	very late
冲击	chōngjī	*v.*	impact
重逢	chóngféng	*v.*	reunite
______	cūxīn	*adj.*	careless, thoughtless
地球	dìqiú	*n.*	the earth, the globe
反对	fǎnduì	*v.*	______
付出	fùchū	*v.*	pay, put in a lot of hard work
改掉	gǎidiào	*v.*	give up, drop
孤身一人	gūshēn-yìrén		all on one's own
______	hànshuǐ	*n.*	sweat
何必	hébì	*adv.*	why do you need to…
激励	jīlì	*v.*	inspire, encourage
降	jiàng	*v.*	lower, decrease, fall
尽可能	jǐnkěnéng	*adv.*	to the best of one's ability
聚	jù	*v.*	gather, meet
聚会	jùhuì	*n.*	get-together, gathering
开阔	kāikuò	*v.*	broaden, open
乐于	lèyú	*v.*	be happy to
离别	líbié	*v.*	part, separate, say goodbye
马虎	mǎhu	*adj.*	______
毛病	máobìng	*n.*	defect
闷热	mēnrè	*adj.*	muggy, sultry
______	mèng	*v.*	dream
面对	miànduì	*v.*	______
______	nǔlì	*adj./v.*	trying hard; make a great effort
偶尔	ǒu'ěr	*adv.*	occasionally
伤感	shānggǎn	*adj.*	melancholy
失落	shīluò	*adj.*	feeling lost
事物	shìwù	*n.*	things, matters
说不定	shuōbudìng	*adv.*	______
突飞猛进	tūfēi-měngjìn		a spurt of progress
突破	tūpò	*v.*	break through
下旬	xiàxún	*n.*	last ten days of the month
______	xǐng	*v.*	wake up
眼界	yǎnjiè	*n.*	horizon
一下子	yíxiàzi	*adv.*	at once, instantly
勇敢	yǒnggǎn	*adj.*	______
______	yǒngqì	*n.*	courage
转眼	zhuǎnyǎn	*v.*	in a flash
走遍	zǒubiàn	*v.*	travel all over

Review 3

Vocabulary

1 Match the words to make phrases.

1 忠实的	a 礼物
2 珍贵的	b 天气
3 孤单的	c 朋友
4 闷热的	d 态度
5 犹豫的	e 生活

2 Circle the odd words out.

1 失落　伤感　惭愧　赶快

2 专心　粗心　关心　开心

3 孤单　无聊　难熬　忍受

4 帮不上　来不及　离不开　说不定

5 修改　设置　刊登　得奖

3 Complete the sentences with the idioms in the box.

求之不得	流连忘返
突飞猛进	异国他乡

1 A: 第一年在 _______ 生活，你一定非常想家吧？

B: 我可不想家。这儿的生活丰富多彩，让我 _______。

2 A: 去美国留学，你的英文水平一定会 _______。

B: 那我真是 _______！

4 Choose the correct words to complete the sentences.

1 这首歌我第一次听，是他的 _______ 吗？

a 原创　b 原始　c 原来

2 没有得到这份工作，让我很 _______。

a 失败　b 失望　c 寂寞

3 他的研究终于有了重大的 _______。

a 突破　b 突然　c 修改

4 上了大学，你应该学会自己 _______ 自己的时间。

a 支配　b 支持　c 花费

5 她不漂亮，可是非常有 _______，所以喜欢她的人特别多。

a 力量　b 魅力　c 能力

5 Match the words with their opposites.

1 反对	a 经常
2 偶尔	b 批评
3 坚持	c 支持
4 表扬	d 放弃
5 无聊	e 熟悉
6 陌生	f 有趣
7 集体	g 个人
8 疏远	h 亲近

Grammar

1 Choose the correct words to complete the sentences.

1 没得到大奖，他 ______ 很失落。

a 听出来　b 看起来　c 看出来

2 这份旅游杂志办得这么好，应该继续办 ______。

a 下来　b 上去　c 下去

3 这些玩具你想跟谁分享 ______。

a 就跟谁分享　b 就跟谁　c 跟谁

4 她的眼睛不太好，总是得戴 ______ 眼镜上 ______ 课，要不然就看不清楚。

a X……着　b 着……X　c 着……着

5 客服部的人找来找去，终于找 ______ 了出错的订单。

a X　b 到　c 下

6 别把钱都 ______ 在买衣服上。

a 用　b 控制　c 支配

7 ______ 生命只剩下一天，我们也应该好好把握每一分钟。

a 虽然　b 即使　c 既然

2 Complete the sentences with the words in the box.

一直	是否	不断	差点儿

1 A: 昨天的辩论比赛，阿曼达表现得怎么样？
B: 她表现得很好，不过对方也非常厉害，她 ______ 就输了。

2 A: 对您来说，坚持梦想 ______ 意味着有的时候要面对困难和孤独？
B: 确实是这样，我相信所有坚持梦想的人都是有勇气的人。

3 A: 马克和安迪的关系很好吗？
B: 是的，他们俩从高中起，就 ______ 是好朋友。

4 A: 我们已经 ______ 地向对方公司保证我们会按时交货，可是他们还是不相信。
B: 那还是让经理来处理吧。

3 Complete the conversations with the words given.

1 A: 她父母本来说周末来给她过生日，可是又突然说不来了。
B: 难怪她今天心情不好，__________ __________ (多……啊)

2 A: 你的照片拍得真好！
B: 哪里哪里，我的水平一般。______ __________ (才……呢)

3 A: 你真的要去留学吗？如果你的家人都反对呢？
B: __________ __________ (即使……也……)

4 A: 听说你参加的夏令营规定又多又严。你能跟父母视频聊天儿吗？
B: 怎么可能，__________ ______(别说……，就是……也……)

4 **Rewrite the sentences using the words given.**

1 他什么都不做，只打游戏。(把……V在……上)

2 这家餐厅的主题是棒球。(以……为……)

3 由于受到了戴维斯的影响，史蒂夫对云南有特殊的感情。(之所以……是因为……)

4 他根本不理解你的想法，你不用跟他解释。(何必……呢)

Integrated skills

2-33

1 **Listen to the short speech and choose the correct answers to the questions.**

1 发言的主要内容是 ______。
   a 大学生的主要问题
   b 大学四年应该怎么过
   c 大学毕业以后找什么工作

2 "读万卷书，行万里路"的意思是 ______。
   a 为了开阔眼界，应该多看书，也应该去很多地方
   b 看很多书，和走很多路一样重要
   c 看书让人变聪明，走路让人身体健康

3 王力决定去英国是为了 ______。
   a 念书，拿学位
   b 有机会旅行，感受不同文化
   c 学会忍受寂寞，适应陌生环境

2 **Listen again and check the correct statements.**

☐ 1 王力是一个成功的人。

☐ 2 在王力看来，年轻人工作要认真仔细，最好不要犯错误。

☐ 3 王力在大学换了专业。他父母和老师开始都不支持他的决定，可是后来他们的看法改变了。

☐ 4 王力认为成功的人一定很幸福。

☐ 5 王力毕业以后去了一家世界知名的公司。

3 **Work in pairs. Discuss what qualities a charismatic person should have and how to cultivate the qualities. You may begin with the adjectives in the box and come up with your own ones.**

美丽	勇敢	幽默	努力
负责	成熟	积极	真诚

Now write down a coherent paragraph using the words you have chosen.

我认为一个有魅力的人首先要……因为……比方说……其次，……

4 **Complete the passage with the correct words in the box.**

失败　得奖　分享　浪费　社交　孤单
坚持　改掉　流连忘返　　突飞猛进

我是一个热爱电脑游戏和网络游戏的人。刚开始我玩得不太好，后来我的水平 ______，最近一年每次参加游戏比赛我都会 ______。玩游戏让我非常有成就感。

可是我的父母却不理解我。他们总是说我把时间都 ______ 在游戏上和虚拟的世界里，说我必须 ______ 玩游戏的坏毛病，否则我以后的人生会很 ______。

可是我觉得虚拟世界也是我生活的一部分。现实生活中，我不会 ______，也没有什么亲近的朋友，常常很 ______；跟陌生人说话更让我紧张。然而在网络上，我有很多和我一样热爱游戏的朋友，他们佩服我、鼓励我，也跟我 ______ 他们的感受。这也是为什么游戏世界那么让我 ______。我的梦想是当一个职业游戏玩家或者游戏开发者。

我应该不应该 ______ 这个梦想？

Now think about the following questions and write a passage expressing your opinions.

1 你支持玩游戏还是反对玩游戏？
2 玩游戏对生活有什么影响？
3 以游戏为梦想值得吗？

Enjoy Chinese

Guess what the ancient Chinese characters resemble.

1	a 休
2	b 好
3	c 分
4	d 并
5	e 车
6	f 鸟

Now match the ancient characters with the modern ones.

Pinyin pronunciation guide

Sound	Words	Example 1	Example 2
Initials			
b	bed	bō 玻	bēi 杯
p	pin	pō 坡	pāi 拍
m	moon	mō 摸	mái 埋
f	fun	fó 佛	fā 发
d	day	dé 得	dā 搭
t	tin	tè 特	tā 他
n	nose	ne 呢	nà 纳
l	long	lè 勒	lā 拉
g	good	gē 哥	gāi 该
k	kind	kē 科	kāi 开
h	hat	hē 喝	hā 哈
j	jug	jī 基	jiāo 交
q		qī 欺	qià 恰
x		xī 希	xiāo 消
zh	bridge	zhī 知	zhā 渣
ch	chin	chī 吃	chá 茶
sh	shirt	shī 诗	shā 沙
r	reduce	rì 日	rén 人
z	"ds" in reads	zī 资	zá 杂
c	"ts" in hats	cí 雌	cā 擦
s	say	sī 思	sè 色
Finals			
a	far	ā 啊	bā 八
o	saw	wō 喔	mò 墨
e	her	é 鹅	chē 车
i	bee	yī 衣	bǐ 比
u	rude	wū 乌	wū 屋
ü	German Fühlen	yū 迂	nǚ 女
ai	eye	āi 哀	bái 白
ei	eight	ēi 欸	féi 肥
ao	cow	áo 熬	bāo 包
ou	oh	ōu 欧	pōu 剖
an	enhance	ān 安	bān 班
en	taken	ēn 恩	běn 本
ang	gang	áng 昂	bāng 邦
eng	sung	hēng 亨	bēng 崩
ong	German Lunge	hōng 轰	dōng 东
ia	yard	ya 呀	xià 夏
ie	yes	yē 耶	bié 别
iao	meow	yāo 腰	jiāo 交
iu	yoga	yōu 优	diū 丢
ian	yen	yān 烟	piān 偏
in	in	yīn 因	bīn 宾
iang	e + yang	yāng 央	niáng 娘
ing	sing	yīng 英	bǐng 丙
iong	German Jünger	yōng 雍	qióng 穷
ua	guano	wā 蛙	guā 瓜
uo	wall	wō 窝	duō 多
uai	why	wāi 歪	guài 怪
uei		wēi 威	wéi 围
uan	wan	wān 弯	duǎn 短
un	won	wēn 温	kūn 昆
uang	u + ongoing	wāng 汪	guāng 光
ueng		wēng 翁	wèng 瓮
üe	ü + eh	yuē 约	quē 缺
üan	ü + an	yuān 冤	xuān 宣
ün	German grün	yūn 晕	qún 群

Combinations of pinyin initials and simple finals

simple finals / Initials	a	o	e	i	u	ü
b	ba	bo		bi	bu	
p	pa	po		pi	pu	
m	ma	mo	me	mi	mu	
f	fa	fo			fu	
d	da		de	di	du	
t	ta		te	ti	tu	
n	na		ne	ni	nu	nü
l	la		le	li	lu	lü
g	ga		ge		gu	
k	ka		ke		ku	
h	ha		he		hu	
j				ji		jü (ju)
q				qi		qü (qu)
x				xi		xü (xu)

Pair work activities for Student A

Unit 1

Read the following job description. Find six differences with Student B's job description.

让我们从这里 **开始**，
汉语教师 **招聘** 广告

》单位介绍

光华国际中学位于北京市朝阳区，是一所为外籍人士子女提供国际化教育的私立中学，共设六个年级，接受12岁到18岁的学生入校学习，使用美式教程和课本。现招聘用英文教授汉语的老师两名。每周课时为二十个小时。待遇从优。

》招聘要求

1. 英文水平高，TOEFL成绩为100分以上
2. 中文为母语
3. 大学及以上文化水平；教育专业、对外汉语专业的毕业生优先
4. 性格活泼开朗、热爱教育、学习能力强
5. 有两年以上对外汉语教学经验
6. 有中学教学经验的老师优先

联系方式	hr@discoverchinagh.edu	

Unit 2

An educational company in China is looking for temporary summer employees to teach English in China. You are very interested in the position. Complete the table with your own information.

姓名	
年龄	
联系方式（电话/电子邮件）	
兴趣、爱好	
教育水平/学校名称	
中文水平/学中文多长时间	
有没有教外国人英文的经验？	
有没有教小孩子的经验？	
有没有教中学生的经验？	
有没有教成年人的经验？	
用三个词介绍你自己	信息

Their HR manager, Student B, schedules an initial phone interview with you.

Act out the interview with Student B. Write down the questions Student B asks. At the end of the interview, you will be told if you will enter the second round of interviews.

Unit 3

You are a travel agent who is helping a group of teenagers from Beijing to plan a one-week trip to your country. This will be their first trip abroad and they want to visit two cities. Student B is the group leader.

1 Pick four cities that you think are worth visiting and have many activities suitable for teenagers.

2 Research the routes and prices of round-trip flights between Beijing and a major city in your country. Make a list of choices.

3 Act out a conversation with Student B and describe the itinerary. Include:

- 决定参观哪两个城市
- 一周的行程
- 在两个城市有哪些活动，参观哪些景点
- 从北京到目的地的往返机票

Unit 4

You and your partner, Student B, are stranded on an island. There is enough food and water but nothing else. Which personal items below do you wish you had brought with you? Explain why. You can choose six items only.

Unit 5

1 **You are working for a consulting firm which advises their clients about business strategies in China. One of your clients, Student B, is seeking your advice about which gifts are suitable for their potential Chinese business partners. Here is your knowledge of gift-giving in China:**

As in the West, gifts in China are given on special occasions and as an expression of gratitude. However, there are many differences which may complicate the exchange of gifts.

Firstly, it is usual for gifts to be presented and received with both hands, as this shows mutual respect. Gifts are commonly wrapped in red and gold, as these colours symbolize good luck.

When giving gifts, there are certain taboos that should be avoided. For example, it is inadvisable to give knives or scissors, as this could be interpreted as a desire to "cut" a friendship. Other examples of unsuitable gifts include clocks and umbrellas, as the Chinese word for "clock" sounds similar to the word for "death" or "end", whilst the Chinese word for "umbrella" sounds similar to the word "lose".

If several gifts are given, it is important to note that six, eight and nine are lucky numbers.

Finally, in Chinese culture it is considered polite to return favours and kindnesses, so if given a gift, it is often best to show your appreciation by reciprocating. (See *Cultural corner* of Unit 6, *Discover China* 3)

2 **Act out a conversation with Student B to help decide what gifts to give.**

Unit 6

It has been ten years since you graduated from university. One week ago, you began working for an international organization in China. Tonight you are attending the organization's annual banquet. Because you do not know many people in the company, you feel a little bit bored. Then you bump into Student B, who was your classmate in the same Chinese class in school.

1 Imagine what has happened in your life (career and family) during the ten years after your graduation.

2 Act out a conversation with Student B. Start with questions about his/her family, his/her life experience after graduation, etc. Be prepared to answer some questions about your life experience too. Make sure you ask Student B about his/her experience with your current employer.

Unit 7

You are the academic director of an ESL school in China. A major part of your job is to deal with students' complaints about your ESL teachers, textbooks or curriculum. Here are some principles you stick to when getting complaints.

- Stay positive.
- Show your sympathy.
- Help the student to analyze the situation.
- Promise to get to the root of the problem and get back to the student quickly.

Now act out a conversation with Student B, who is a Chinese student who goes to your school. Try to help him/her with his/her complaints. You will need to make apologies if necessary.

Unit 8

Student B and you are good friends. You have just graduated from college, and you have received two job offers. Right now you are tempted by the second one, but you want to consult Student B before making the final decision:

- The first one is a corporate job. The salary is good, but the location is in a big city where the living expenses are high. There will always be a lot of pressure and competition at work, but there is also great potential in terms of career development.
- The second one is at an educational institute. The salary is low, but the location is in a suburb of a big city where the living expenses are relatively low. It offers more stability than the first job, but there is less room for career development. You will have lots of free time if you take this job.

1 List the pros and cons of both positions.

2 Act out a casual discussion with Student B. You are trying to convince Student B that the second choice suits you better.

Unit 9

Look at the picture. Find differences with Student B's picture.

Unit 10

Look at the statements and check if you agree or disagree.

☐ 大城市比小城镇/郊区的生活更好。

☐ 出去旅游的时候不必省钱。

☐ 买二手的衣服比买新衣服更好。

☐ 网络让人和人的交流变得更少。

☐ 让孩子做家务活应该给钱。

☐ 学外语是为了工作的机会更多。

Now go through the statements with Student B, and mark the ones from which your opinions differ. Pick one and carry out a mini-debate with Student B. Support your opinions with examples.

Unit 11

You are passionate about other countries. You plan to travel the world and visit 20 countries. You think you can always support yourself by teaching English. Student B is a good friend who likes to stay home. He/She thinks spending more than ten days on the road is unbearable.

1 Make a list of reasons why you love travelling to a foreign country and living there for an extended period of time.

2 Carry out a debate with Student B.

Unit 12

It has been ________ months/years since you started learning Chinese. You have been through many difficulties, but at the same time you have made substantial progress. It is time to reflect on your learning journey and share it with your teachers and classmates.

1 Discuss your learning experience with Student B, who is also a Chinese language learner. Find out what you had in common in learning Chinese. For example:

- Did you have the same native language?
- Did you encounter similar difficulties?
- Did you both enjoy learning about Chinese culture?
- Did you both find writing characters a challenging task?

Add to the list more questions you want to ask.

2 Share the most rewarding/interesting experience you have had while learning Chinese.

Pair work activities for Student B

Unit 1

Read the following job description. Find six differences with Student A's job description.

让我们从这里**开始**，
汉语教师**招聘**广告

》单位介绍

光华国际中学位于上海市碧云社区，是一所为外籍人士子女提供国际化教育的私立中学，共设六个年级，接受12岁到18岁的学生入校学习，使用美式教程和课本。现招聘用英文教授汉语的老师两名。每周课时为十五个小时。待遇从优。

》招聘要求

1. 英文水平高，TOEFL成绩为100分以上
2. 中文为母语
3. 大学及以上文化水平；中文专业或对外汉语专业的毕业生优先
4. 性格活泼开朗、热爱教育、学习能力强
5. 有两年以上国际学校教学经验
6. 有海外留学经历者优先

联系方式 021-XXXX4785 ☎

Unit 2

You are the HR manager of an educational company in China. You are looking for temporary summer employees to teach English in China. Below is a checklist of the credentials and characteristics the ideal candidate will have.

汉语教师招聘要求

- 英文好，最好为母语
- 有教学经验
- 喜欢帮助别人
- 中文水平不错，可以跟中国人进行日常对话
- 性格独立，可以在中国独立生活
- 去过很多地方，适应新环境能力很强

Student A is one of the many applicants for the position, and you will conduct an initial phone interview with him/her. Prepare a list of questions about the applicant's background information, past working experience and personality.

Act out the telephone interview with Student A. Take notes while Student A is answering your questions. Make a decision at the end of the interview and tell Student A if your company will invite him/her for a second interview.

Unit 3

You are the team leader of a group of teenagers from Beijing who are going to visit a foreign country for one week. This will be the group's first trip abroad and they want to visit two cities. Below is information about the group.

- 你带的团一共有十个学生，都是高中一年级的学生。
- 你们的钱不太多，希望飞机票尽量经济、便宜。不一定要直飞。
- 除了参观景点以外，希望可以参观国外的高中，有机会跟当地的学生交谈。

Student A is a travel agent and will help you plan the trip. He/She will suggest four cities to visit, as well as routes and prices of round-trip flights. You will have to make decisions based on the information Student A provides and the budget/purpose of the group visit.

Act out a conversation with Student A about the itinerary and respond to:

- 决定参观哪两个城市
- 一周的行程
- 在两个城市有哪些活动，参观哪些景点
- 从北京到目的地的往返机票

Unit 4

You and your partner, Student A, are stranded on an island. There is enough food and water but nothing else. Which personal items below do you wish you had brought with you? Explain why. You can choose six items only.

Unit 5

1 **Your company has decided to enter the Chinese market. A consulting firm is helping develop your company's business strategies in China. You are going to ask one of the consulting firm's associates, Student A, about which gifts are suitable for your potential Chinese business partners. Here is a list of items you have come up with. Complete the list with other gifts.**

1 绿色的棒球帽

2 瑞士军刀

3 印有公司 logo 的伞

4 一瓶红酒

5 有公司 logo 的 T 恤衫

6 一块手表

7 印有公司 logo 的笔、笔记本

8 ________________

9 ________________

10 ________________

2 **Act out a conversation with Student A, going over the items one by one. Make a decision about which gifts to take.**

Unit 6

It has been ten years since you graduated from university. One week ago, you began working for an international organization in China. Tonight you are attending the organization's annual banquet. Because you do not know many people in the company, you feel a little bit bored. Then you bump into Student A, who was your classmate in the same Chinese class in school.

1 Imagine what has happened in your life (career and family) during the ten years after your graduation.

2 Act out a conversation with Student A. Start with questions about his/her family, his/her life experience after graduation, etc. Be prepared to answer some questions about your life experience too. Make sure you ask Student A about his/her experience with your current employer.

Unit 7

You are a Chinese student who attends an ESL school to improve your English. Recently you have been unhappy about your class, because:

- Unlike the previous ESL teacher you had, the current teacher speaks too fast, and does not seem to focus on grammar much.
- The textbook is too difficult for your level.
- The teacher often puts you on the spot by asking for your opinions.
- You are not used to doing presentations in English in front of many people.

You may also add some other problems to the list.

Now act out a conversation with Student A, who is the academic director of the school. Choose three complaints and continue to complain until you are happy about Student A's solution.

Unit 8

Student A and you are good friends. Student A has just graduated from college, and he/she has received two job offers.

- The first one is a corporate job. The salary is good, but the location is in a big city where the living expenses are high. There will always be a lot of pressure and competition at work, but there is also great potential in terms of career development.
- The second one is at an educational institute. The salary is low, but the location is in a suburb of a big city where the living expenses are relatively low. It offers more stability than the first job, but there is less room for career development. He/She will have lots of free time if he/she takes this job.

1 List the pros and cons of both positions.

2 Act out a casual discussion with Student A. Student A is trying to convince you that the second choice suits him/her better, but you think Student A should definitely take the first offer and try to make him/her change his/her mind.

Unit 9

Look at the picture. Find differences with Student A's picture.

Unit 10

Look at the statements and check if you agree or disagree.

- ☐ 大城市比小城镇/郊区的生活更好。
- ☐ 出去旅游的时候不必省钱。
- ☐ 买二手的衣服比买新衣服更好。
- ☐ 网络让人和人的交流变得更少。
- ☐ 让孩子做家务活应该给钱。
- ☐ 学外语是为了工作的机会更多。

Now go through the statements with Student A, and mark the ones from which your opinions differ. Pick one and carry out a mini-debate with Student A. Support your opinions with examples.

Unit 11

You do not hate travelling but you prefer to be close to home. You think spending more than ten days on the road is unbearable. Student A is a good friend of yours who is passionate about other countries. It is his/her plan to travel the world and visit 20 countries. Student A thinks that he/she can always support him/herself by teaching English.

1 Make a list of challenges and practical difficulties that people face while travelling and living abroad, especially for an extended period of time.

2 Carry out a debate with Student A.

Unit 12

It has been ________ months/years since you started learning Chinese. You have been through many difficulties, but at the same time you have made substantial progress. It is time to reflect on your learning journey and share it with your teachers and classmates.

1 Discuss your learning experience with Student A, who is also a Chinese language learner. Find out what you had in common in learning Chinese. For example:

- Did you have the same native language?
- Did you encounter similar difficulties?
- Did you both enjoy learning about Chinese culture?
- Did you both find writing characters a challenging task?

Add to the list more questions you want to ask.

2 Share the most rewarding/interesting experience you have had while learning Chinese.

Grammar reference

Unit 1

Expressing "not at all", "not even one", "not a single…" with 一……都/也 不/没……

(yī … dōu / yě bù / méi …)

一……都/也 不/没…… is used to express "not at all", "not a single …" or "not even one". After "一", the phrase can either be "一点儿", which modifies uncountable nouns, or "一 + measure word", which precedes countable nouns. Sometimes, an object is moved to the very beginning of the sentence to serve as a topic, thus showing a strong emphasis.

	Subject	yī 一 ……	Noun	dōu 都/ yě 也	bù 不/ méi 没……
	Tā 他	yìdiǎnr 一点儿	xiūxi de 休息 的 shíjiān 时间	dōu 都	méiyǒu 没有。
Cóng zǎo- 从 早 shang dào 上 到 xiànzài 现在	tā 她	yìdiǎnr 一点儿	shuǐ 水	yě 也	méi hē 没 喝。
Zhèxiē shū 这些 书，	wǒ 我	yì běn 一 本		yě 也	bù xiǎng 不 想 kàn 看。
Zài zhèli 在 这里	tā 他	yí gè 一个	péngyou 朋友	dōu 都	méiyǒu 没有。
Nàxiē 那些 yǐqián de 以前 的 shìqing 事情，	tā 他	yí jiàn 一 件		dōu 都	bú jìde 不记得 le 了。

Emphasizing details of a past action using 是……的

(shì … de)

是……的 is used to emphasize the time, place, manner, purpose or agent of a particular action in the past. What the speaker wants to highlight should be put between 是 and 的. Sometimes, 是 can be omitted, but 的 must not be.

Tā (shì) zuótiān dào de Lúndūn.
1 她（是）昨天 到 的 伦敦。(Time)

Tā (shì) zuò huǒchē qù de Lúndūn.
2 她（是）坐 火车 去 的 伦敦。(Manner)

Tā (shì) zài Lúndūn xué de jiànzhùxué.
3 她（是）在 伦敦 学 的 建筑学。(Place)

Tā (shì) wèile xué jiànzhùxué cái qù Lúndūn de.
4 她（是）为了 学 建筑学 才 去 伦敦 的。(Purpose)

(Shì) tā de gāozhōng tóngxué qù chēzhàn jiē de tā.
5（是）她 的 高 中 同学 去 车 站 接 的 她。(Agent)

Showing direction of movement with 回/进/上/下+来/去

(huí / jìn / shàng / xià + lái / qù)

回, 进, 上 and 下 can combine with either 来 or 去 to show the direction of movement. That is, in words such as 回来, 上去, 下来, etc., 来 and 去 serve as directional complements. 来 indicates the action moves towards the speaker, while 去 indicates the action moves away from the speaker. If there is an object showing location or destination, it is placed between 回/进/上/下 and 来/去, e.g. 回北京来, 进房间去, etc.

	Verb	Object	Directional complement	
Wǒ fùmǔ shàng 我 父母 上 gè xīngqī jiù 个 星期 就	huí 回	jiāxiāng 家乡	qù 去	le 了。
Nǐ juéde tā 你 觉得 他 míngnián hái huì 明 年 还 会	huí 回	zánmen 咱们 gōngsī 公司	lái 来	ma 吗？
Wàimian wèidào bú 外面 味道 不 tài hǎo, nǐ kuài 太 好，你 快	jìn 进	wūzi 屋子	qù 去。	
Wǒ zhù zài sān céng, 我 住 在 三 层， nǐ néng bù néng 你 能 不 能	shàng 上	lóu 楼	lái 来？	

	Verb	Object	Directional complement	
Zhème gāo 这么高， nǐ shì bú shì yǒu- 你是不是有 diǎnr hàipà 点儿害怕？ Yào wǒ bāng nǐ 要我帮你	xià 下		qu 去	ma 吗？

Introducing an extreme case using 连……都/也……
(lián … dōu / yě …)

连……都/也…… means "even" and expresses that information or an event is unexpected or surprising. In order to express that something is unexpected or surprising, an extreme case is placed between **连** and **都/也**. In this structure, **连** and **都/也** are both necessary; neither may be dropped.

	lián 连	Extreme case	dōu 都/ yě 也	Verb
Nǐ zhēn xíng 你真行！	Lián 连	Tángshī 唐诗	yě 也	huì bèi ya 会背呀。
Zuìjìn kuài yào 最近快要 mángsǐ le 忙死了，	lián 连	shàng cèsuǒ de 上厕所的 shíjiān 时间	dōu 都	kuài méiyǒu 快没有 le 了。
Zài Lúndūn shēng- 在伦敦生 huóle liǎng nián 活了两年 le kěshì tā 了，可是他	lián 连	Dàyīng 大英 Bówùguǎn 博物馆	yě 也	méi qùguo 没去过。
Gōngzuòle yì tiān 工作了一天， wǒ bà lèi de 我爸累得	lián 连	shuōhuà de 说话的 lìqi 力气	dōu 都	méiyǒu le 没有了。
Nǐ bú shì hěn xǐ- 你不是很喜 huan yīnyuèjù 欢音乐剧 ma zěnme 吗，怎么	lián 连	Māo 《猫》	dōu 都	méi tīng- 没听 shuōguo 说过？

Unit 2

Indicating a very high degree of something with 不得了
(bùdéliǎo)

……不得了 is a complement and is used to indicate a very high degree of an adjective or an emotional verb. They form the structure "adj./emotional verb **得不得了**". The adjectives or emotional verbs can be either negative or positive in meaning.

	Adj. / Verb	de 得	bùdéliǎo 不得了
Wūzi li méiyǒu 屋子里没有 kōngtiáo 空调，	rè 热	de 得	bùdéliǎo 不得了。
Tā de nǚpéngyou gēn 他的女朋友跟 tā fēnshǒu le tā 他分手了，他	nánguò 难过	de 得	bùdéliǎo 不得了。
Nà jiā fànguǎnr de 那家饭馆儿的 Shànghǎicài 上海菜，	hǎochī 好吃	de 得	bùdéliǎo 不得了。
Tīngshuō zhōumò yào qù 听说周末要去 diàoyú Xiǎo Lín 钓鱼，小林	gāoxìng 高兴	de 得	bùdéliǎo 不得了。
Nàge míngxīng tā 那个明星，她	xǐhuan 喜欢	de 得	bùdéliǎo 不得了。

Repeated actions with 再 or 又
(zài / yòu)

Both **再** and **又** can serve as adverbs meaning "again", thus indicating the repetition of an action or activity. **再** indicates that an action which has occurred in the past is to be repeated in the future. In contrast, **又** indicates that the repeated action has already occurred. In some circumstances, **又** can also be used to indicate the future recurrence of an action which can be expected or anticipated.

	zài yòu 再/又	Verb phrase
Nǐ néng 你能	zài 再	gěi tā fā fēng yóujiàn ma 给她发封邮件吗？

	zài yòu 再/又	Verb phrase
Wǒmen kěyǐ 我们可以	zài 再	gěi tā yí cì jīhuì 给他一次机会。
Wǒ guò jǐ tiān 我过几天	zài 再	qù tāmen xuéxiào 去他们学校。
Wǒ hé wǒ gē zuótiān 我和我哥昨天	yòu 又	kànle yí biàn zhège 看了一遍这个 diànyǐng 电影。
Tā 他	yòu 又	mèngjiàn fùmǔ le 梦见父母了。
Míngtiān 明天	yòu 又	yào kǎoshì le 要考试了。

Expressing "a little bit" using 一下 (yíxià) or 一点儿 (yìdiǎnr)

一下 and **一点儿** can both be used to moderate a statement to mean "a little bit". **一点儿** is used to show that an action is carried out to a minor extent or "a little bit", and refers to the action verb itself rather than the object of the verb. **一点儿** can also be used as a qualifier to modify the object of the verb and denote that the quantity is small. In contrast, **一下** is only used in an imperative sentence or when the speaker wants to make a suggestion or request.

	Verb	yíxià 一下/ yìdiǎnr 一点儿	Object	
Zhè shìr 这事儿 wǒ bú tài 我不太 qīngchu nǐ 清楚，你 háishi 还是	wèn 问	yíxià 一下	biérén ba 别人吧。	
Wǒ néng 我能 bù néng 不能	jiè 借	yíxià 一下	nǐ de 你的 Zhōngwénshū 中文书？	
Nǐ hǎohǎo 你好好 gēn tā 跟他	jiěshì 解释	yíxià 一下，		bié zài chǎo- 别再吵 jià le 架了。

	Verb	yíxià 一下/ yìdiǎnr 一点儿	Object	
Wǒ 我	mǎile 买了	yìdiǎnr 一点儿	shūcài 蔬菜 hé ròu 和肉，	wǎnshang 晚上 zánmen zì- 咱们自 jǐ zuòfàn 己做饭 ba 吧。
Tā 他	zhīdào 知道	yìdiǎnr 一点儿	Zhōngguó de 中国的 lìshǐ 历史。	
Qù Xībānyá 去西班牙 lǚyóu zuì- 旅游，最 hǎo néng 好能	dǒng 懂	yìdiǎnr 一点儿	Xībānyáwén 西班牙文。	

Indicating the beginning of an action or the start of a new state with 起来 (qǐlai)

起来 is used after an action verb to indicate the beginning of an action or after an adjective to indicate the start of a new state. Even though **起来** still serves as a complement, its literal meaning of "upward movement" as a directional complement has been lost. If the verb takes an object, the object should be inserted between **起** and **来**.

	Verb 起 (qǐ) (object) 来 (lái) / Adj. 起来 (qǐlai)
Nǐ bú zuò gōngkè zěnme 你不做功课，怎么	xiě qǐ xiǎoshuō lái le 写起小说来了？
Tā de gǒu hé línjūjiā 她的狗和邻居家 de gǒu 的狗	dǎle qǐlái 打了起来。
Tā gēnzhe yīnyuè 他跟着音乐	chàng qǐ gē lái 唱起歌来。

	qǐ lái Verb 起 (object) 来 / qǐlai Adj. 起来
Yì xiǎngdào yào zài dàjiā 一想到要在大家 miànqián shuōhuà tā jiù 面前说话，他就	jǐnzhāng qǐlai 紧张起来。
Kànjiàn yòu piàoliang yòu hǎo- 看见又漂亮又好 chī de dàngāo háizi yí- 吃的蛋糕，孩子一 xiàzi jiù 下子就	gāoxìng de tiào qǐlai le 高兴得跳起来了。

Unit 3

Introducing a new subject using 至于 (zhìyú)

至于 as a preposition means "as to" or "with regard to". It is used to introduce a new subject or raise a new topic. The new subject must be related to the topic of the previous statement, or be a new aspect of the previous topic. The new subject could be a noun phrase, a verb phrase, or a clause. 至于 and its new subject are followed by a further comment.

Previous statement	zhìyú 至于 + new subject matter	Further comment
Tīngshuō tā yào líkāi 听说他要离开 gōngsī le 公司了，	zhìyú yuányīn 至于原因，	wǒ bú tài 我不太 qīngchu 清楚。
Tīngshuō tā yào líkāi 听说他要离开 gōngsī le 公司了，	zhìyú shénme 至于什么 shíhou líkāi 时候离开，	xiànzài hái bú 现在还不 tài qīngchu 太清楚。
Tīngshuō tā yào líkāi 听说他要离开 gōngsī le 公司了，	zhìyú tā yǐ- 至于他以 hòu qù nǎr 后去哪儿 gōngzuò 工作，	wǒ jiù bù zhī- 我就不知 dào le 道了。
Nà jiā cānguǎn fàn- 那家餐馆，饭 cài wèidào tèbié hǎo 菜味道特别好， fúwù yě hěn bàng 服务也很棒，	zhìyú jiàgé 至于价格，	dāngrán yě 当然也 shì xiāngdāng 是相当 gāo de 高的。
Duì wǒ láishuō néng 对我来说，能 cānjiā zhè cì bǐsài jiù 参加这次比赛就 shì hěn hǎo de jīnglì 是很好的经历，	zhìyú bǐsài 至于比赛 chéngjì 成绩，	qíshí bìng 其实并 bú shì hěn 不是很 zhòngyào 重要。

Comparative structures using 不如 (bùrú)

The comparative structure using 不如 means "A is not as ... as B". The adjectives or verb phrases in the comparison using 不如 must be words with a positive connotation. If the adjectives appear at the start of the sentence, they do not need to be repeated at the end. If there is no specific adjective mentioned, the default meaning "(not as) good" applies.

Context	A	bùrú 不如	B	Adj.
	Xiāngjiāo 香蕉	bùrú 不如	píngguǒ 苹果	hǎochī 好吃。
	Wǒ gōngzuò 我工作	bùrú 不如	tā 他	nǔlì 努力。
	Wǒ mèimei 我妹妹 chànggē 唱歌 chàng de 唱得	bùrú 不如	wǒ 我	hǎo 好。
Tā tīqiú tī 他踢球踢 de nàme hǎo 得那么好，	wǒ 我	bùrú 不如	tā 他。	
	Zuò fēijī 坐飞机	bùrú 不如	zuò 坐 huǒchē 火车。	

Expressing fractions and percentages with ……分之……

……分之…… is used to express fractions or percentages. The order is the reverse of that used in English. So, when expressing a fraction, the denominator precedes 分之, while the numerator follows 分之, e.g. ¾ is read 四分之三. When expressing a percentage, the idea of "parts per hundred" is expressed first, with 百分之……, e.g. 25.9% is read 百分之二十五点九. "A 占 B 的……分之……" is a particular structure used to express fractions or percentages, often appearing in formal and written expression.

Huǒchēpiào chàbuduō bǐ fēijīpiào piányi sì fēn zhī sān
1 火车票差不多比飞机票便宜四分之三。

Shǐyòng gōnggòng jiāotōng shàng-xiàbān de rén zhàn chéngshì zǒngrénkǒu de sān fēn zhī yī
2 使用公共交通上下班的人占城市总人口的三分之一。

Shìjiè shang yuē yǒu wǔ fēn zhī yī de rén hē bú dào gānjìng de shuǐ
3 世界上约有五分之一的人喝不到干净的水。

Dìqiú shang dàyuē bǎi fēn zhī jiǔshíqī de shuǐ shì xiánshuǐ
4 地球上大约百分之九十七的水是咸水。

Liùshíwǔ suì yǐshàng de lǎorén zhàn Lúndūn zǒngrénkǒu de bǎi fēn zhī shísān diǎn qī
5 六十五岁以上的老人占伦敦总人口的百分之十三点七。

Moderating positive adjectives with 还

还 as an adverb is used to moderate or weaken the positive tone of adjectives. As such, the meaning of 还 is similar to "quite" or "reasonably" in English. Even though 还 moderates the positive tone of adjectives, the speaker in fact still wants to convey a positive comment. If there are some other degree adverbs modifying the positive adjectives, they often follow 还 rather than precede it.

	hái 还	Positive adjective
Tā juéde Xiǎo Lín rén 他觉得小林人	hái 还	búcuò 不错。
Zhè jiā lǚguǎn de fúwù 这家旅馆的服务	hái 还	xíng 行。
Dìtiě yuèpiào 地铁月票	hái 还	suàn piányi 算便宜。
Zuótiān de kǎoshì 昨天的考试	hái 还	bǐjiào róngyì 比较容易。
Zhè fùjìn jiùsuàn dàole wǎnshang yě 这附近就算到了晚上也	hái 还	suàn ānquán 算安全。

Unit 4

Verb + object as a separable compound

"Verb + object" compounds (V-O compounds) are a group of verbs whose internal structure is "verb + object". A V-O compound is not a combination of two words; it is considered one word only, and the English translation is usually one word, e.g. 睡觉=sleep; 唱歌=sing. The V-O compounds can be separated by inserting the aspectual particles 了, 过, or 着, or by duration, frequency, and quantifiers. Because V-O compounds already contain an object, they cannot be directly followed by another object; this is why, e.g. *我要见面他 is ungrammatical. The correct expression is 我要跟他见面.

	Verb		Object	
Wèile fùxí, tā zuótiān zhǐ 为了复习，她昨天只	shuì 睡	le liǎng gè xiǎoshí de 了两个小时的	jiào 觉。	
Wǒ bàba zuì xǐhuan gěi wǒ hé mèimei 我爸爸最喜欢给我和妹妹	zhào 照		xiàng 相。	
Nǐ néng bu néng guòlai 你能不能过来	bāng 帮	yíxià 一下	máng 忙？	

	Verb		Object	
Tā 他	bì 毕	le 了	yè 业	jiù bāndào Shēnzhèn qù le 就搬到深圳去了。
Tiānqì tài rè le, tā jīntiān 天气太热了，他今天	xǐ 洗	le wǔ cì 了五次	zǎo 澡。	

tōngguò 通过 as a preposition

通过 as a preposition means using a certain method to achieve a desired outcome. The structure is "通过 + method, subject + VP" or "Subject + 通过 + method + VP". The method introduced by 通过 should be a noun phrase or substantivized verb phrase.

	tōngguò 通过	Method	
	Tōngguò 通过	shèjiāo wǎngluò 社交网络，	niánqīngrén zhījiān jìnxíngzhe gèzhǒng-gèyàng de jiāoliú 年轻人之间进行着各种各样的交流。
Niánqīngrén zhījiān 年轻人之间	tōngguò 通过	shèjiāo wǎngluò 社交网络	jìnxíngzhe gèzhǒng-gèyàng de jiāoliú 进行着各种各样的交流。
	Tōngguò 通过	yǎnjing、ěrduo、bízi 眼睛、耳朵、鼻子，	rénmen kěyǐ gǎnshòudào wàibù shìjiè 人们可以感受到外部世界。
Rénmen 人们	tōngguò 通过	yǎnjing、ěrduo、bízi 眼睛、耳朵、鼻子，	kěyǐ gǎnshòudào wàibù shìjiè 可以感受到外部世界。
Tāmen shì 他们是	tōngguò 通过	biérén de jièshào 别人的介绍	cái rènshi de 才认识的。

	tōngguò 通过	Method	
Zhōngguó de yìxiē shǎoshù mínzú xǐhuan 中国的一些少数民族喜欢	tōngguò 通过	chànggē huò tiàowǔ de fāngshì 唱歌或跳舞的方式	lái biǎodá tāmen xīnli de xiǎngfǎ 来表达他们心里的想法。

Introducing the agent or performer of an action using yóu 由

由 as a preposition is used to introduce and emphasize the agent or doer who performs a certain action. The structure is "Topic + 由 + agent + verb". The agent introduced by 由 should be a noun or a pronoun indicating a person or an organization.

Object	yóu 由	Agent	Verb	
Zhè cì gōngsī niánhuì 这次公司年会，	yóu 由	Wáng jīnglǐ 王经理	fùzé 负责。	
1931 nián de kēxué kǎochá duì shì 1931年的科学考察队是	yóu 由	Wáng jiàoshòu 王教授	dàilǐng 带领	de 的。
Guójiā de wèilái yīnggāi 国家的未来应该	yóu 由	rénmín 人民	juédìng 决定。	
2012 nián de xiàjì Àoyùnhuì shì 2012年的夏季奥运会是	yóu 由	Lúndūn 伦敦	zhǔbàn 主办	de 的。
Lǚxíng xiànlù 旅行线路	yóu 由	nǐ 你	ānpái 安排	ba 吧。

Disyllabic words that become monosyllabic in formal style

In written Chinese or formal speech, some disyllabic words like modal verbs, conjunctions, adverbs, etc. may appear in their monosyllabic form. The monosyllabic forms rarely appear in oral Chinese or informal style.

	Disyllabic words	
Wǒmen 我们	yīng (gāi) 应（该）	bǎ kèhù de xūyào fàng 把客户的需要放 zài dì-yī wèi 在第一位。
	Rú (guǒ) 如（果）	yǒu rènhé xūyào qǐng 有任何需要，请 jíshí liánxì wǒ bùmén 及时联系我部门。
Kèhù 客户	kě (yǐ) 可（以）	tōngguò kèfúbù gēn wǒ 通过客服部跟我 gōngsī liánxì 公司联系。
Jiào shǎo yùn- 较少运 dòng de rén 动的人 yīng shǎo chī 应少吃	huò (zhě) 或（者）	bù chī tài duō tiánshí 不吃太多甜食。
Zhèxiē gōng- 这些公 yuán hé yì- 园和艺 shùguǎn 术馆	yǐ (jīng) 已（经）	quánbù kāifàng 全部开放。

Unit 5

Concessive clauses with 倒 (dào)

倒 is an adverb that shows a turning point or concession in a sentence. 倒 may appear either in the first clause or in the second. If the first clause expresses negative comments, then the second clause uses 倒 to show the change in meaning and introduce positive comments. In contrast, if the first clause uses 倒 to show a concession to introduce positive comments, then the second clause should express negative comments. The comments in the second clause are what the speaker wants to emphasize or highlight. The second clause will often contain 不过, 但是, or 可是.

Clause 1 (negative)	Clause 2 (dào 倒 positive)
Zài Nèiměnggǔ dāng lǎoshī 在内蒙古当老师， shōurù díquè bù gāo 收入的确不高，	búguò Mǎ lǎoshī dàoshì 不过马老师倒是 zhēnde xǐhuan zhè zhǒng shēng- 真的喜欢这种生 huó fāngshì 活方式。
Nǐ mǎi de píngguǒ yǒudiǎnr 你买的苹果有点儿 xiǎo 小，	wèidào dào hái búcuò 味道倒还不错。
Wǒ nǎinai yǐjīng bāshí duō 我奶奶已经八十多 suì le yá yě diàoguāng 岁了，牙也掉光 le ěrduo yě bú tài tīng 了，耳朵也不太听 de jiàn le 得见了，	búguò jīngshen dào hěn hǎo 不过精神倒很好。

Clause 1 (dào 倒 positive)	Clause 2 (negative)
Mǎ lǎoshī dào hěn xǐhuan zài 马老师倒很喜欢在 Nèiměnggǔ de shēnghuó 内蒙古的生活 fāngshì 方式，	búguò tā jiārén juéde tā 不过她家人觉得她 shōurù tài dī le 收入太低了。
Nǐ mǎi de píngguǒ wèidào 你买的苹果味道 dào hái búcuò 倒还不错，	jiùshì yǒudiǎnr xiǎo 就是有点儿小。
Wǒ nǎinai jīngshen dào hái 我奶奶精神倒还 hǎo 好，	kěshì tā yá yě diàoguāng 可是她牙也掉光 le ěrduo yě bú tài tīng 了，耳朵也不太听 de jiàn le wǒmen dōu hěn 得见了，我们都很 dānxīn tā 担心她。

Expressing "doing well" with 好好 (hǎohǎo)

好好 as an adverbial modifies the verb phrase which follows it, expressing the meaning of "doing something thoroughly" or "doing something as well as possible". Sometimes model verbs like 想 / 会 / 应该 / 得 / 要

appear before 好好 and help to emphasize the tone or the attitude of the speaker. In colloquial expression, the second "好 hǎo" changes to "hāo" and the "er" sound is also added, giving "hǎohāor".

	hǎohǎo 好好 + verb phrase
Zhè jiàn shìqing wǒmen děi 这件事情，我们得	hǎohǎo tán yì tán 好好谈一谈。
Qǐng nǐmen 请你们	hǎohǎo kǎolǜ yíxià wǒ 好好考虑一下我 de jiànyì 的建议。
Míngtiān jiù shì zhōumò le 明天就是周末了， nǐ yě 你也	hǎohǎo fàngsōng fàngsōng 好好放松放松 ba 吧。
Wǒ de péngyou xiǎng 我的朋友想	hǎohǎo yánjiū yíxià chá 好好研究一下茶 de lìshǐ hé wénhuà 的历史和文化。
Yào xiǎng jiànkāng yídìng yào 要想健康，一定要	hǎohǎo duànliàn shēntǐ 好好锻炼身体。

Making deductions with 既然 (jìrán)

既然 is a conjunction used in the structure "既然 + fact / reason / premise, 那 / 就 / 为什么 + inference / suggestion". 既然 appears in the first clause to restate a known fact, reason or premise, while the second clause, as the main clause, presents a logical inference or suggestion deduced from the fact, reason or premise mentioned in the first clause. The second clause often has 那 or 就, meaning "then", to show the inference or suggestion is drawn naturally and logically. The second clause may also contain a rhetorical question, indicated by 为什么, to show a strongly questioning tone.

	jìrán Clause 1 (既然)	Clause 2
	Jìrán Xiǎo Lín xǐ- 既然小林喜 huan huàhuà 欢画画，	tā yīnggāi yuàn- 他应该愿 yì qù shàng huà- 意去上画 huàkè 画课。
	Jìrán zhèli de 既然这里的 dōngxi dōu bú tài 东西都不太 héshì 合适，	wǒmen háishi 我们还是 qù biéde shāngdiàn 去别的商店 kànkan ba 看看吧。
	Jìrán nǐ duì nà 既然你对那 jiā gōngsī hěn gǎn 家公司很感 xìngqù 兴趣，	wèi shénme hái bù 为什么还不 shēnqǐng ne 申请呢？
Mǎkè qǐng A: 马克请 wǒ cānjiā tā de 我参加他的 shēngrì wǎnhuì 生日晚会， kěshì nàtiān wǒ 可是那天我 tài máng zěnme 太忙，怎么 bàn ya 办呀？	Jìrán nǐ méi B: 既然你没 shíjiān 时间，	nà jiù bié qù le 那就别去了。
Wǒ fùmǔ bú A: 我父母不 tài xīwàng wǒ bān 太希望我搬 dào Guǎngzhōu zhù 到广州住。	Jìrán nǐ fù- B: 既然你父 mǔ bù tóngyì 母不同意，	nǐ jiù liú zài Xī- 你就留在西 ān ba 安吧。

Stressing an extreme degree with 再……不过了 (zài … bú guò le)

再……不过了 is used to stress an extreme degree, and means "nothing is more … than". The words inserted between 再 and 不过了 may be either adjectives or emotional verbs. The adjectives or emotional verbs usually have positive connotations.

	zài bú guò le 再……不过了
Zhè jiàn yīfu chuān zài 这件衣服穿在 nǐ shēn shang 你身上	zài héshì bú guò le 再合适不过了。

	zài bú guò le 再……不过了	
Tā shuō tā hěn máng 他说他很忙， kǒngpà méi shíjiān cān- 恐怕没时间参 jiā tóngxué jùhuì Wǒ 加同学聚会。我 juéde tā de yìsi 觉得他的意思	zài qīngchu bú guò le 再清楚不过了。	
Yòng shǒujī pāi zhàopiàn 用手机拍照片	zài jiǎndān bú guò le 再简单不过了。	
Néng bǎ tā qǐnglái 能把她请来 chànggē 唱歌	zài hǎo bú guò le 再好不过了。	
Xīhóngshì chǎo jīdàn 西红柿炒鸡蛋 shì yí gè 是一个	zài pǔtōng bú guò 再普通不过	de jiā- 的家 chángcài 常菜。

Unit 6

Indicating an extreme degree with ……死了 (sǐ le)

死了 is used as a degree complement to intensify the adjectives preceding it, indicating an extreme degree of the adjective in question. 死了 is similar to "deadly" or "… to death" in English. For example, 冷死了 means "deadly cold". Usually, the adjectives preceding 死了 have negative meanings, but occasionally, 死了 is used to intensify emotional adjectives with positive connotations, e.g. 高兴, 开心, 兴奋. In addition, if the speaker uses 死了 to express that they personally are affected to an extreme degree, 我 can be inserted in between 死 and 了.

	sǐ le Adj. + 死了
Lóushàng de yīnyuè zhème dà shēng 楼上的音乐这么大声， zhēnshì 真是	chǎosǐ le 吵死了。
Bié mǎi le zhè jiā shāngdiàn de 别买了，这家商店的 píngguǒ 苹果	guìsǐ le 贵死了。
Zhōumò yìzhí xià dàyǔ nǎr dōu 周末一直下大雨，哪儿都 qù bù liǎo dāi zài jiāli 去不了，呆在家里	wúliáo sǐ le 无聊死了。 yùmèn sǐ wǒ le 郁闷死我了。 kùnsǐ wǒ le 困死我了。
Nǐ gěi nǐ mèimei mǎile zhème piào- 你给你妹妹买了这么漂 liang de lǐwù tā yídìng 亮的礼物，她一定	gāoxìng sǐ le 高兴死了。

Expressing wishes and hopes with 要是/如果……就好了 (yàoshi rúguǒ … jiù hǎo le)

要是/如果……就好了 is a subjunctive expressing a wish or hope. It is similar in meaning to "It would be great, if only …". Sometimes, 要是/如果 can be dropped.

	yàoshi rúguǒ (要是/如果) clause	jiù hǎo le 就好了
Zhēn 真 kěxī 可惜，	yàoshi míngtiān wǎnshang nǐ néng 要是明天晚上你能 lái gēn wǒmen yìqǐ kàn qiúsài 来跟我们一起看球赛	jiù hǎo le 就好了。
	Rúguǒ wǒmen de dàxué zài tóng 如果我们的大学在同 yí gè chéngshì 一个城市	jiù hǎo le 就好了。
	Míngtiān méiyǒu kǎoshì 明天没有考试	jiù hǎo le 就好了。
	Zhè jiàn yīfu piányi yìdiǎnr 这件衣服便宜一点儿	jiù hǎo le 就好了。

	yàoshi rúguǒ (要是/如果) clause	jiù hǎo le 就好了
Zěnme xià- 怎么下 yǔ le 雨了？	Yàoshi chūmén de shíhou dài- 要是出门的时候带 shang sǎn 上伞	jiù hǎo le 就好了。

Expressing emphasis using 可 (kě)

可 as an adverb is used to emphasize a statement. Without 可, the meaning of the statement doesn't change, but the tone of the statement is weakened. 可……了 can also be employed to intensify an adjective. It is similar to 很, but its tone is slightly stronger than 很. The emphatic 可 is mainly used in colloquial expression.

Subject	kě 可	Verb phrase
Zuò huǒchē 坐火车	kě 可	bǐ zuò fēijī shūfu 比坐飞机舒服。
Nǐ 你	kě 可	bié wàngle jiāo fángzū 别忘了交房租。
Xué Zhōngwén 学中文	kě 可	děi zhùyì shēngdiào 得注意声调。
Tā 她	kě 可	bù xiāngxìn nǐ shuō de zhèxiē huà 不相信你说的这些话。
Wǒ 我	kě 可	méiyǒu shíjiān péi nǐ guàngjiē 没有时间陪你逛街。

Subject	kě 可	le Adj. + 了
Jīnglǐ 经理	kě 可	shēngqì le 生气了。
Zhège yóuxì 这个游戏	kě 可	yǒu yìsi le 有意思了。

Justifying an opinion or decision using 反正 (fǎnzhèng)

反正 as a modal adverb means "anyway" or "anyhow". The clause involving 反正 indicates a reason which is used to support the speaker's subjective attitude or judgment of a situation. The situation usually involves options or choices, e.g. 去 vs. 不去; 见面 vs. 不见面.

		fǎnzhèng 反正 + justification	
Méi xiǎng- A: 没想 dào zhè mén 到这门 kè zhème 课这么 nán zěnme 难，怎么 bàn ya 办呀？		Fǎnzhèng xiàn- B: 反正现 zài hòuhuǐ yě 在后悔也 láibují le 来不及了，	nǔlì hǎo- 努力好 hǎo xué ba 好学吧。
	Nà nǐ jiù B: 那你就 huàn yì mén 换一门 bié de kè ba 别的课吧，	fǎnzhèng xuǎn- 反正选 kè de shíjiān 课的时间 hái méi guò 还没过。	
	Wǒmen duō 我们多 mǎi jǐ zhǒng 买几种 shuǐguǒ ba 水果吧，	fǎnzhèng zhèxiē 反正这些 shuǐguǒ de jià- 水果的价 qián dōu shì yí- 钱都是一 yàng de 样的，	zhǐ chī yì 只吃一 zhǒng shuǐ- 种水 guǒ duō méi 果多没 yìsi 意思。
Wǒ xiǎng A: 我想 mǎi gè xīn 买个新 zhàoxiàngjī 照相机， kě tài guì 可太贵 le 了！	Wǒ kàn B: 我看 nǐ háishi bié 你还是别 mǎi le 买了，	fǎnzhèng yòng 反正用 shǒujī yě kě- 手机也可 yǐ pāi zhàopiàn 以拍照片。	
		Fǎnzhèng yí B: 反正一 bù hǎo zhào- 部好照 xiàngjī kěyǐ 相机可以 yòng hěn jiǔ 用很久，	guì diǎnr 贵点儿 yě zhídé 也值得。

Unit 7

Expressing "how come" with 怎么 (zěnme)

怎么 is a question word used to ask for a reason or explanation. 怎么 has a similar tone and connotation to "how come" in English. It not only asks "why", but also expresses a tone of surprise. 怎么 often appears after the subject of a sentence.

Nǐ zěnme huì zài zhèr Bú shì Wáng Yúnyún lái jiē wǒ ma
1 你怎么会在这儿？不是王云云来接我吗？

Tā zěnme bǎ tā nǚpéngyou de shēngrì wàng le
2 他怎么把他女朋友的生日忘了？

Hǎixiān zěnme yuè lái yuè guì le
3 海鲜怎么越来越贵了？

Tā bù lái zěnme yě bù gěi wǒmen dǎ gè diànhuà
4 她不来，怎么也不给我们打个电话？

Nǐ zài Běijīng zhùle sì nián zěnme hái méi qùguo Chángchéng
5 你在北京住了四年，怎么还没去过长城？

dàodǐ jiūjìng
Emphasizing an inquiry with 到底/究竟

到底 and **究竟** express an intensity or incredulity similar to the phrase "on earth". They are adverbs used to emphasize a question or to press the other speaker to give an answer or tell the truth. **到底/究竟** can precede the subject of the sentence. **到底** and **究竟** emphasize three question forms: questions beginning with wh-words; questions posed by a verb (V-not-V questions); and questions which offer an "either … or …" alternative. They can also be used in embedded questions. However, **究竟** is more formal than **到底**.

Jiūjìng shì shénme yuányīn ràng nǐ duì wǒmen méiyǒule xìnxīn
1 究竟是什么原因让你对我们没有了信心？

Hěn duō dàxuéshēng dōu xiǎng bù qīngchu zìjǐ jiūjìng yīnggāi xuǎn shénme zhuānyè
2 很多大学生都想不清楚自己究竟应该选什么专业。

Wǒmen dàodǐ zài nǎge fángjiān kāihuì
3 我们到底在哪个房间开会？

Nǐ dàodǐ rèn bú rènshi tā
4 你到底认不认识他？

Bìyè yǐhòu tā dàodǐ xiǎng dú yánjiūshēng háishi xiǎng mǎshàng gōngzuò
5 毕业以后，他到底想读研究生还是想马上工作？

Liǎng gè dōu shì tā de hǎopéngyou tā shízài bù zhīdào dàodǐ gāi bāng shéi
6 两个都是他的好朋友，他实在不知道到底该帮谁。

(zhǐ) búguò zhǐ (shì) bàle
Minimizing a situation with (只)不过/只(是)……罢了

不过/只不过/只/只是……罢了 is a pattern used to trivialize or downplay the thing, the situation, or the number they modify. **不过/只不过/只/只是** means "merely". **罢了** is a modal particle which also means "merely". **罢了** either appears at the end of the clause or can be dropped.

	búguò 不过/ zhǐbuguò 只不过/ zhǐ zhǐshì 只/只是	Verb phrase	bàle 罢了	
Zhège cài 这个菜 qíshí bù 其实不 nán zuò 难做，	zhǐbuguò 只不过	bǐjiào huā 比较花 shíjiān 时间	bàle 罢了。	
	Búguò 不过	shì yí 是一 gè xiǎo 个小 wánjù 玩具，		huàile jiù 坏了就 huàile ba 坏了吧， méi guānxi 没关系 de 的。
Tā 他	zhǐshì 只是	xìnggé 性格 yǒudiǎnr 有点儿 nèixiàng 内向，		bìng bú shì 并不是 bù xiǎng gēn 不想跟 nǐ shuōhuà 你说话。
Wǒ hái hǎo 我还好，	zhǐbuguò 只不过	yǒudiǎnr 有点儿 gǎnmào 感冒	bàle 罢了，	bié dānxīn 别担心。
Nǎli nǎ- 哪里哪 li wǒ nǎ 里，我哪 yǒu nǐ shuō 有你说 de nàme 的那么 lìhai Wǒ 厉害。我	zhǐshì 只是	yùnqi 运气 hěn hǎo 很好	bàle 罢了，	yàoburán 要不然 yě jìn bù liǎo 也进不了 zhème hǎo 这么好 de gōngsī 的公司。

búdàn bùzhǐ bùjǐn bùguāng érqiě hái yě

Indicating "not only ..., but also ..." with 不但 / 不只 / 不仅 / 不光……而且 / 还 / 也……

不但……而且…… is the most commonly used structure to express "not only …, but also …". Besides 不但…… 而且……, there are some other structures which are also used to express the same meaning. 不但 can be replaced by 不仅 / 不只 / 不光; 而且 can be replaced by 还 / 也. In addition, 而且 can also be used in conjunction with 还 or 也. Unlike their English counterparts, 不但 / 不只 / 不仅 / 不光 and 而且 / 还 / 也 can only be followed by an adjective or a verb phrase; they cannot be followed by a noun phrase. Thus, a sentence like *他会说不但法文，而且中文 is ungrammatical.

Subject	búdàn bùzhǐ 不但 / 不只 / bùjǐn bùguāng 不仅 / 不光 + adj./verb phrase	érqiě hái yě 而且 / 还 / 也 + adj./verb phrase
Qí zìxíngchē 骑自行车	búdàn kěyǐ duànliàn 不但可以锻炼 shēntǐ 身体，	érqiě hái néng bǎo- 而且还能保 hù huánjìng 护环境。
Tā 他	bùzhǐ jìde dàjiā 不只记得大家 de míngzi 的名字，	yě zhīdào měi gè 也知道每个 rén de shēngrì hé 人的生日和 xìngqù àihào 兴趣爱好。
Zhè jiā chāoshì 这家超市 de shūcài 的蔬菜	bùjǐn pǐnzhǒng fēngfù 不仅品种丰富，	érqiě jiàgé yě bǐ 而且价格也比 biéde chāoshì yào 别的超市要 piányi 便宜。
Xǐyījī de 洗衣机的 fāmíng 发明	bùjǐn ràng rénmen bú 不仅让人们不 zài xīnkǔ de yòng 再辛苦地用 shǒu xǐ yīfu 手洗衣服，	hái ràng rénmen yǒu- 还让人们有 le gèng duō xiūxi 了更多休息、 yúlè de shíjiān 娱乐的时间。
Tā 她	bùguāng cōngming 不光聪明，	hái fēicháng nǔlì 还非常努力。

Unit 8

hòulái ránhòu

Comparing 后来 and 然后

后来 is a time noun referring to a certain period of time long ago in the past. 后来 can only be used to give the sequence of past events. It is similar to "afterwards" or "later on" in English.

Unlike 后来, 然后 is a conjunction and is often used together with 先 and 最后 to indicate the sequence of actions. It is similar to "and then" or "after that" in English. In addition, 然后 can be used to indicate the sequence of future actions as well as past ones.

Past event 1	hòulái 后来 + past event 2
Tā gāng rènshi Xiǎo Lín de 他刚认识小林的 shíhou juéde Xiǎo Lín bú tài 时候觉得小林不太 ài shuōhuà 爱说话，	hòulái cái zhīdào Xiǎo Lín qí- 后来才知道小林其 shí tèbié xǐhuan liáotiānr 实特别喜欢聊天儿。
Wǒ yì nián qián jìn zhège 我一年前进这个 bùmén de shíhou hái jiànguo 部门的时候还见过 tā jǐ cì 他几次，	hòulái jiù zài yě méi jiàn- 后来就再也没见 dào tā shì bú shì líkāi 到，他是不是离开 zhège bùmén le 这个部门了？
Zhè běn xiǎoshuō yì chūlái 这本小说一出来 jiù fēicháng shòu huānyíng 就非常受欢迎，	hòulái hái bèi pāichéngle 后来还被拍成了 diànyǐng 电影。

Action 1	ránhòu 然后 + action 2
Wǒ bù néng gàosu nǐ dá- 我不能告诉你答 àn Nǐ zìjǐ zài zǐxì 案。你自己再仔细 dú yí biàn 读一遍，	ránhòu hǎohǎo xiǎng yi 然后好好想一 xiǎng ba 想吧。
Xiān bǎ zhèxiē cài qiēchéng 先把这些菜切成 xiǎokuàir 小块儿，	ránhòu zài fàngjìn guō li 然后再放进锅里 chǎo yi chǎo 炒一炒。
Tāmen xiàtiān xiān qùle 他们夏天先去了 Hā'ěrbīn 哈尔滨，	ránhòu yòu qùle Xī'ān hé 然后又去了西安和 Lìjiāng 丽江。

Expressing “no matter what / how / whether” with
wúlùn búlùn bùguǎn dōu
无论/不论/不管……都……

无论, 不论 and 不管 mean “no matter what / how / whether …” and appear in the first part of the sentence to introduce the circumstances. 都 appears in the second part of the sentence to emphasize that the result won’t change. 无论/不论/不管 is always used with 1) wh-words, 2) questions which offer “either ... or ...” alternatives (是 X 还是 Y), or 3) questions in the “verb-not-verb” form. Among the three words, 无论 is the most formal and is generally used in written language; 不论 is less formal than 不管, and is used in both oral and written language; 不管 is the most informal, and generally used in oral language.

wúlùn búlùn bùguǎn 无论/不论/不管 + circumstances	dōu 都 + result
Wúlùn shì kēxué háishi 无论是科学还是 yìshù 艺术，	dōu lí bù kāi rénlèi de 都离不开人类的 sīkǎo 思考。
Wúlùn fàngqì shénme 无论放弃什么，	dōu búyào fàngqì xīwàng 都不要放弃希望。
Búlùn wèntí duōme fùzá 不论问题多么复杂，	tā dōu néng zhǎodào jiějué 他都能找到解决 de bànfǎ 的办法。
Bùguǎn nǐ tóngyì bù tóngyì 不管你同意不同意 tā de shuōfa 他的说法，	nǐ dōu děi chéngrèn tā 你都得承认他 de huà háishi yǒu yídìng de 的话还是有一定的 dàoli de 道理的。
Bùguǎn shéi zhǎo nǐ 不管谁找你，	nǐ dōu bù yīnggāi shàngkè 你都不应该上课 de shíhou jiē diànhuà 的时候接电话。

yuánlái guǒrán jìngrán
Expressing tones with adverbs 原来, 果然, 竟然

原来 is used for recently discovered information. The tone is that of sudden realization.

果然 is used to confirm that the fact indeed corresponds to the previous statement, assumption or expectation.

竟然 is used to indicate that the fact or the situation is unexpected from the speaker’s point of view, or is an unusual situation. 竟 is interchangeable with 竟然, but more literary than 竟然.

原来 can only be placed at the start of a sentence. 果然 can be placed both at the beginning of a sentence or after the subject. 竟然 can only appear after the subject.

yuánlái 原来
Tīngshuō tā tèbié gāo zuótiān jiànle cái zhīdào yuán- 听说他特别高，昨天见了才知道，原 lái tā hái méiyǒu wǒ gāo 来他还没有我高。
Yuánlái zhè zhǒng yú jiù shì sānwényú a yǐ- 原来这种鱼就是三文鱼 (salmon) 啊，以 qián hái zhēn bù zhīdào 前还真不知道。
Wǒmen dōu yǐwéi nǐ yǐjīng xiàbān huíjiā le yuánlái nǐ 我们都以为你已经下班回家了，原来你 hái méi zǒu a 还没走啊。

guǒrán 果然
Péngyou shuō zài nà jiā diàn kěyǐ mǎidào xīn shǒujī guǒ- 朋友说在那家店可以买到新手机，果 rán wǒ jiù mǎidào le 然我就买到了。
Wǒ tīngshuō tā bú yuànyì hé wǒmen yìqǐ zhù wǒ qù 我听说他不愿意和我们一起住，我去 wèn tā le tā guǒrán bú yuànyì bānlái 问他了，他果然不愿意搬来。
Zuótiān wǒ zài dìtiě shang kàndào yí gè rén hěn xiàng Xiǎo 昨天我在地铁上看到一个人，很像小 Lín jīntiān yí wèn nàge rén guǒrán shì tā 林，今天一问，那个人果然是他。

jìngrán 竟然
Zhēn bù gǎn xiāngxìn yì zhāng yóupiào jìngrán màidào liǎng 真不敢相信，一张邮票竟然卖到两 wàn yuán 万元。

jìngrán 竟然
Tōuzǒu tā xiézi de jìngrán shì yì zhī dà māo 偷走她鞋子的竟然是一只大猫。
Méi xiǎngdào tā jìngrán néng yòng fěnbǐ huàchū zhème měi de huà 没想到他竟然能用粉笔画出这么美的画。

Expressing personal judgments with 算 (是)
suàn(shì)

算 means "to be considered as" or "to count as". As a verb, it introduces the speaker's subjective judgment about a person, a thing or an event. 算 prevents a judgment, positive or negative, from sounding absolute. Adverbs like 就, 也 and 还 often precede 算. 是 is optional.

Topic	suàn (shì) 算 (是) + judgment
Hángzhōu 杭州	suàn(shì) wǒ qùguo de zuì piàoliang de chéngshì le 算(是)我去过的最漂亮的城市了。
Zhè tiáo yú 这条鱼	hái suàn(shì) xīnxian 还算(是)新鲜。
Xīhóngshì 西红柿	néng suàn(shì) shuǐguǒ ma 能算(是)水果吗?
Xǐhuan tīng biérén liáotiānr 喜欢听别人聊天儿	yě suàn(shì) yì zhǒng tècháng ba 也算(是)一种特长吧。
Duì hěn duō rén láishuō yǒu gōngzuò yǒu shíwù yǒu zhù de dìfang 对很多人来说，有工作、有食物、有住的地方	jiù suàn(shì) xìngfú le 就算(是)幸福了。

Unit 9

Expressing "seem to be" with 看起来
kàn qǐlai

看起来 is used to express "it looks like …" or "sb/sth seems to be …". The sentence subject should precede 看起来. The predicate after 看起来 indicates what the subject appears to be like. Usually the predicate contains adjectives which may appear with degree adverbs or in different comparative structures. 看起来 has a connotation of subjective description and comparison; therefore it indicates how the observer feels.

	Subject	kàn qǐlai 看起来	Predicate
	Lǎoshī jīntiān 老师今天	kàn qǐlai 看起来	tǐng lěi de 挺累的。
	Zhège xiàngmù 这个项目	kàn qǐlai 看起来	bǐ qùnián nàge xiàngmù kùnnan duō le 比去年那个项目困难多了。
Wǒ yě bù zhīdào zhè liàng chē shì shénme páizi de. Búguò 我也不知道这辆车是什么牌子的。不过，	tā 它	kàn qǐlai 看起来	bìng bú shì hěn guì 并不是很贵。
Nǐ māma zhēn niánqīng 你妈妈真年轻，	tā 她	kàn qǐlai 看起来	jiù xiàng shì nǐ de jiějie 就像是你的姐姐。
	Ài xiào de rén 爱笑的人	kàn qǐlai 看起来	gèng kě'ài yě gèng hǎokàn 更可爱，也更好看。

Expressing "nearly" with 差点儿
chàdiǎnr

差点儿 literally means "differing a little bit". It is an adverb and means "nearly", expressing an event or action almost happened (but did not). Since 差点儿 is used to describe something which has already occurred, 就 and 了 often appear with the affirmative form of verb phrases that are modified by 差点儿.

If the action or event was good and desired by the subject, 差点儿 implies that "it nearly happened, and it was a pity that it didn't". On the other hand, if the action or event was bad and not desired by the subject, 差点儿 implies that "it nearly happened, but luckily it didn't".

	chàdiǎnr 差点儿	jiù (就) + verb phrase
Fùmǔ 父母	chàdiǎnr 差点儿	wàngle xiǎo nǚ'ér 忘了小女儿 de shēngrì 的生日。
Yóuyú liǎng tiān dōu zhǎo 由于两天都找 bú dào tā tā de 不到他，他的 péngyoumen 朋友们	chàdiǎnr 差点儿	jiù gěi jǐngchá dǎ 就给警察打 diànhuà le 电话了。
Jīntiān xiàwǔ de kè wǒ 今天下午的课，我	chàdiǎnr 差点儿	chídào le 迟到了。
Tā 他	chàdiǎnr 差点儿	dāngshang zǒngtǒng 当上总统。
Wèile ràng zìjǐ 为了让自己 de sùshè hé jiāli yí- 的宿舍和家里一 yàng shūfu tā 样舒服，她	chàdiǎnr 差点儿	bǎ jiāli suǒ- 把家里所 yǒu de dōngxi dōu 有的东西都 bāndào sùshè 搬到宿舍。

Exclamations with 多……啊 (duō … a)

多 and 啊 are used together to intensify an adjective. This forms an exclamation and expresses a strong feeling on behalf of the speaker. Adjectives or noun phrases that are modified by adjectives should be placed between 多 and 啊. In the structure, 多 is necessary while 啊 is optional. 多……啊 is usually used in oral expressions when the speaker expresses feelings or impressions about something.

	duō 多 + adj. …… (a) (啊)	
	Duō hǎo de zhǔyi 多好的主意 a 啊，	zánmen jiù tīng tā 咱们就听他 de ba 的吧。
	Duō dìdao de 多地道的 Shànghǎicài a 上海菜啊！	Zhēn méi xiǎngdào zài 真没想到在 Lúndūn yě néng chīdào 伦敦也能吃到 zhème hǎochī de Shàng- 这么好吃的上 hǎicài 海菜。
Nǐ dìdi 你弟弟	duō dúlì 多独立，	tā gēnběn bù xūyào 他根本不需要 nǐ lái zhàogù tā 你来照顾他。
Zuò dìtiě 坐地铁	duō fāngbiàn a 多方便啊，	érqiě hái hěn piányi 而且还很便宜。
Nǐ de sùshè 你的宿舍	duō gānjìng a 多干净啊。	Wǒ de sùshè kě méi 我的宿舍可没 nǐ de hǎo 你的好。

Expressing "whether or not" with 是否 (shìfǒu)

是否 means "whether or not". However, it is an adverb and is not always interchangeable with 是不是. 是否 is used either in a question or in a clause that serves as the object of verbs like 考虑, 犹豫, 想, etc. 是否 is always placed before the verb phrases that it modifies. It is often used in formal oral or written expression.

	shìfǒu 是否	Verb phrase
Jiàoshòu hái zài kǎolǜ 教授还在考虑	shìfǒu 是否	yào jìnxíng zhè cì shíyàn 要进行这次实验。
Zhèngfǔ réng zài yóuyù 政府仍在犹豫	shìfǒu 是否	yào zài běndì xīnjiàn yì 要在本地新建一 jiā yīyuàn 家医院。
Nǐ 你	shìfǒu 是否	hái bǎ wǒ dàngchéng nǐ 还把我当成你 zuì hǎo de péngyou 最好的朋友？

	shì fǒu 是否	Verb phrase
Cānsàizhě rúhé zhī- 参赛者如何知 dào zìjǐ 道自己	shì fǒu 是否	déjiǎng le 得奖了?

Unit 10

Continual repetition of an action with Verb 来 verb 去 (lái qù)

V 来 V 去 is used to express continual repetition of an action. Here 来 and 去 have lost their directional meanings, and instead they indicate that a certain action is done over and over again. Very often a verb-complement structure follows V 来 V 去 in order to indicate the result of the repetitive action. A complement may be either resultative, or the negative form of a potential complement. If the verb has an object, the object should be placed after the verb and its complement.

Subject	lái qù Verb 来 verb 去	Verb + complement (+ object)
Nǐ 你	wènlái-wènqù 问来问去	yě wèn bù chū shénme jiéguǒ de 也问不出什么结果的。
Wǒ 我	xiǎnglái-xiǎngqù 想来想去，	dōu xiǎng bù míngbai māo shì zěn- 都想不明白猫是怎 me bǎ nàge hézi dǎkāi de 么把那个盒子打开的。
Wǒ 我	xiǎnglái-xiǎngqù 想来想去，	yě xiǎng bù qǐlái tā jiào shén- 也想不起来她叫什 me míngzi 么名字。
Tāmen 他们	zhǎolái-zhǎoqù 找来找去，	zǒng suàn zhǎodàole nà běn shū 总算找到了那本书。
Tā 他	kànlái-kànqù 看来看去，	zěnme yě kàn bù qīngchu hēibǎn 怎么也看不清楚黑板 shang jiūjìng shì shénme zì 上究竟是什么字。

Indicating a continuing action with the complement 下去 (xiàqu)

下去 literally means "go down", and is often used as a directional complement. However, it has also developed a more abstract meaning, in which it serves as a complement to indicate a continuing action. The verbs that precede 下去 are action verbs which can continue (or not). The negative form is 不 V 下去, which means the subject is not able to continue the action. For example, 讨论下去 means "to continue to discuss" or "to carry on discussing", while 讨论不下去 means "not able to carry on discussing".

	bú xiàqù Verb (不)下去	
Zhè jiàn shìqing wǒmen bú- 这件事情，我们不 yào zài 要再	tǎolùn xiàqu 讨论下去	le 了。
Měi gè yuè shōurù duōshǎo cái 每个月收入多少才 néng zài zhè zuò chéngshì 能在这座城市	shēnghuó xiàqu 生活下去?	
Zhège huódòng duō yǒu 这个活动多有 yìyì a yīnggāi 意义啊，应该	jìxù xiàqu 继续下去。	
Zhǐ shuōle jǐ jù tā jiù 只说了几句，她就	shuō bú xiàqù 说不下去	le 了。
Měi tiān liù diǎn qǐlai zhēn- 每天六点起来，真 de tài zǎo le wǒ juéde 的太早了，我觉得 wǒ kěndìng 我肯定	jiānchí bú xiàqù 坚持不下去	le 了。

Talking about disposal of time/money/energy with 把 (bǎ)

把……V 在……上 is used to express how one disposes of one's time, money, or energy. In the structure, the verbs usually are 花, 用, 放 or 浪费. The phrases that are inserted between 在……上 can be either nouns or verbs.

Subject	bǎ 把	Time/ money/energy	zài shang Verb 在…… 上
Tā 他	bǎ 把	shíjiān 时间	dōu làngfèi zài kàn wúliáo de diànshìjù shang le 都浪费在看无聊的电视剧上了。
Xiǎo Lín 小林	bǎ 把	shíjiān 时间	dōu yòng zài xué Yīngyǔ shang le 都用在学英语上了。
Fùmǔ bù ràng wǒ 父母不让我	bǎ 把	qián 钱	làngfèi zài mǎi mànhuà-shū shang le 浪费在买漫画书上了。
Wǒ jiějie 我姐姐	bǎ 把	qián 钱	dōu huā zài mǎi piàoliang yīfu shang le 都花在买漂亮衣服上了。
Tā 她	bǎ 把	jīnglì 精力	dōu fàng zài jiāo péngyou shang le 都放在交朋友上了。

jíshǐ yě Expressing "even if" with 即使……也……

The conjunctive structure 即使……也…… means "even if ..., still...". It is used to mean that even if the condition in the first clause were realized, the situation in the second clause would not change. 即使……也…… has the same meaning and function as 就算……也……, but it is more formal than the latter. 即使 is different from 虽然 because 即使 introduces a hypothetical condition, while 虽然 introduces a fact.

	(jíshǐ) (即使) clause 1	(yě) (也) clause 2
	Jíshǐ tā duì nǐ yǒu hǎogǎn 即使他对你有好感，	yě bújiàndé jiù zhēnde huì àishang nǐ 也不见得就真的会爱上你。
Zhème duō de nèiróng 这么多的内容，	jíshǐ jīntiān dōu jìzhù le 即使今天都记住了，	míngtiān yě huì wàng de 明天也会忘的。
	Jíshǐ huàn yì jiā gōngsī 即使换一家公司，	lǎobǎn yě bù yídìng hǎo 老板也不一定好。
	Jíshǐ zài hēi-yè zhōng 即使在黑夜中，	zhè kuǎn xiàngjī yě néng pāi-chū wánměi de zhàopiàn 这款相机也能拍出完美的照片。
	Jíshǐ shībài 即使失败，	yě búyào fàngqì 也不要放弃。

Unit 11

xiǎng jiù Expressing "as one pleases" with 想……就……

"想+V+question word+就+V+question word" (or "想+question word+V+就+question word+V") is used to express that someone can do something as he/she pleases. The two "V+wh" (or "wh+V") structures following 想 and 就 must be the same and are necessary for both. The "question words" in this structure are used as indefinite references. The subjects preceding 想 and 就 may not be the same.

Subject 1	xiǎng 想 + verb + question word	Subject 2	jiù 就+ verb + question word	
Nǐ 你	xiǎng kàn shénme biǎoyǎn 想看什么表演，		jiù kàn shénme biǎoyǎn 就看什么表演。	
Tā 他	xiǎng jǐ diǎn huílai 想几点回来，		jiù jǐ diǎn huílai 就几点回来。	Nǐ bú-yào guǎn tā 你不要管他。

	Subject 1	xiǎng 想 + verb + question word	Subject 2	jiù 就 + verb + question word	
	Nǐ 你	xiǎng qù 想 去 nǎr 哪儿，	wǒmen 我们	jiù qù 就 去 nǎr 哪儿。	
Yǒuqián 有 钱 de hǎo- 的 好 chu jiù 处 就 shì 是		xiǎng 想 zěnme 怎么 huāqián 花 钱，		jiù zěnme 就 怎么 huāqián 花 钱。	
	Zǒng- 总 jīnglǐ 经理	xiǎng zhāo- 想 招 pìn shéi 聘 谁，	gōngsī 公司	jiù zhāo- 就 招 pìn shéi 聘 谁。	

Emphasizing a particular manner of carrying out an action using Verb 1 着 (zhe) + verb 2

"V1 着 (o1)+v2 (o2)" is used to mean "to conduct an action in a particular manner or state". "V1 着 (o1)" is not the main action, but is used to indicate a particular manner or state. "V2 (o2)" is the main action, which is conducted in the particular manner or state of "v1 着 (o1)".

Subject	Verb 1 着 (zhe) (object 1)	Verb 2 (object 2)
Tā xǐhuan 他 喜欢	zhànzhe 站着	chī fàn 吃饭。
Tāmen 他们	zhuīzhe nàge 追着 那个 míngxīng 明 星	yào tā de qiānmíng 要 他的 签 名。
Tā 她	bàozhe shòushāng 抱着 受 伤 de xiǎogǒu 的 小狗	dàkū qǐlai 大哭 起来。

Subject	Verb 1 着 (zhe) (object 1)	Verb 2 (object 2)
Gěi nǐ tuījiàn yì 给 你 推荐 一 běn shū jiào 本 书，叫	Dàizhe Yǎnjìng 《带着 眼镜 hé Xīn 和 心	Qù Lǚxíng 去 旅行》。
Yì qún háizi 一 群 孩子	xiàozhe nàozhe 笑着 闹着	pǎojìn wūzi 跑进 屋子。

Emphasizing the reason for a result with 之所以 (zhīsuǒyǐ)…… 是因为 (shì yīnwèi)……

之所以……是因为…… is used to show result and reason. 之所以 introduces the result, which is caused by the reason introduced by 是因为. Compared with 因为……所以……, 之所以……是因为…… is a formal expression and often appears in written language. The subject or topic should go before 之所以.

Subject	zhīsuǒyǐ 之所以……	shì yīnwèi 是 因为……
Zhège dìfang 这个 地方	zhīsuǒyǐ huì xīyǐn 之所以 会 吸引 dàliàng de yóukè 大量 的 游客，	shì yīnwèi tā sìjì-rú- 是 因为 它 四季如 chūn fēngjǐng-rúhuà 春 、风景如画 。
Tā 他	zhīsuǒyǐ néng 之所以 能 zài duǎnduǎn jǐ nián 在 短 短 几年 nèi qǔdé zhème 内 取得 这么 dà de chénggōng 大 的 成 功，	shì yīnwèi tā cóng 是 因为 他 从 bú huì wèi yìdiǎndiǎn 不 会 为 一点点 chéngjiù jiù gǎndào 成就 就 感到 jiāo' ào 骄傲。
Yí gè rén 一个人	zhīsuǒyǐ huì jué- 之所以 会 觉 de lèi 得 累，	shì yīnwèi duì suǒyǒu 是 因为 对 所有 de shìqing dōu tài guò 的 事情 都 太 过 zàihu 在乎。
Zhège guójiā 这个 国家 de jīngjì 的 经济	zhīsuǒyǐ néng kuài- 之所以 能 快 sù fāzhǎn 速 发展，	shì yīnwèi zhèngfǔ shí- 是 因为 政府 实 xíngle bǐjiào yǒuxiào 行了 比较 有效 de jīngjì zhèngcè 的 经济 政策 。

Subject	zhīsuǒyǐ 之所以……	shì yīnwèi 是因为……
Háizi 孩子	zhīsuǒyǐ kě'ài 之所以可爱，	shì yīnwèi tāmen jiǎn- 是因为他们简 dān yòu zhēnchéng 单又真诚。

Expressing "to regard A as B" using 以……为……
(yǐ wéi)

以……为…… is used to express "to regard A as B". For example, 以北京时间为准 means "to regard Beijing time as the reference". 以……为…… is a formal expression. Its informal counterpart is 把……当作…….

Subject	yǐ 以 A	wéi 为 B
Huàxué yánjiū 化学研究	yǐ shíyàn 以实验	wéi jīchǔ 为基础。
Hěn duō guójiā 很多国家 dōu 都	yǐ háomǐ límǐ fēn- 以毫米、厘米、分 mǐ mǐ qiānmǐ 米、米、千米	wéi chángdù 为长度 dānwèi 单位。
Hěn duō shèhuì 很多社会 réngrán 仍然	yǐ nánxìng 以男性	wéi zhōngxīn 为中心。
Shēnghuó shìfǒu 生活是否 yīnggāi 应该	yǐ kuàilè 以快乐	wéi mùdì 为目的？
Shìjiè Dìqiúrì 世界地球日	yǐ zhǐ yǒu yí gè dìqiú 以"只有一个地球"	wéi zhǔtí 为主题。

Unit 12

Expressing an emphatic tone using 才……呢
(cái ne)

才……呢 is used to show that the speaker wants to emphasize a fact or situation when responding to the first speaker's question or statement. It can be used to emphasize both the positive form and the negative form of an adjective or verb.

	cái ne Subject + 才……呢
Zhè jiā diàn de kāfēi kě A: 这家店的咖啡可 hǎohē le 好喝了！	Nà jiā diàn de kāfēi cái B: 那家店的咖啡才 hǎohē ne 好喝呢。
Nǐmen xuéxiào de tǐyù- A: 你们学校的体育 guǎn zhēn búcuò a 馆真不错啊！	Tāmen de tǐyùguǎn cái B: 他们的体育馆才 hǎo ne 好呢！
Zuótiān Xiǎo Lín méi qù- A: 昨天小林没去 wǎn ba 晚吧？	Tā cái zhǔnshí ne Bié- B: 他才准时呢。别 rén dōu hái méi dào tā jiù 人都还没到，他就 dào le 到了。
Nǐ bié xiāngxìn tā shuō A: 你别相信他说 de huà 的话。	Wǒ cái bú huì xiāngxìn B: 我才不会相信 tā bèi tā piàn ne 他，被他骗呢。
Tīngshuō zuò dìtiě qù jī- A: 听说坐地铁去机 chǎng hěn bù fāngbiàn 场很不方便。	Bú huì ya zuò dìtiě qù B: 不会呀，坐地铁去 jīchǎng cái fāngbiàn ne 机场才方便呢。

Expressing unnecessariness using 何必……呢
(hébì ne)

何必……呢 is used in a rhetorical question to express the idea that there is no need to do something or that something is unnecessary. This is similar to the way we use "Why …?" in English. 何必……呢 appears in the second clause, where 何必 means 没有必要, while the first clause introduces a reason or premise which explains why there is no need to do the thing. 呢 can sometimes be dropped.

Clause 1	hébì ne 何必……呢
Wǒ kěyǐ děng xià gè xīngqī 我可以等下个星期 yǒu shíjiān le zài qù yóujú 有时间了再去邮局，	hébì yídìng yào zhège 何必一定要这个 xīngqī qù ne 星期去呢？
Nǐ bú shì yǐjīng tōngguò nà- 你不是已经通过那 ge kǎoshì le ma Suīrán fēn- 个考试了吗？虽然分 shù yǒudiǎnr dī 数有点儿低，	kěshì hébì zài kǎo yí 可是何必再考一 cì ne 次呢？

Clause 1	hébì ne 何必……呢
Jìrán tā yǐjīng gēn nǐ fēn- 既然他已经跟你分 shǒu le 手了，	nǐ hébì hái gēn tā lián- 你何必还跟他联 xì ne 系呢？
Nǐ bú shì zhù sān lóu ma 你不是住三楼吗？	Wǒmen zǒu lóutī jiù xíng 我们走楼梯就行 le hébì zuò diàntī 了，何必坐电梯？
Tā yào pāi shǎoshù mínzú 他要拍少数民族 de zhàopiàn qù Běijīng de 的照片，去北京的 Zhōnghuá Mínzúyuán jiù kěyǐ 中华民族园就可以，	hébì fēiyào qù yí tàng 何必非要去一趟 Yúnnán 云南？

Expressing “let alone” with 别说 A, 就是B, 也/都……

(biéshuō jiù shì yě dōu)

别说 means “let alone”, “not to mention”. Topic A and topic B are related, but B is a more extensive case than A in terms of the comment following 也/都. The structure indicates that in most cases if the comment can be applied to topic B, then the comment can also be applied to topic A.

	biéshuō 别说 A	jiùshì 就是 B	yě dōu 也/都 + comment
Wǒ yéye shuō 我爷爷说， tā xiǎo de shíhou 他小的时候	biéshuō diànnǎo 别说电脑 hé wǎngluò 和网络，	jiùshì hǎo- 就是好 kàn de shū 看的书，	yě méiyǒu 也没有 duōshǎo 多少。
Zhège fángjiān 这个房间 juéduì ānquán 绝对安全，	biéshuō shì 别说是 rén le 人了，	jiùshì 就是 wénzi 蚊子，	yě jìn 也进 bù lái 不来。
	Biéshuō zǒu yí 别说走一 gè xiǎoshí 个小时，	jiùshì 就是 zǒu liù gè 走六个 xiǎoshí 小时，	tā dōu méi 他都没 wèntí 问题。
Zhème qítè de 这么奇特的 shuǐguǒ 水果，	biéshuō chī 别说吃 le 了，	jiùshì kàn 就是看，	wǒ dōu méi 我都没 kànguo 看过。

	biéshuō 别说 A	jiùshì 就是 B	yě dōu 也/都 + comment
Zhǐyào ràng wǒ gēn 只要让我跟 nǐmen yìqǐ qù 你们一起去 Yúnnán 云南，	biéshuō wèi nǐ- 别说为你 men kāichē 们开车，	jiùshì bāng 就是帮 nǐmen zuò 你们做 gèng duō de 更多的 shìqing 事情，	wǒ yě 我也 yuànyì 愿意。

Indicating “constantly” or “non-stop” with 一直 or 不断

(yìzhí búduàn)

Both 一直 and 不断 are adverbs used to indicate that the action is continuous. But they do not always apply to the same context. 一直 means “all along” or “all the time”, which expresses the continuation of an action or an unchangable circumstance within a certain period of time. The verbs or adjectives modified by 一直 are usually durative; 一直 can also be used together with structures indicating ongoing actions such as 在V or V着.

However, 不断 literally means “nonstop” or “unceasingly”. The verbs modifed by 不断 are usually those that express a single occurrence, so 不断 is used to indicate that the action is repeated again and again.

In addition, 不断 often requires the adverbial particle 地 to follow it, while 一直 does not. If 一直 and 不断 appear in one sentence, 一直 goes before 不断.

Subject	yìzhí 一直/ búduàn de 不断(地)	Verb phrase
Zhèxiē nián 这些年 lái tā 来，她	yìzhí 一直	bǎ dàngchéng zìjǐ de 把Amy当成自己的 jiějie 姐姐。
Zhège guójiā 这个国家	yìzhí 一直	fēicháng zhòngshì értóng de 非常重视儿童的 jiàoyù 教育。
Yàshēn gōngsī 亚深公司	búduàn de 不断地	bǎ huòwù cóng Shēnzhèn yùn- 把货物从深圳运 dào quánguó gèdì 到全国各地。

Subject	yìzhí 一直 / búduàn de 不断 (地)	Verb phrase
Zhè xiàng huán- 这 项 环 jìng zhèngcè 境 政策	búduàn 不断	shòudào gè fāngmiàn de pīpíng 受 到 各 方 面 的批评。
Rén de 人 的 yìshēng yào 一生，要	yìzhí bú- 一直 不 duàn de 断 地	jìnxíng gèzhǒng-gèyàng de 进行 各种 各样 的 xuǎnzé 选择。

Picture captions

Unit 1 p15 Traditional dragon boat racing at the Dragon Boat Festival / pp22–23 Shenzhen Bay Bridge, Shenzhen, Guangdong Province

Unit 2 p27 Lion dancing at the Spring Festival / pp34–35 Flying cranes, Heilongjiang Province

Unit 3 p39 Modern Chinese girl in traditional cheongsam / p43 St Sophia Cathedral, Dragon Tower, Songhua River Highway Bridge, Entrance of Zhongyang Street, Harbin, Heilongjiang Province / p44 Flood Control Monument by the Songhua River, Harbin, Heilongjiang Province / p46–47 Sun Island Park in winter, Harbin, Heilongjiang Province

Unit 4 p51 Entrance to the Earth God Worship House of Ditan Park, Beijing / p55 Girl looking through battlements at the Jiankou Great Wall, Beijing / pp58–59 Songhua River at dusk, Harbin, Heilongjiang Province

Unit 5 p74–75 Tianchi Lake, Changbai Mountain, Jilin Province

Unit 6 p79 Young couple riding a tandem bicycle in a hutong, Beijing / pp86–87 Cityscape of Shenzhen, Guangdong Province

Unit 7 p96 Busy streets in Shenzhen featuring Shun Hing Square, or Diwang Building, Shenzhen, Guangdong Province / p100 Round and square decoration on a carved wooden door, Chengde Summer Resort, Chengde, Hebei Province

Unit 8 p103 Three White Pagodas and Cangshan Mountain at night, Dali, Yunnan Province / p107 Paper cutting featuring a dancing girl of the Dai ethnic group / p108 Stone Forest in Kunming, Lijiang, Shangri-La County and Mainri Snow Mountain, Yunnan Province / pp110–111 Rural scene at Dali, Yunnan Province

Unit 9 p119 Cityscape of Lijiang, Yunnan Province / pp126–127 Yangtze River, Shangri-La, Yunnan Province

Unit 10 p131 The Giant Stone Buddha at Leshan Mountain, Sichuan Province / p138–139 Harbin Park Bridge, Harbin, Heilongjiang Province

Unit 11 pp150–151 Xi'an ancient city wall at dusk, Shaanxi Province

Unit 12 p155 Stupa at Fragrant Hill in autumn, Beijing / p164 Chinese traditional paper cutting featuring fish and a character for "happiness"

Review 3 p170 Chinese writing brush on a brush rack beside tea ware

Pair work activities pp174–175 Pair of pagodas on Fir Lake in Guilin, Guangxi Zhuang Autonomous Region / p176 Laoniuwan, part of the Yellow River between Shanxi Province and the Inner Mongolia Autonomous Region / p177 Gingko leaves by the side of a traditional building roof in autumn, Beijing / pp180–181 Limestone karst skyline over the Lijiang River, Guilin, Guangxi Zhuang Autonomous Region / p182 Bamboo rafts on the Lijiang River, Yangshuo, Guangxi Zhuang Autonomous Region / p183 Paddy rice field, East China

English translations

Unit 1

Vocabulary and listening

Mark: Yeong-min, how was your winter vacation?

Yeong-min: Very good. I went back to South Korea to see my parents and friends. It was so good to be with my parents. I ate well and have put on some weight. How about you? Where did you go for your vacation?

Mark: I didn't go anywhere. I just stayed at school studying Chinese. Next week I have an interview to attend.

Yeong-min: What kind of interview? Are you looking for a job?

Mark: Just a post for an internship. Since I want to stay and work in China after graduation, I need to gain some work experience in China by interning during the summer vacation.

Yeong-min: Excellent! You've made such an early start in preparing for job hunting. What kind of company and post is it?

Mark: It's an international trading company, and their Customer Service Department are looking for an interpreter. I am a people person, and I also understand Chinese culture, which I hope will meet their requirements.

Yeong-min: You are quite capable. With good preparation, it shouldn't be a problem.

Mark: Thanks for your encouragement. However, they say that a lot of people are applying for this post, and the competition is fierce. I have no confidence at all.

Yeong-min: Don't worry. You'll be fine. By the way, where did you see the information for the job?

Mark: On a website. I'll send you the link this evening. Oh yes, Amanda went back to Brazil. Did you know?

Yeong-min: She sent me an email. Ah, so many friends have left Beijing. Wang Yu has also gone to the States to study.

Mark: Yes. Anyway, we can still contact them online. Recently I came across a line from an old poem: "A bosom friend afar brings a distant land near".

Yeong-min: Great, you even know some old poetry!

Reading and writing

Home Job search Company search Print

Current page: Yashen International Trading Co Ltd

Industry: import and export

Size: 100–150 employees

Location: the mainland of China

Company description: Yashen International Trading Co Ltd specializes in the import and export of children's toys and clothing products. Founded in 2000, the company has branches in Beijing, Chongqing and Shenzhen.

Position	Location	Issue date
1 Customer service intern	Shenzhen	28 March
2 Branch sales manager	Chongqing	15 March

Home Job search Company search Print

Current page: Interpreter intern, Customer Service Department, Yashen International Trading Co Ltd (2)

Location: Shenzhen (frequent business trips required)

Duties: Assist in receiving American and European customers; provide interpretation service in Chinese and English; assist in arranging work schedules, visits and sightseeing activities for customers.

Requirements: Undergraduate students; priority will be given to those majoring in English, economics or management who have strong communication skills and experience of English-Chinese translation or of secretarial work.

Benefits: Free accommodation and internship wages; those with an excellent standard of performance during the internship may become employees after graduation.

How to apply: Please send your CV to the company's mailbox; notice for interview will be issued in one week.

Contact person: Miss Wen

The International Exchange Centre is looking for summer volunteers

Number of people required: 2

Project: The 4th International Secondary School Students' Summer Camp

Time period: 15 July to 15 August

Location: Beijing and Harbin

Duties: Assist the International Exchange Centre in organization and student management at the International Summer Camp for Secondary School Students.

Benefits: Food, accommodation and transport during the summer camp will be provided by the International Exchange Centre; there will also be a small living allowance.

Applicant requirements: International students of the university (all nationalities welcome) must have fluent English and Chinese, with strong communication skills.

Application method: Fill in and submit the application form to Mr Wang at the International Students Office before 30 March; interview notice will be issued by 20 April.

Contact: Room 203, International Exchange Centre

Unit 2

Vocabulary and listening

Wang Yu: Mark! How's the interview preparation for the company you last mentioned going? Do you want me to help you practise it again?

Mark: No, thanks, Wang Yu. The interview was last Wednesday, and since then I have been waiting for the outcome.

Wang Yu: How do you feel about it?

Mark: Not too bad, and I'm fairly satisfied with my performance.

Wang Yu: What kind of questions did they ask you?

Mark: What they were most interested in is why, as a foreigner, I want to stay and work in China. Then they asked me to present my previous work experience, and my plans for the future. In general, they didn't ask any complicated questions.

Wang Yu: How did you present your work experience?

Mark: I said I had helped my classmates translate some papers, and I had done some volunteering in a retirement home during high school in Australia.

Wang Yu: Did you emphasize your adaptability and conscientious attitude to work?

Mark: I didn't say that directly, but they should be able to sense that. When the interview was coming to an end, they were already talking about the benefits of the internship with me.

Wang Yu: Your chances are good! By the way, can you work in China while you hold a student visa?

Mark: Oops! Thanks for reminding me. I forgot to ask. Tomorrow I will write a letter to ask about this. Enough about me. How are you finding living in the States?

Wang Yu: I still haven't got used to it. I miss my home very much. My Chinese stomach doesn't seem to be able to consume American food. Besides, with the huge pressure from studying and trying to cope with my inadequate English, my feelings are quite complicated.

Mark: Don't worry. All these difficulties are just temporary. I felt the same way as you when I first arrived in Beijing. But now hasn't everything turned out well? I've made lots of new friends, and I have also fallen in love with Chinese food. Now I even want to stay and work here. I think you will definitely get used to your new life soon.

Reading and writing

Dear Miss Wen,

How are you? I would like to thank you for taking the time to read my application letter.

My name is Mark, and I am from Australia. I am an international student majoring in modern Chinese at Beijing Foreign Studies University, and will graduate next year. I am hoping that I can stay and work in China after graduation, so I would like to gain some relevant work experience during the summer vacation. I'm very interested in the interpreter intern post in the Customer Service Department in your company. I believe I can adapt to the job and become a competent interpreter very quickly.

My mother tongue is English, but my current major is modern Chinese, with a minor in economics. In the last two years, I have helped my classmates translate various types of articles. Although I haven't had a chance to work as a business interpreter formally, I did receive and assist my Australian friends who came to China to explore business development.

I have an open and optimistic personality, and I love sports and travelling. I'm sympathetic and responsible, and enjoy dealing with various people. In high school, I spent two years as a volunteer in a retirement home in Brisbane, mainly helping with documentation, recording notes for meetings, and organizing a lot of activities. While working on this job, I honed my abilities in organization, planning and communication, and performed tasks with diligence and detailed planning. During the several years I have spent studying and living in China, I have learnt a great deal not only about Chinese history and culture, but also about cultural differences between the East and the West. I think all these have helped to qualify me for the role of an interpreter in the Customer Service Department in your company.

I really hope I get the opportunity to work as an intern at your company, which will also lay a good foundation for my future career. Attached please find my CV.

I look forward to hearing from you.

Regards,
Mark
4 March, 2014

Unit 3

Vocabulary and listening

CSO = Customer Service Officer YM = Yeong-min

CSO: Hello, Qingfeng Travel Service Ticket Centre. How may I help you?

YM: Hi, I'm from Beijing Foreign Studies University. Our university will have a group with 15 people travelling from Beijing to Harbin in mid-July. I want to know roughly how much plane tickets and train tickets will cost during that period of time.

CSO: Wait a minute, and I will check that for you. May I know your surname please?

YM: My surname is Jin.

CSO: Mr Jin, because July is peak season for tourism, the plane tickets will be full price. As for the train tickets, you have a lot more choices. You can choose a regular or an express train, a sleeping berth or a hard seat.

YM: Excuse me, could you explain in more detail?

CSO: Certainly, Mr Jin: a regular train from Beijing to Harbin takes from 10 to 20 hours, and a ticket for a sleeping berth is two or three times that of a hard seat. A hard seat is of course not as comfortable as a sleeping berth, but the price is much cheaper. An express train is a high-speed train, and the fastest one takes only 8 hours to get to Harbin. There are only seats on a high-speed train, but the seats are more comfortable than those on a regular train. A first-class ticket for a high-speed train is nearly half of the full price for an air ticket, while a second-class ticket is cheaper, by about a third.

YM: Train tickets are not very expensive. However, I still need to discuss it with our team leader. By the way, is there any discount for group tickets, and can you deliver the tickets to us?

CSO: Mr Jin, I suggest you allow our travel consultant to help you. They will make the most economical and sensible travel plan to suit your requirements, including your tickets, food and accommodation, and any other arrangements for the trip. That way, you can enjoy a worry-free trip. Shall I put you through to our travel consultant?

YM: That would be great! Thank you!

Reading and writing

Four-day trip from Beijing to Harbin during summer

Price: RMB 2000*

Departure date: Every Tuesday and Friday from 1 July to 15 September

Main transport: train — Departure: Beijing; Destination: Harbin

Local transport: air-conditioned coach

Day 1:

- Take the train from Beijing Railway Station to Harbin

Day 2:

- Climb the highest iron tower in Asia, Dragon Tower, and take in a bird's-eye view of Harbin.
- See the St Sophia Cathedral and Square, and visit the Harbin Municipal Architectural Art Museum.
- Stroll along the longest pedestrian precinct in Asia, Central Street. Walk on the cobblestone pavement, appreciate the European-style buildings and get a sense of the last hundred years of history.

Day 3:

- Visit Heilongjiang Provincial Museum and learn about the history and culture of Northeast China.
- Free time in the afternoon. You can go for a walk along the Songhua River, enjoy the shows at Harbin's Summer Concert, or go shopping in the downtown area and try some of the local cuisine.

Day 4:

- Visit the Sun Island summer resort, a national AAAAA scenic place of interest. You can also buy a ticket to visit the largest indoor snow and ice art gallery in Asia, and view the beautiful ice lanterns and snow sculptures.
- Take the train at night and get back to Beijing the next morning.

Notes for visiting Harbin in summer:

1 The temperature difference between day and night is substantial, so please make sure that you bring enough clothes to avoid getting cold.

2 The sunshine is strong in summer, so make sure you apply sun cream to avoid getting sunburnt.

* Price includes transport, accommodation, breakfast and lunch each day, tickets for places of interest and a tour guide. Personal activities, dinner and travel insurance are not included in the price.

Unit 4

Vocabulary and listening

Mr Qian: Hello, everyone, welcome to the Beijing Foreign Studies University International Summer Camp for Secondary School Students. I'm your team leader, and my surname is Qian. Today is our camp's opening ceremony. First of all, let's welcome Director Wang of the International Exchange Centre to make a welcome speech and announce the opening of the camp.

Wang: All students from far and wide, on behalf of the Beijing Foreign Studies University International Exchange Centre, I welcome you here to attend the International Summer Camp for Secondary School Students. Beijing Foreign Studies University is a very famous higher education institution for language majors in China, and it was also one of the first universities to provide a programme to teach Chinese as a foreign language. We have already held three summer camps for international secondary school students. The theme of this year's camp is using Chinese to tell Chinese stories. I believe, through the rich and diverse language practice activities, your Chinese proficiency will be much improved by the time you leave the camp, and your understanding of China will be much enriched, just like the students of the previous three camps. I hereby announce the International Summer Camp for Secondary School Students formally open!

Mr Qian: Thank you very much, Director Wang, for the speech. Next, I would like to introduce you to the two assistants who will stay with you for the duration of the summer camp. Both of them are students at our university: Sun Xiaowen and Jin Yeong-min.

Xiaowen: Hello everyone, I'm Xiaowen. I'm very happy to have the opportunity to stay with you for your summer in China.

Yeong-min: I'm Yeong-min, how are you doing? I hope you have an enjoyable and very productive stay at the camp. Feel free to contact me whenever you need anything!

Reading and writing

Summer Camp Rules

1. Listen to and follow the instructions and arrangements of the camp teachers and staff. Strict observation of daily schedules is required.
2. Take good care of your personal belongings, and report the loss of valuables to the team leader or assistant immediately.
3. Be mindful of food and water hygiene and sudden weather changes. Report immediately to the team leader or assistant if you feel ill, and, accompanied by them, go to see the doctor.
4. Go to class on time. If you cannot attend the class because of illness, ask the teacher for time off in advance.
5. Finish your homework on time. If you have any questions about the lessons, you may raise them with the teacher on duty during the evening self-study class.
6. Try your best to speak Chinese. Do not speak other languages, or speak them less.
7. Take an active part in the extracurricular activities and the tours and sightseeing activities. If you have a special reason for not attending, inform the team leader in advance.
8. No unaccompanied activities will be allowed during free time. Try to avoid going to places you are not familiar with. Remember the frequently used telephone numbers, and if an emergency occurs, make the phone call immediately.
9. Cooperate with other members of the camp, and show team spirit by caring for and supporting each other.

Frequently used telephone numbers:

Emergency call: 110 Fire service: 119
Medical emergency service: 120

Daily schedule

08:00–10:00	Language lesson
10:00–12:00	Culture lesson
12:00–14:00	Lunch and noon recess
14:00–17:30	Extracurricular activities, tours and sightseeing
17:30–19:30	Dinner and free time
19:30–21:30	Evening self-study

Things to pack for the Harbin tour:

- summer clothes (you are also advised to bring long-sleeved shirts and trousers)
- sun protection (sun cream, hat and sunglasses)
- personal prescription medicines
- toiletries for personal use
- watch, torch, mug, umbrella, notebook, pen
- cash (RMB)

Unit 5

Vocabulary and listening

Mark: Manager Tang, were you looking for me?

Tang Yu: Mark, come here. Sit on the sofa. How's it going? How are you coping with the work in the first week of your internship?

Mark: Thanks for your concern. I like my job very much, and have been learning from my colleagues from the moment I arrived.

Tang Yu: That's great. Talk to your colleagues if you have any questions. In the next two weeks, we are going to receive a delegation from Australia, and you will be accompanying them everywhere and will be responsible for the main interpretation work.

Mark: Oh… I will try my best.

Tang Yu: But there's no need to be nervous, since the other colleagues in the Customer Service Department will help you in every way possible. I have seen your CV, and have confidence in you.

Mark: Thank you for your trust. It is a lot of pressure, but it is a good opportunity for me to practise. I will make good use of it.

Tang Yu: Good. There are two more things on which I need your advice. We plan to hold a welcome dinner banquet for the delegation. Which do you think is more appropriate, Western food or Chinese food?

Mark: I think since they have come to China, wouldn't they like to try local Chinese cuisine?

Tang Yu: Sounds reasonable. In addition, we want to give each of them a souvenir. Do you have any suggestions?

Mark: I don't think it is necessary to give an expensive gift. Oh wait, I saw our company makes a panda toy made from environmentally friendly materials, which not only reflects our company's mission to protect the environment, but also looks very Chinese. We could not find a better gift than that! What do you think?

Tang Yu: Yes, that sounds good, too. Let's further discuss issues concerning this delegation at Friday's regular meeting.

Mark: OK, Manager Tang. I will think about whether there are other issues to consider. If there's nothing else, I will go back to work.

Tang Yu: OK.

Reading and writing

Memo

Mark,

Manager Tang has asked you to go to her office when you get back. It's mainly about arrangements for the Australian delegation. In addition, the company's invitation card needs an English version. Please translate with reference to the Chinese invitation card on your desk. Please send me the translation via email no later than noon tomorrow. Thank you.

Xie Yue
10:15 am, 2 July

Meeting Notice

The Customer Service Department is going to have the regular monthly meeting on 5 July (this Friday), with the following arrangements:

Time: registration from 9:50 am, meeting begins at 10:00 am.

Venue: the big conference room beside the General Manager's office

Participants: all staff of the Customer Service Department

Meeting agenda:

1) Team leaders report on this month's work progress and the work plan for next month. Need to include an analysis of any unfinished work and propose specific suggestions for improvement.
2) Manager Tang delivers the summary of the Customer Service Department's work.
3) Discuss arrangements for the reception of the Australian delegation.
4) Discuss customer feedback on the new customer service system.

Yashen (Shenzhen) Customer Service Department
2 July

Invitation card

Dear (Mr/Ms) __________ ,

Yashen International Trading Co Ltd Shenzhen Branch requests the pleasure of your company

At an event for __________________

On ____________________ (date and time)

At ____________________________ (address)

Telephone: _________________

Li Shuqing, General Manager
_____________ (D/M/Y)

Unit 6

Vocabulary and listening

Xie Yue: Mark, you did a good job today!

Mark: Thanks! Actually I was very nervous and afraid of missing important information because I had misheard or hadn't translated accurately.

Xie Yue: Really? No one could tell.

Mark: That's good. Fortunately, Zhou Xiang had prepared the material for me in advance, or I would have performed very badly today.

Zhou Xiang: You are too modest, Mark. Colleagues are supposed to help each other.

Xie Yue: Yes, you two have cooperated very well.

Zhou Xiang: Thanks for the compliment. Mark, I really admire you: you have learnt Chinese so well! If only I could speak English as well as you speak Chinese.

Mark: Your English is already very good. I would like to learn about international trade from you.

Xie Yue: Yes, Zhou Xiang is a very talented student majoring in foreign trade studies. You two can certainly learn from each other and improve together.

Mark: We should really learn from you and others in the company who have so much experience. Practical experience is more important than information learnt from books.

Zhou Xiang: That's absolutely right. Xie Yue, have you been working in the Customer Service Department since you joined the company?

Xie Yue: No, when I first came here I worked in the Sales Department. But later I found that I was more suited to customer service work, so less than a year later I was transferred to the current department.

Zhou Xiang: I see. If there is an opportunity, I would also like to intern in the Sales Department.

Xie Yue: Really? Then I will recommend you for a position there to gain experience at some point.

Zhou Xiang: That would be great!

Xie Yue: How are you both feeling? Are you tired? Do you still have the energy to sing karaoke?

Mark: Now? Zhou Xiang, it's up to you. If you go, I will go.

Zhou Xiang: Tomorrow is the weekend anyway, and there's no need to go to sleep early. Let's go. Afterwards, I will take you out for a midnight snack.

Reading and writing

Mark,

Attached are two documents for the evening banquet the day after tomorrow, one being the individual arrangements and agenda for the banquet, the other the outline of the General Manager's speech. The General Manager's speech is not long this time and there's no need to prepare a speech draft, so there is only an outline. Please let me know immediately if there is anything else you need, and I will help you prepare it.

Zhou Xiang

Attachment 1: Evening banquet agenda and arrangements.doc view download

Attachment 2: General Manager's speech (outline).doc view download

Evening banquet welcome speech (outline)

1 Opening speech: "Dear delegates from Australia, colleagues from Shenzhen, ladies and gentlemen, good evening. On behalf of all the staff of Yashen Company Shenzhen Branch, I would like to extend our warmest welcome to the Australian delegation here to visit our company!"

2 A simple review of the history of Yashen's development; focus on introducing Shenzhen Branch's current main business and international partners.

3 Introduce the company's plan for business development and seeking new partners in Australia in the next two years. Wish the delegation great success in its visit to China.

4 Concluding remarks: "Lastly, I would like to propose a toast to our friendship and future cooperation, and to the health of all the ladies and gentlemen present. Cheers!"

Evening banquet agenda for the Australian delegation

Time: 18:30 – 22:00, 12 July 2014

Venue: Banquet Hall, ground floor, Shenzhen Hotel

Received by: Reception team, Customer Service Department

Interpreter: Mark

Hostess: Tang Yu

18:30 Guests of the banquet start to arrive, and reception staff lead them to their seats.

18:45 Members of the Australian delegation and the main leaders of the company take their seats.

19:00 The hostess introduces the company leaders and the VIPs.

19:10 The General Manager makes a welcome speech.

19:20 The Australian delegation makes a speech of thanks in response.

19:30 The evening banquet formally begins, interspersed with performances of Chinese folk music for guests to enjoy.

22:00 The evening banquet ends.

Unit 7

Vocabulary and listening

Xie Yue: Mark, you are the only one left in the office. Why haven't you left? Are you planning to work overtime?

Mark: Ah, working overtime might not be enough to solve the problem.

Xie Yue: Do you want to talk about it with me?

Mark: OK. I received a phone call from the factory yesterday, saying that one of our customers' orders cannot be completed on time. I then sent an email to the customer informing them of the situation. Unexpectedly, they were very angry, and criticized us for not keeping our promise, saying that they would cancel the order. Have I caused a lot of trouble?

Xie Yue: Don't worry. Relax and calm down first. What exactly is the reason why the factory cannot complete the order on time?

Mark: They say that recently they have not been able to find enough qualified workers in the labour market.

Xie Yue: Hmm, that is quite possible. Did you mention any solutions in your email?

Mark: No, I just explained the situation.

Xie Yue: Dealing with this kind of problem does require experience, so don't put the blame all on yourself. But if I were the customer, I would think that you were just finding excuses.

Mark: Then what should I do now?

Xie Yue: "The customer is always right." You should not only apologize sincerely to the customer, but also propose solutions, for example, shortening the delivery time, or giving the customer a discount, and so on. However, you should consult Manager Tang on how to handle this specifically. Remember, if you come across similar problems in the future, do consult your supervisor immediately.

Mark: Thank you very much. Do you think Manager Tang will forgive me?

Xie Yue: Don't worry about it. Just stop work for now.

Reading and writing

Wang Yu,

How are you doing?

Nowadays people are used to sending emails and chatting online, and basically do not write letters any more. But I still think writing letters by hand is very engaging, and by doing this I can also practise my handwriting.

I have been working as an intern in the Shenzhen company for one month. Being at work feels very different from being at university. I leave home early and return late, with endless amounts of information to check, emails to reply to and phone calls to make. In addition, my colleagues often come to ask me questions about English and about cultural differences. My brain doesn't stop working even after work, and it is always excited! But I feel myself becoming smarter because the busy schedule every day gives me many opportunities to learn new things.

For example, last week I went on a business trip for the first time, accompanying a customer on a visit to the factory. I had to handle everything by myself, from booking the hotel, buying the plane tickets and arranging the itinerary to interpreting. Although I'm in a flurry, doing these things is really helping me to exercise my skills.

I consider myself very lucky. My boss and colleagues are very kind to me, and I can consult them whenever I have questions. Just yesterday, I made a not-so-small mistake due to my lack of experience. My boss not only didn't criticize me, but also gave me some very good suggestions. This meant a lot to me. I really hope I can continue working for this company after graduation.

Also, I often sing karaoke with my colleagues in my spare time. Already I can sing a few Chinese songs. Next time you come back, we can go and sing songs together.

Enclosed, please find a photo I took. It's a street view of Shenzhen. This city is full of energy, and I like it very much.

How are you doing in the States? Have you made many new friends? Write to me when you have time.

Hoping everything goes well, and may all your wishes come true.

Your friend, Mark

24 July, Shenzhen

Unit 8

Vocabulary and listening

Steve: Hello! My name is Steve. How should I address you?

Da Liu: You can call me Da Liu. Your Chinese is very good! Is this the first time you've come to Lijiang?

Steve: Thanks, Da Liu. Yes, this is my first time in Yunnan. I just arrived from Kunming yesterday. Yunnan is really a great place. Are you from here? You are so lucky to be able to live here!

Da Liu: I'm not from here. I came here for a holiday seven years ago, and, after arriving, I didn't want to leave. Later, I quit my job and moved to Lijiang.

Steve: What did you do in the past?

Da Liu: I used to work in Shanghai, a typical white-collar employee. The job seemed decent, but in fact there was too much pressure. I often suffered from insomnia. At the time I wondered whether that was the life I really wanted. When I came to Lijiang for a holiday, I suddenly experienced the pleasure of enjoying life. I asked myself: why not change my lifestyle? I really hated my previous life.

Steve: I see. I once interviewed a teacher, who had also given up the life in Beijing and moved to Inner Mongolia.

Da Liu: So you are a journalist. Are you here to interview people?

Steve: I'm here for a holiday. I heard long ago that the scenery in Yunnan is like a postcard and that it is a paradise for amateur photographers. Clearly it lives up to its reputation.

Da Liu: What do you think of Lijiang?

Steve: Lijiang is a very beautiful little town. However, it is more commercialized than I imagined. I haven't thought about where to go next. Do you have any suggestions?

Da Liu: You have asked the right person! Wait a minute, and I will go to get a map. Then I'll tell you some places you don't want to miss!

Steve: That's great! I will buy you a beer afterwards!

Reading and writing

Yeong-min,

I'm in Kunming, Yunnan now. It's as warm as spring no matter what season it is in Kunming, so it is also known as "Spring City". In the picture is the famous "Stone Forest". There are a lot of delicacies here, and the one I like most is Dai food. Dai is an ethnic group in Yunnan, and their peacock dance is very beautiful. The Dai also have a musical instrument called the cucurbit flute, the sound of which is very distinct. I'm sure you would like it.

Steve, in Kunming, Yunnan

Wang Yu,

Is everything going well with you in the States? Currently I'm in Lijiang, Yunnan, a very small and sweet town. Life can be very slow and lazy here, and time seems to have stopped. If only you could be here too, we could enjoy the sunshine and daydream together…

In Lijiang I met group after group of young people from the big cities; they often mentioned a phrase "man shenghuo" (slow life). Have you heard of this?

Steve, in Lijiang, Yunnan

Amanda,

I haven't heard from you for a long time, and I hope everything has been going well since you have returned to Brazil. I'm now in Zhongdian, Yunnan, the legendary "Shangri-La". Here everything is awash with Tibetan religious and cultural features, which is quite different from the world outside. Tomorrow I'm leaving for Mainri Snow Mountain, and I'm very excited about it. I hope this "holy mountain" can bring me good luck!

Steve, in Zhongdian, Yunnan

Mark,

I have been in Yunnan for two weeks, and haven't had time to go to many places. Unfortunately, I'm leaving here today. What impressed me most was the trip on horseback to Yubeng Village behind the Mainri Snow Mountain. Although in some places the road was very narrow and a bit dangerous, and my altitude sickness was serious, I thought it was worthwhile after I got to Yubeng. It is a Shangri-La, an amazing retreat from the world!

Steve, at Kunming Airport, Yunnan

Unit 9

Vocabulary and listening

Wang Yu: Steve, you look thinner and have a nice tan.

Steve: Do I look smarter?

Wang Yu: Haha, you look fine.

Steve: I just came back from Yunnan. Although the temperature was not high, the UV rays were strong. While at Mainri Snow Mountain, my altitude sickness was so serious that I was nearly hospitalized. That's why I look thinner and tanned now.

Wang Yu: Fortunately you are OK, otherwise the trip wouldn't have been worthwhile.

Steve: It would still have been worthwhile even if I had got sick. I enjoyed Yunnan so much as to not want to go home!

Wang Yu: Then send me a couple of photos you're pleased with now.

Steve: I haven't had a chance to sort out the photos in my camera. I am sending you two photos from my mobile phone. They were taken at the foot of Mainri Snow Mountain.

Wang Yu: The snow mountain in your pictures has a calming effect.

Steve: It's even more beautiful if you see it with your own eyes. But the quality of my photos this time is really good. Honestly, they could match those taken by a professional photojournalist.

Wang Yu: Really? Then you should try to submit them to a travel magazine.

Steve: Actually, I've been considering whether to participate in a photography contest. The theme is "Yunnan through My Eyes".

Wang Yu: What a good opportunity! Why are you hesitating then?

Steve: The closing date is coming soon. I'm worried that I may not have enough time to choose the photos. In addition, there are so many talented photographers, which definitely makes it difficult to win an award.

Wang Yu: Didn't you say just now that you are very professional? Why, are you afraid of failure and too scared to compete with them?

Steve: I'm not afraid at all. Winning or losing is not important. Participation is what really matters.

Wang Yu: Invite me for dinner if you win an award.

Steve: Only too glad to!

Reading and writing

"Yunnan through My Eyes" Photography Contest Calling for Submissions

In order to provide a platform for amateur photographers to display their work, and to reflect the charm of Yunnan and promote tourism development, *Yunnan Travel* magazine and the Yunnan Photographers Association have decided to jointly hold a photography contest entitled "Yunnan through My Eyes".

1 Contest schedule

1) Submission of work: From now until 31 July 2014

2) Evaluation: three weeks after closing of submission

3) Result announcement: *Yunnan Travel*, the September 2014 volume

2 Submission requirements

1) The contest is open to all amateur photographers.

2) The photographs must be taken in Yunnan after June 2013, with no limitation on style.

3) Each person can submit up to six photos, each of which must be accompanied by a title and information about the photo, including the time when the photo was taken, the place and its content.

4) Participants must send their printed photos by post first, and then send electronic files as required after being selected for the contest. The photos must be original images and should not have been altered in any way.

5) The work should be original photos which have not been published before. All legal liability for the works shall be the sole responsibility of the participants. The participants must agree to abide by the above regulations.

3 Prizes

First prize: one winner, with a cash reward of 5000 yuan

Second prize: five winners, with a cash reward of 2000 yuan each

Third prize: ten winners, with a cash reward of 500 yuan each

All prize winners will be issued with a certificate by Yunnan Photographers Association, and all volumes of *Yunnan Travel* magazine in 2015.

4 Submission address: "Yunnan through My Eyes" Contest, *Yunnan Travel* Magazine Press, Kunming, Yunnan, Postal code: 650000

All participants should provide their names and contact information.

Yunnan Photographers Association

Yunnan Travel magazine

15 May 2014

Unit 10

Vocabulary and listening

Yeong-min: It's nice and cool here. Let's sit down.

Xiaowen: OK. Yeong-min, about the topics for the speech and debate competition, I can only think of three. The first is "Why I study Chinese". This should not be difficult for the students of the summer camp, and they will definitely have something to say.

Yeong-min: Having something to say doesn't guarantee that they will be interested. Our topics have to be ones that participants are happy to talk about and the audience is willing to listen to. What other topics do you have in mind?

Xiaowen: The second topic is "The development of science and technology and modern life". What do you think?

Yeong-min: Isn't this topic too broad? Even if students have opinions on this, they may not be able to explain them clearly in Chinese. A more specific topic would be better.

Xiaowen: The third topic then is very specific: "The influence of the Internet on daily life". I remember on the opening day, several students looked quite disappointed after learning from the timetable that there would be few opportunities to go online. Is this topic good?

Yeong-min: Yeah, it is better than the previous two, definitely. However…

Xiaowen: Ah, nothing works! If we keep going like this, we are not going to get a result, even if we continue this discussion for three days!

Yeong-min: Xiaowen, don't worry. Let me finish first. I think this is a very good topic for the speech competition, but as a topic for debate, it is not controversial enough.

Xiaowen: That's right. I've got a new idea! How about this: "Can money bring happiness?"

Yeong-min: You are very smart! There are many possible answers to this question, and no fixed conclusion. No matter what stand you take, you will always find something to say. I think it works!

Xiaowen: Really? Sorry, Yeong-min, I've got a bad temper…

Yeong-min: I don't think so at all. I think you are quite direct, and say what you think, which is really adorable!

Reading and writing

The Fourth International Summer Camp for Secondary School Students

Model composition: The Internet and Me

A Summer without the Internet

I used to think that the Internet was my best friend, with which I could do anything. For example, I watched sports programmes on the Internet almost every day. Every now and then, I would log in to social networking websites to update my status, and get the latest news about my friends. Before going out for dinner, I would check out the comments on the website. When going to a place I didn't know, I would check the map online in advance. Before leaving for someplace far away, I would also check the weather, buy plane tickets and book hotels online, etc.

This summer I came to Beijing to attend a summer camp, where it was not convenient to go online. I thought that this summer was going to be boring. However, when the summer camp ended, I found that, even though it was not easy without the Internet, there were some positive changes in my life.

First of all, I participated in many group activities, got close to nature and had more communication with the teachers and other students. This not only enabled us to develop deeper connections, but also helped me to improve my Chinese a lot. Second, since it was not convenient to send emails or log in to social networking websites, the way I kept in touch with my friends in the States was mainly through making phone calls. I also sent them typical Chinese postcards, which made them very happy because they could see the messages and my wishes to them written by hand. In addition, as I couldn't go online to listen to music and watch videos, I had much more time to focus on reading books quietly.

The experiences of this summer have made me realize that the Internet alienates people from the real world while making our lives easier. Now, although the Internet is still an indispensable part of my life, I will not waste all my time on the web. I will not allow the Internet to allocate my time, but will make it serve me better.

Comments:

1 Congratulations for stepping out of the virtual world and entering the real world. ☺

2 The language is smooth, the structure is clear, and the main idea is profound. It is a good essay.

3 Not allowing the Internet to allocate our time, but making it serve us better - that is a very good conclusion!

Unit 11

Vocabulary and listening

Steve: Wang Yu, I didn't expect you to come back home now. This is a surprise!

Wang Yu: It's a school holiday. All the students around were gone, and I was really bored being alone. It feels so good to be home! I can eat whatever I want, and sleep as long as I wish.

Steve: You must have found these six months very difficult, living abroad, away from home, by yourself.

Wang Yu: I couldn't get used to it when I first got there, and I cried a lot. Honestly, I can deal with the difficulties and pressure of life and of study. The most difficult thing to overcome is the feeling of loneliness and of being isolated. Because of the time difference, I cannot call my family any time I want. There is no one to share my happiness, and when I feel sad I often deal with it by myself.

Steve: Actually you can call me at any time. Although I cannot give you any concrete help, at least I can be a good listener.

Wang Yu: I know. But the hardest time has already passed. Enough about me, how about you? Has the result of the photography contest been announced?

Steve: Haha, I have good news to tell you. I got the second prize, and I'm the only foreigner to get a prize.

Wang Yu: Great! Congratulations! Show me your masterpiece! ... The photos look really nice. Why didn't you put them on your blog?

Steve: It's not that I didn't want to. The copyright of these photos has been purchased by a photo agency, and they no longer belong to me. Hey, we made a deal and I owe you a dinner. It can be your welcome home dinner as well. Tell me, what do you want to eat?

Wang Yu: And it can be a celebration for you getting the prize! I do happen to be hungry–in fact, I'm dying for hot pot now. Let's go eat hot pot!

Reading and writing

Footsteps

By Special correspondent Xiao'ai

In the Dai restaurant near Beijing Nationality University, I recognized my interviewee at a glance: Steve, a young man from London, UK, who is also the only foreigner to win a prize in the "Yunnan through My Eyes" photography contest. Nearsighted, Steve's wearing a pair of glasses, but his blue eyes are bright and friendly. Steve's handshake is sincere and strong. His Chinese is very good, uttered at a moderate speed.

Steve decided to stay and live in Beijing after he graduated from university two years ago. During this period of time, he took a part-time job as a journalist for a British magazine while continuing his study of Chinese. What Steve likes to do most is to travel to different places in China, bringing along his beloved camera. The Yangtze River, the Great Wall, the Shaolin Temple in Songshan Mountain, the grasslands in Inner Mongolia... He takes photos everywhere throughout these places. In his own words, he's recording his footsteps through photography.

Steve tells me he had not been confident enough to take part in the "Yunnan through My Eyes" contest at the beginning, and it was because of the encouragement of a Chinese friend that he finally decided to participate. Steve felt very happy about winning the prize. He likes China, and he likes Chinese people in particular. The theme of Steve's winning photos is the variety of people in different parts of Yunnan. The Yunnan trip also introduced him to many other friends who, like him, have fallen in love with Yunnan.

During the interview, Steve makes particular mention of a British man, H. R. Davis. Over one hundred years ago, this British scholar paid four visits to Yunnan in six years, using words and photos to record in detail the climate, produce, culture and geography of various places in Yunnan, leaving a record for us. "If the opportunity arises, I really hope I can live in Yunnan for some period of time, and not just be a passer-by who leaves after seeing the scenery and taking some photos." At the end of the interview, Steve says that he has one wish, which is to go to Yunnan again, following in the footsteps of Davis.

Unit 12

Vocabulary and listening

Yeong-min: Our last gathering was last summer, wasn't it? One year has passed in a flash!

Wang Yu: Yes. And everyone looks more mature.

Steve: I think we have all had some experiences. We should talk about them.

Mark: Me first. Actually you all know that I went to Shenzhen for an internship. Although occasionally I found it hard, I have learnt a lot, and got rid of my bad habit of carelessness. The manager said that I would be welcome to work there after graduation.

Steve: Mark, that's great!

Mark: Stop it. You're really the great one. A few casual photos taken during your travels ended up winning a prize!

Wang Yu: Mark, I don't agree with what you're saying. Steve is not someone who takes casual photos. He has been trying hard to improve his photography skills. No pain, no gain.

Steve: Thank you, Wang Yu. It wasn't easy for you either, being alone in the States and having to handle everything by yourself.

Wang Yu: I often saw you all in my dreams while I was in the States, and felt lost when I woke up. But now here we are together again. Yeong-min, how about you?

Yeong-min: I feel ashamed to say this: I only went to help out at the school's summer camp. But I have good news: Xiaowen, who worked together with me at the summer camp, is now my girlfriend!

Mark: You're shocked us, Yeong-min! Come on, tell us how you go after girls. Don't keep it to yourself!

Yeong-min: As a man, by being brave!

Steve: Great, Yeong-min! Why didn't you bring Xiaowen today?

Yeong-min: She's a bit shy. Maybe next time.

Wang Yu: It seems that everyone has gained a lot.

Mark: I think Yeong-min is the one who has gained the most!

Reading and writing

Reunion in August

It is very muggy in Beijing this summer. It's already late August now, but the temperature is still high. There was rain this morning, and it finally feels cool now, with a taste of autumn.

Before I went to my friends' gathering today, my feelings were quite complicated. I was quite excited about seeing my old friends, but I felt sad when I thought of having to go back to the States soon, not knowing when we will next be able to see each other. During the get-together, some friends proposed that we would meet once every two years, and it could be anywhere in the world. This made me happy again. Yes, every parting leads to the next reunion, so why should I be upset!

It is not easy to study in the States, and I have shed a lot of sweat and tears in the past six months. But whenever I think of these friends, I have courage and energy. Several years ago when they first came to China, they were also alone. In addition to differences in language and food, they also faced various kinds of cultural impacts. But they've all adapted to their new life quickly and well. M decided to work and live in China after graduation. S participated in a photography contest held by a Chinese magazine and won a prize. Y has found a Chinese girlfriend. Their Chinese has all improved a lot too.

The best thing I can learn from them is their optimistic and open attitude, and their willingness to accept new things. For example, they all love travelling. During their two to three years in China they have been to many more places than I have been to. Even distant places like Inner Mongolia and Yunnan bear their footprints, not to mention big cities like Shenzhen and Xi'an. They also plan to travel all over China!

I'm very lucky to have such friends in my life, who inspire me to push myself incessantly and achieve more. From now on, I will be more positive and optimistic when facing difficulties and problems in my life. Even if I cannot go round the world, I will try my best to see more and travel more to broaden my horizons.

Comments:

It's so good for you all to get together! I miss you very much, and will definitely attend the gathering next time!

Amanda, we all miss you too! Maybe our next reunion will be in Brazil with you! ☺

Vocabulary List

	WORD	PINYIN	PART OF SPEECH	MEANING	UNIT
A	爱好者	àihàozhě	*n.*	hobbyist, enthusiast, fan	8
	爱上	àishang	*v.*	fall in love	2
	安排	ānpái	*v.*	arrange	1
B	把握	bǎwò	*v.*	grasp, seize	5
	白领	báilǐng	*n.*	white-collar worker	8
	颁发	bānfā	*v.*	award, confer, issue	9
	版本	bǎnběn	*n.*	version	5
	帮不上	bāng bú shàng		cannot help	11
	保密	bǎomì	*v.*	keep secret	12
	保险	bǎoxiǎn	*n.*	insurance	3
	保证	bǎozhèng	*v.*	guarantee	10
	报告	bàogào	*v./n.*	report	4
	倍	bèi	*num.*	times (multiply)	3
	必须	bìxū	*adv.*	must	8
	避暑胜地	bìshǔ shèngdì		summer resort	3
	遍	biàn	*measure word*	(for number of times)	11
	辩论	biànlùn	*v.*	debate	10
	表达	biǎodá	*v.*	express	1
	表扬	biǎoyáng	*v.*	praise, commend	12
	冰灯	bīngdēng	*n.*	ice lantern	3
	并且	bìngqiě	*conj.*	and	2
	不但	búdàn	*conj.*	not only	5
	不断	búduàn	*adv.*	nonstop, incessantly	12
	不过……罢了	búguò...bàle		just, only	7
	不见得	bújiàndé	*adv.*	not necessarily	10

	WORD	PINYIN	PART OF SPEECH	MEANING	UNIT
	不限	búxiàn	*v.*	no limit	1
	补助	bǔzhù	*n.*	subsidy	1
	不得了	bùdéliǎo		extremely	2
	不等	bùděng	*adj.*	varied	3
	不通	bùtōng	*v.*	blockage, barrier	12
	不许	bùxǔ	*v.*	not allow, must not, prohibit	12
	不足	bùzú	*adj.*	not enough	7
	布里斯班	Bùlǐsībān	*n.*	Brisbane	2
	布置	bùzhì	*v.*	arrange for	5
	步行街	bùxíngjiē	*n.*	pedestrian precinct	3
C	材料	cáiliào	*n.*	material	5
	踩	cǎi	*v.*	tread on	3
	参考	cānkǎo	*v.*	refer to	5
	参与	cānyù	*v.*	participate in	9
	惭愧	cánkuì	*adj.*	ashamed, abashed	12
	策划	cèhuà	*v.*	plan	2
	曾经	céngjīng	*adv.*	ever	2
	差异	chāyì	*n.*	differences	2
	差点儿	chàdiǎnr	*adv.*	nearly	9
	馋	chán	*v./adj.*	covet; covetous	11
	产品	chǎnpǐn	*n.*	product	1
	长城	Chángchéng	*n.*	The Great Wall	11
	长江	Cháng Jiāng	*n.*	The Yangtze River	11
	长期	chángqī	*n.*	long term	12
	长袖	chángxiù	*n.*	long sleeves	4
	尝	cháng	*v.*	taste	5
	常用	chángyòng	*adj.*	frequently used	4

WORD	PINYIN	PART OF SPEECH	MEANING	UNIT
场	chǎng	*measure word*	(for rain/snow)	12
成立	chénglì	*v.*	establish	1
成熟	chéngshú	*v./adj.*	mature	12
承担	chéngdān	*v.*	bear, assume	9
诚恳	chéngkěn	*adj.*	sincere	7
诚意	chéngyì	*n.*	sincerity	5
程度	chéngdù	*n.*	degree	8
吃不惯	chī bú guàn	*v.*	not get used to eating	2
吃惊	chījīng	*v.*	be startled, be shocked, be taken aback	12
迟迟	chíchí	*adv.*	very late	12
冲击	chōngjī	*v.*	impact	12
充满	chōngmǎn	*v.*	be filled with	7
重	chóng	*adv.*	again, afresh	11
重逢	chóngféng	*v.*	reunite	12
重庆	Chóngqìng	*n.*	Chongqing	1
抽时间	chōu shíjiān		make time	2
出发	chūfā	*v.*	take off	3
出远门	chūyuǎnmén		go far	10
闯祸	chuǎnghuò	*v.*	make trouble	7
辞职	cízhí	*v.*	quit one's job	8
聪明	cōngming	*adj.*	smart	7
从事	cóngshì	*v.*	be engaged in	1
粗心	cūxīn	*adj.*	careless, thoughtless	12
错误	cuòwù	*n.*	mistake, error	7
D 答谢	dáxiè	*v.*	acknowledge, return thanks	6
打印	dǎyìn	*v.*	print	1
大巴	dàbā	*n.*	chartered bus	3
傣族	Dǎizú	*n.*	Dai ethnic group	8
待遇	dàiyù	*n.*	treatment, remuneration	1
戴	dài	*v.*	wear	11
戴维斯	Dàiwéisī		Davis	11
单独	dāndú	*adj.*	alone, by oneself	4
当	dāng	*prep.*	when	4
当前位置	dāngqián wèizhì		current page	1
导致	dǎozhì	*v.*	cause	7
倒	dào	*adv.*	nevertheless	5
道歉	dàoqiàn	*v.*	apologize	7
得奖	déjiǎng	*v.*	win an award	9
得意	déyì	*adj.*	proud, pleased	9
登	dēng	*v.*	climb	3
登录	dēnglù	*v.*	log in	10
地点	dìdiǎn	*n.*	location	1
地理	dìlǐ	*n.*	geography	11
地球	dìqiú	*n.*	the earth, the globe	12
典型	diǎnxíng	*adj.*	typical	8
电子版	diànzǐbǎn	*n.*	electronic version	9
订单	dìngdān	*n.*	order (form)	7
丢失	diūshī	*v.*	get lost	4
动车	dòngchē	*n.*	bullet train	3
对外汉语	duìwài Hànyǔ		Chinese for speakers of other languages	4
对于	duìyú	*prep.*	as for	11
顿	dùn	*measure word*	(for meals)	11
多次	duōcì	*adv.*	many times	2
多亏	duōkuī	*v.*	owing to; fortunately	6
E 饿	è	*adj.*	hungry	11

WORD	PINYIN	PART OF SPEECH	MEANING	UNIT
儿童	értóng	*n.*	children	1
F 发表	fābiǎo	*v.*	publish (original work)	9
发布	fābù	*v.*	issue, release	1
发呆	fādāi	*v.*	stare blankly, daydream	8
发言	fāyán	*n./v.*	speech; give a speech	4
发扬	fāyáng	*v.*	carry on (spirit)	4
翻译	fānyì	*n./v.*	translator; translate	1
反对	fǎnduì	*v.*	object, oppose	12
反而	fǎn' ér	*adv.*	on the contrary	10
反馈	fǎnkuì	*v.*	feedback	5
反正	fǎnzhèng	*adv.*	anyway, all the same	6
犯	fàn	*v.*	commit (an error, crime)	7
方案	fāng' àn	*n.*	plan	3
防晒	fángshài		sunblock	3
防晒霜	fángshài-shuāng	*n.*	sun cream	4
放弃	fàngqì	*v.*	give up	8
费用	fèiyong	*n.*	expense	3
分工	fēngōng	*v./n.*	divide work; division of labour	6
分公司	fēngōngsī	*n.*	branch	1
分析	fēnxī	*v.*	analyze	5
分享	fēnxiǎng	*v.*	share (good things)	11
丰富多彩	fēngfù--duōcǎi	*adj.*	rich and colourful	4
风格	fēnggé	*n.*	style	9
风景如画	fēngjǐng-rú-huà		picturesque landscape	8
否则	fǒuzé	*conj.*	otherwise	9
服务	fúwù	*v./n.*	serve; service	10
符合	fúhé	*v.*	accord with	1
俯瞰	fǔkàn	*v.*	overlook	3
辅修	fǔxiū	*v.*	minor	2
付出	fùchū	*v.*	pay, put in a lot of hard work	12
负责	fùzé	*v.*	take charge of	5
附	fù	*v.*	attach	2
附件	fùjiàn	*n.*	attachment	6
复杂	fùzá	*adj.*	complicated	2
富有	fùyǒu	*v.*	be rich in	2
G 改掉	gǎidiào	*v.*	give up, drop	12
改进	gǎijìn	*v.*	improve	5
干杯	gānbēi	*v.*	empty one's glass	6
赶上	gǎnshàng	*v.*	catch up	9
敢	gǎn	*v.*	dare	9
感动	gǎndòng	*v.*	touch	7
感情	gǎnqíng	*n.*	feelings	10
感受	gǎnshòu	*v.*	feel for, experience	3
感谢	gǎnxiè	*v.*	thank heartily	2
刚好	gānghǎo	*adv.*	it so happened that	11
高材生	gāocáishēng	*n.*	top student	6
高速	gāosù	*adj.*	high speed	3
高原反应	gāoyuán fǎnyìng		altitude sickness	8
隔	gé	*v.*	every other; separate	10
各位	gèwèi	*pron.*	everyone	4
更新	gēngxīn	*v.*	update	10
工厂	gōngchǎng	*n.*	factory	7
工人	gōngrén	*n.*	worker	7
公布	gōngbù	*v.*	make publicly known, announce	9

WORD	PINYIN	PART OF SPEECH	MEANING	UNIT
公司	gōngsī	*n.*	company	1
功课	gōngkè	*n.*	homework	4
供	gōng	*v.*	for	5
恭请	gōngqǐng	*v.*	humbly invite	5
共同	gòngtóng	*adv.*	together	6
沟通	gōutōng	*v.*	communicate	1
孤单	gūdān	*adj.*	lonely	11
孤身一人	gūshēn-yìrén		all on one's own	12
鼓励	gǔlì	*v.*	encourage	1
固定	gùdìng	*adj.*	fixed	10
顾客	gùkè	*n.*	customer	7
顾问	gùwèn	*n.*	consultant	3
怪	guài	*v.*	put the blame on	7
关键	guānjiàn	*adj.*	key, crux	9
管理	guǎnlǐ	*v.*	administer	1
广场	guǎngchǎng	*n.*	square	3
广大	guǎngdà	*adj.*	numerous, enormous	9
逛	guàng	*v.*	stroll	3
规模	guīmó	*n.*	size, scale	1
贵	guì	*adj.*	honourable	2
贵重	guìzhòng	*adj.*	valuable	4
国际	guójì	*adj.*	international	1
果然	guǒrán	*adv.*	sure enough	8
过	guò	*v.*	over	6
过	guò	*v.*	spend	10
过客	guòkè	*n.*	passer-by	11
过去	guòqù	*n.*	past	2
H 害怕	hàipà	*v.*	be afraid of, fear	9
寒假	hánjià	*n.*	winter break	1
汗水	hànshuǐ	*n.*	sweat	12

WORD	PINYIN	PART OF SPEECH	MEANING	UNIT
行业	hángyè	*n.*	industry	1
好好	hǎohǎo	*adv.*	making a great effort	5
好在	hǎozài	*adv.*	fortunately	9
合格	hégé	*adj.*	qualified	7
合理	hélǐ	*adj.*	reasonable	3
合作	hézuò	*v.*	cooperate	6
何必	hébì	*adv.*	why do you need to …	12
黑	hēi	*adj.*	dark, tanned	9
后顾之忧	hòugùzhīyōu		worries	3
后悔	hòuhuǐ	*v.*	regret	8
后来	hòulái	*n.*	later on	2
后天	hòutiān	*n.*	the day after tomorrow	6
忽然	hūrán	*adv.*	all of a sudden	8
葫芦丝	húlusī	*n.*	cucurbit flute	8
互相	hùxiāng	*adv.*	each other	4
怀疑	huáiyí	*v.*	doubt, suspect	8
坏	huài	*adj.*	bad	10
环保	huánbǎo	*adj.*	environmentally friendly	5
回答	huídá	*v./n.*	answer	10
回顾	huígù	*v.*	review, retrospect	6
汇报	huìbào	*v.*	report	5
会议	huìyì	*n.*	meeting, conference	2
活力	huólì	*n.*	energy	7
火锅	huǒguō	*n.*	hot pot	11
火警	huǒjǐng	*n.*	fire department	4
伙伴	huǒbàn	*n.*	partner	6
获得	huòdé	*v.*	win, acquire	9
J 积极	jījí	*adj./adv.*	active; actively	4
积累	jīlěi	*v.*	accumulate	1

WORD	PINYIN	PART OF SPEECH	MEANING	UNIT
激动	jīdòng	*v.*	excite	8
激励	jīlì	*v.*	inspire, encourage	12
激烈	jīliè	*adj.*	fierce	1
即日	jírì	*n.*	this very day	9
即使	jíshǐ	*conj.*	even if	10
急救	jíjiù	*v.*	give first aid	4
集体	jítǐ	*n.*	group	10
记录	jìlù	*v./n.*	record	2
季节	jìjié	*n.*	season	8
既然	jìrán	*conj.*	since	5
既……也……	jì...yě...	*conj.*	both … and …	2
寄	jì	*v.*	mail	7
加班	jiābān	*v.*	work overtime	7
加上	jiāshang	*v.*	plus	2
兼职	jiānzhí	*v./n.*	part-time	11
简历	jiǎnlì	*n.*	résumé, CV	1
建立	jiànlì	*v.*	establish	10
建筑	jiànzhù	*n.*	architecture	3
将来	jiānglái	*n.*	future	2
讲	jiǎng	*v.*	tell, speak	4
讲稿	jiǎnggǎo	*n.*	speech notes, script	6
讲信用	jiǎng xìnyòng		care about one's trustworthiness	7
奖金	jiǎngjīn	*n.*	prize money, bonus	9
奖项	jiǎngxiàng	*n.*	prize	9
降	jiàng	*v.*	lower, decrease, fall	12
交朋友	jiāo péngyou		make friends	2
阶段	jiēduàn	*n.*	phase	6
接待	jiēdài	*v.*	receive (clients)	1
接风	jiēfēng	*v.*	give a reception in a guest's honour	11
节目	jiémù	*n.*	programme	10
结论	jiélùn	*n.*	conclusion	10
截止日期	jiézhǐ rìqī		deadline	9
解决	jiějué	*v.*	solve	7
届	jiè	*measure word*	session, class (for meetings, graduating classes, etc.)	4
届时	jièshí	*v.*	at that time	5
借口	jièkǒu	*n.*	excuse	7
今后	jīnhòu	*n.*	from now on	6
金钱	jīnqián	*n.*	money	10
尽管	jǐnguǎn	*conj.*	even though	2
尽可能	jǐnkěnéng	*adv.*	to the best of one's ability	12
紧急	jǐnjí	*adj.*	urgent	4
进出口	jìn-chūkǒu		import and export	1
尽力而为	jìnlì'érwéi		try one's best to finish a task	5
近视	jìnshì	*adj.*	nearsighted	11
经济	jīngjì	*adj.*	economical	3
经理	jīnglǐ	*n.*	manager	1
经历	jīnglì	*n.*	experience	1
竞争	jìngzhēng	*v.*	compete	1
竟然	jìngrán	*adv.*	surprisingly	8
镜片	jìngpiàn	*n.*	lens	11
究竟	jiūjìng	*adv.*	what on earth, what exactly	7
就	jiù	*adv.*	as soon as; (if)…then; only, just	6
就座	jiùzuò	*v.*	be seated	6
举办	jǔbàn	*v.*	host, hold	4
举行	jǔxíng	*v.*	host, hold	5
具有	jùyǒu	*v.*	have (an abstract quality)	5

WORD	PINYIN	PART OF SPEECH	MEANING	UNIT
聚	jù	v.	gather, meet	12
聚会	jùhuì	n.	get-together, gathering	12
K				
开场白	kāichǎngbái	n.	opening note	6
开阔	kāikuò	v.	broaden, open	12
开朗	kāilǎng	adj.	extrovert	2
开营	kāiyíng	v.	open (a summer camp)	4
刊	kān	n.	issue (periodical)	9
看出来	kàn chūlai		discern, make out	6
考察	kǎochá	v.	investigate	2
客户	kèhù	n.	client	1
课外	kèwài	n.	extracurricular	4
孔雀舞	kǒngquèwǔ	n.	peacock dance	8
口译	kǒuyì	v./n.	interpret; interpreter	1
苦	kǔ	adj.	bitter, difficult	11
夸奖	kuājiǎng	v.	praise, compliment	6
昆明	Kūnmíng	n.	Kunming	8
困难	kùnnan	n.	difficulty	2
L				
来宾	láibīn	n.	guest	6
来不及	láibují	v.	have no time	8
来得及	láidejí	v.	be able to make it in time	9
……来……去	... lái ... qù		(doing something) over and over	10
懒	lǎn	adj.	lazy	8
浪费	làngfèi	v.	waste	10
劳务	láowù	n.	labour	7
老人院	lǎorényuàn	n.	retirement home	2
乐于	lèyú	v.	be happy to	12

WORD	PINYIN	PART OF SPEECH	MEANING	UNIT
类似	lèisì	v.	similar	7
冷静	lěngjìng	adj.	calm; cool down	7
离别	líbié	v.	part, separate, say goodbye	12
离不开	lí bù kāi		cannot do without	10
理念	lǐniàn	n.	belief	5
力量	lìliàng	n.	power	9
立场	lìchǎng	n.	standing, position	10
丽江	Lìjiāng	n.	Lijiang	8
例会	lìhuì	n.	regular meeting	5
联合	liánhé	adj.	united, joint	9
链接	liànjiē	v.	link	1
良多	liángduō	num.	quite a lot	4
凉快	liángkuai	adj.	nice and cool	10
亮	liàng	adj.	bright, shining	11
列车	lièchē	n.	train	3
零用钱	língyòngqián	n.	petty cash	4
领队	lǐngduì	n.	team leader	3
流程	liúchéng	n.	programme	6
流利	liúlì	adj.	fluent	1
流连忘返	liúlián-–wàngfǎn		enjoy so much as to not want to go home	9
留言	liúyán	v.	leave a message	5
流眼泪	liú yǎnlèi		shed tears	11
龙塔	Lóng Tǎ		Dragon Tower	3
漏掉	lòudiào	v.	miss	6
旅行社	lǚxíngshè	n.	travel agent	3
旅游业	lǚyóuyè	n.	tourism	9
M				
马虎	mǎhu	adj.	careless, perfunctory	12
满意	mǎnyì	v.	satisfy	2

WORD	PINYIN	PART OF SPEECH	MEANING	UNIT
忙碌	mánglù	*adj.*	busy	7
毛病	máobìng	*n.*	defect	12
帽子	màozi	*n.*	hat	4
美食	měishí	*n.*	cuisine	3
魅力	mèilì	*n.*	charm, charisma, glamour	9
闷热	mēnrè	*adj.*	muggy, sultry	12
梦	mèng	*v.*	dream	12
面对	miànduì	*v.*	face	12
面试	miànshì	*v.*	interview	1
面向	miànxiàng	*v.*	be geared towards	9
民乐	mínyuè	*n.*	Chinese folk music	6
名不虚传	míngbù-xūchuán		live up to one's name	8
陌生	mòshēng	*adj.*	strange, unfamiliar	10
默默	mòmò	*adv.*	silently	11
母语	mǔyǔ	*n.*	mother tongue	2
目的地	mùdìdì	*n.*	destination	3
目前	mùqián	*n.*	for the time being	2
N 难熬	nán' áo	*adj.*	hard to endure	11
难得	nándé	*adj.*	rare, hard to get	5
脑子	nǎozi	*n.*	brain	7
能力	nénglì	*n.*	capacity, competence	1
拟	nǐ	*v.*	propose	5
年轻人	niánqīngrén	*n.*	young people	8
弄	nòng	*v.*	manage to get	10
努力	nǔlì	*adj./v.*	trying hard; make a great effort	12
O 哦	ò	*interj.*	oh (expressing understanding)	5
欧式	Ōushì	*n.*	European style	3
偶尔	ǒu' ěr	*adv.*	occasionally	12
P 陪	péi	*v.*	accompany	4
陪同	péitóng	*v.*	accompany	5
佩服	pèifú	*v.*	admire	6
配合	pèihé	*v.*	cooperate	5
批评	pīpíng	*v.*	criticize, blame	7
啤酒	píjiǔ	*n.*	beer	8
票务	piàowù	*n.*	ticket service	3
品尝	pǐncháng	*v.*	taste	3
平台	píngtái	*n.*	platform	9
评价	píngjià	*v./n.*	review	10
评审	píngshěn	*v.*	judge, grade, review	9
Q 期待	qīdài	*v.*	look forward to	2
期间	qījiān	*n.*	period	1
骑	qí	*v.*	ride (a horse/a bike)	8
启事	qǐshì	*n.*	notice, announcement	9
谦虚	qiānxū	*adj.*	modest, humble	6
签到	qiāndào	*v.*	sign in	5
签证	qiānzhèng	*v./n.*	visa	2
前辈	qiánbèi	*n.*	senior	6
欠	qiàn	*v.*	owe	11
强调	qiángdiào	*v.*	emphasize	2
亲近	qīnjìn	*v.*	get close to	10
亲眼	qīnyǎn	*adv.*	with one's own eyes	9
请	qǐng	*v.*	hire	7
请假	qǐngjià	*v.*	ask for time off	4
请柬	qǐngjiǎn	*n.*	invitation card	5
请教	qǐngjiào	*v.*	ask for help (from one's seniors)	7

WORD	PINYIN	PART OF SPEECH	MEANING	UNIT
请示	qǐngshì	v.	ask for opinion (of one's supe-rior)	7
求之不得	qiúzhī-bùdé		all that one could wish for	9
求职信	qiúzhíxìn	n.	application letter	2
取长补短	qǔcháng-bǔduǎn		complement one another	6
全部	quánbù	n.	all	3
全程	quánchéng	n.	the whole trip	1
全价	quánjià	n.	full price	3
全力	quánlì	n.	full strength	5
全体	quántǐ	n.	the whole, all	5
群	qún	measure word	group, flock	8
R 然而	rán' ér	conj.	however	10
热烈	rèliè	adj.	warm	6
人民币	rénmínbì	n.	Renminbi	4
人士	rénshì	n.	person, people (formal)	11
人文	rénwén	n.	humanities, culture	11
忍受	rěnshòu	v.	tolerate	11
认出	rènchū	v.	recognize	11
任何	rènhé	pron.	any	4
如下	rúxià		as follows	5
入场	rùchǎng	v.	enter	6
S 三分之一	sān fēn zhī yī		one third	3
伞	sǎn	n.	umbrella	4
散步	sànbù	v.	take a walk	3
色彩	sècǎi	n.	colour	8
沙发	shāfā	n.	sofa, couch	5
伤感	shānggǎn	adj.	melancholy	12

WORD	PINYIN	PART OF SPEECH	MEANING	UNIT
商量	shāngliang	v.	discuss, negotiate	3
商业	shāngyè	n.	commerce	3
上门	shàngmén	v.	home delivery	3
上司	shàngsi	n.	supervisor	7
稍等	shāoděng	v.	wait a minute	3
稍微	shāowēi	adv.	slightly	10
设置	shèzhì	v.	set up	9
社交	shèjiāo	v.	socialize	10
摄影	shèyǐng	v./n.	take a photograph; photography	8
申请	shēnqǐng	v./n.	apply; application	1
深	shēn	adj.	deep	10
深圳	Shēnzhèn	n.	Shenzhen	1
神山	shénshān	n.	holy mountain	8
声音	shēngyīn	n.	sound, voice	8
圣·索菲亚教堂	Shèngsuǒ-fēiyà Jiàotáng		St Sophia Cathedral	3
胜任	shèngrèn	v.	be competent at (a job)	2
剩	shèng	v.	remain, be left	7
失败	shībài	v.	fail	9
失落	shīluò	adj.	feeling lost	12
失眠	shīmián	v.	insomnia	8
失望	shīwàng	adj.	disappointed	10
十分	shífēn	adv.	very	8
石林	Shílín	n.	the Stone Forest	8
时差	shíchā	n.	time difference	11
实践	shíjiàn	n.	practice	4
实习	shíxí	v.	internship	1
实在	shízài	adv.	indeed, truly	8
食宿	shísù	v.	food and lodging	3
使	shǐ	v.	make	10

WORD	PINYIN	PART OF SPEECH	MEANING	UNIT
市场	shìchǎng	*n.*	market	7
世外桃源	shìwài--táoyuán	*n.*	a Shangri-La	8
视频	shìpín	*n.*	video clips	10
事情	shìqing	*n.*	matter, affair	5
事物	shìwù	*n.*	things, matters	12
事项	shìxiàng	*n.*	item, matter	3
适应	shìyìng	*v.*	adapt to	2
是否	shìfǒu	*adv.*	whether	1
室内	shìnèi	*n.*	indoor	3
手表	shǒubiǎo	*n.*	watch	4
手忙脚乱	shǒumáng--jiǎoluàn		in a flurry, in a rush	7
手写	shǒuxiě	*v.*	handwrite	7
守则	shǒuzé	*n.*	rules	4
首页	shǒuyè	*n.*	home page	1
疏远	shūyuǎn	*v.*	alienate; become distant	10
输	shū	*v.*	lose	9
熟悉	shúxī	*v.*	get familiar with	4
属于	shǔyú	*v.*	belong	11
顺便	shùnbiàn	*adv.*	while you are at it, conveniently	10
说不定	shuōbudìng	*adv.*	perhaps	12
死	sǐ	*adj.*	extreme	6
似乎	sìhū	*adv.*	seemingly; as if	8
松花江	Sōnghuā Jiāng		Songhua River	3
送货	sònghuò	*v.*	deliver goods	7
搜索	sōusuǒ	*v.*	search	1
随	suí	*v.*	go with	2
随时	suíshí	*adv.*	anytime	7
缩短	suōduǎn	*v.*	shorten	7

WORD	PINYIN	PART OF SPEECH	MEANING	UNIT
所	suǒ	*measure word*	(for institutions)	4
T 太阳岛	Tàiyáng Dǎo		Sun Island	3
太阳镜	tàiyángjìng	*n.*	sunglasses	4
态度	tàidu	*n.*	attitude	2
谈到	tándào		talking about	2
探访	tànfǎng	*v.*	visit, investigate	11
趟	tàng	*measure word*	(for trips)	8
讨厌	tǎoyàn	*v.*	dislike, loathe	8
特点	tèdiǎn	*n.*	feature	8
特色	tèsè	*n.*	special feature	5
特殊	tèshū	*adj.*	special	4
特约记者	tèyuē jìzhě		special reporter	11
提到	tídào	*v.*	mention	8
提纲	tígāng	*n.*	outline	6
提醒	tíxǐng	*v.*	remind	2
提议	tíyì	*v.*	propose	6
体会	tǐhuì	*v./n.*	experience	8
体面	tǐmiàn	*adj.*	decent, respectable	8
天堂	tiāntáng	*n.*	heaven	8
条	tiáo	*n.*	note	5
铁	tiě	*n.*	iron	3
听从	tīngcóng	*v.*	listen to and obey	4
听众	tīngzhòng	*n.*	listener	11
停止	tíngzhǐ	*v.*	stop	8
通过	tōngguò	*prep.*	via, through	4
通知	tōngzhī	*n./v.*	notice; notify	1
同情	tóngqíng	*v.*	sympathize	2
同时	tóngshí	*conj.*	at the same time	10
投稿	tóugǎo	*v.*	submit for publication	9

WORD	PINYIN	PART OF SPEECH	MEANING	UNIT
突飞猛进	tūfēi-měngjìn		a spurt of progress	12
突破	tūpò	v.	break through	12
突然	tūrán	adj.	all of a sudden	11
图像	túxiàng	n.	image	9
团	tuán	n.	group	3
团队精神	tuánduì jīngshén		team spirit	4
团体票	tuántǐpiào	n.	group tickets	3
推动	tuīdòng	v.	push forward, promote	9
W 外籍	wàijí	n.	foreign nationality	11
外贸	wàimào	n.	foreign trade	6
完成	wánchéng	v.	complete, accomplish	4
玩具	wánjù	n.	toy	1
晚宴	wǎnyàn	n.	dinner banquet	5
网站	wǎngzhàn	n.	website	1
忘	wàng	v.	forget	2
旺季	wàngjì	n.	peak season	3
危险	wēixiǎn	adj./n.	dangerous; danger	8
唯一	wéiyī	adj.	the one and only	11
卫生	wèishēng	n.	hygiene	4
未	wèi	adv.	not yet	5
胃	wèi	n.	stomach	2
温差	wēnchā	n.	difference in temperature	3
温度	wēndù	n.	temperature	9
温暖如春	wēnnuǎn-rú-chūn		as warm as springtime	8
文件	wénjiàn	n.	document, file	6
文秘	wénmì	n.	secretary	1
文章	wénzhāng	n.	article	2
卧铺	wòpù	n.	berth	3
握手	wòshǒu	v.	handshake	11
无法	wúfǎ	v.	be unable, be incapable	7
无聊	wúliáo	adj.	boring	10
午休	wǔxiū	v.	lunch break	4
物产	wùchǎn	n.	produce	11
物品	wùpǐn	n.	item, thing	4
X 洗漱用品	xǐshù yòngpǐn		toiletries	4
系统	xìtǒng	n.	system	5
下面	xiàmiàn	n.	following	4
下旬	xiàxún	n.	last ten days of the month	12
下载	xiàzǎi	v.	download	6
夏令营	xiàlìngyíng	n.	summer camp	1
相处	xiāngchǔ	v.	get along	4
相反	xiāngfǎn	adj.	opposite	10
香格里拉	Xiānggélǐlā	n.	Shangri-La	8
详细	xiángxì	adj.	detailed	3
享受	xiǎngshòu	v.	enjoy	8
想法	xiǎngfǎ	n.	ideas, thoughts	10
想象	xiǎngxiàng	v.	imagine	8
消息	xiāoxi	n.	news	8
销售	xiāoshòu	v.	sell	1
小伙子	xiǎohuǒzi	n.	young guy	11
协会	xiéhuì	n.	association	9
协助	xiézhù	v.	help, assist	1
心情	xīnqíng	n.	mood, feelings	2
心想事成	xīnxiǎng-shìchéng		May all your wishes come true!	7
欣赏	xīnshǎng	v.	enjoy, appreciate	3
信	xìn	n.	letter	7

WORD	PINYIN	PART OF SPEECH	MEANING	UNIT
信任	xìnrèn	v.	trust	5
信息	xìnxī	n.	information	1
信心	xìnxīn	n.	confidence	1
兴奋	xīngfèn	adj.	excited	7
行程	xíngchéng	n.	itinerary	1
醒	xǐng	v.	wake up	12
兴致	xìngzhì	n.	mood to enjoy	6
幸福	xìngfú	adj./n.	happy; happiness	1
幸运	xìngyùn	adj.	lucky	7
修改	xiūgǎi	v./n.	revise; revision	9
宣布	xuānbù	v.	announce	4
学历	xuélì	n.	academic qualification	2
雪雕	xuědiāo	n.	snow sculpture	3
寻求	xúnqiú	v.	seek, explore	6
Y 沿着	yánzhe	prep.	along, following	11
眼界	yǎnjiè	n.	horizon	12
演讲	yǎnjiǎng	n.	speech	10
阳光	yángguāng	n.	sunshine	3
养成	yǎngchéng	v.	cultivate (habits)	2
药品	yàopǐn	n.	medicine	4
业界同仁	yèjiè tóngrén		colleagues	6
业务	yèwù	n.	business	6
夜宵	yèxiāo	n.	night snack or refreshment	6
一等	yīděng		first class	3
医疗	yīliáo	v.	medical	4
一切	yíqiè	pron.	everything	7
一下子	yíxiàzi	adv.	at once, instantly	12
仪式	yíshì	n.	ceremony	4
以为	yǐwéi	v.	assumed (incorrectly)	10

WORD	PINYIN	PART OF SPEECH	MEANING	UNIT
一眼	yìyǎn		at a glance	11
异国他乡	yìguó tāxiāng	n.	foreign land	11
意外	yìwài	n.	accident	3
引导	yǐndǎo	v.	guide	6
饮食	yǐnshí	n.	food and drink	4
营员	yíngyuán	n.	camper	4
应付	yìngfù	v.	deal with	11
硬座	yìngzuò	n.	hard seat	3
永远	yǒngyuǎn	adv.	forever	7
勇敢	yǒnggǎn	adj.	brave	12
勇气	yǒngqì	n.	courage	12
优先	yōuxiān	v.	be given priority	1
犹豫	yóuyù	v.	hesitate	9
邮政编码	yóuzhèng biānmǎ		postal code	9
游览	yóulǎn	v.	tour	1
友好	yǒuhǎo	adj.	friendly	4
友谊	yǒuyì	n.	friendship	6
有力	yǒulì	adj.	with force	11
有限公司	yǒuxiàn gōngsī		limited company	1
于是	yúshì	conj.	thereupon	6
雨崩村	Yǔbēng Cūn	n.	Yubeng Village	8
预防	yùfáng	v.	prevent	3
员工	yuángōng	n.	employee, staff	5
原创	yuánchuàng	v.	original, creative	9
原来	yuánlái	adv.	as it turns out to be	8
原谅	yuánliàng	v.	forgive	7
原始	yuánshǐ	adj.	raw, original, primitive	9
远道而来	yuǎndào' ér-lái		coming from far away	4

WORD	PINYIN	PART OF SPEECH	MEANING	UNIT
愿望	yuànwàng	*n.*	wish	11
云南	Yúnnán	*n.*	Yunnan Province	8
杂志	zázhì	*n.*	magazine, periodical	9
在座	zàizuò	*v.*	be present	6
暂时	zànshí	*adj.*	temporary	2
藏族	Zàngzú	*n.*	Tibetan ethnic group	8
糟糕	zāogāo	*adj.*	terrible	6
责任	zérèn	*n.*	responsibility	2
窄	zhǎi	*adj.*	narrow	8
展现	zhǎnxiàn	*v.*	unfold, display	9
招聘	zhāopìn	*v.*	recruit	1
朝夕相处	zhāoxī–xiāngchǔ		be together day and night	4
召开	zhàokāi	*v.*	call (a meeting)	5
照相机	zhàoxiàngjī	*n.*	camera	9
折扣	zhékòu	*n.*	discount	3
珍贵	zhēnguì	*adj.*	valuable	11
真诚	zhēnchéng	*adj.*	sincere	11
争议性	zhēngyìxìng	*n.*	argumentativeness	10
征稿	zhēnggǎo	*v.*	solicit contributions	9
整理	zhěnglǐ	*v.*	sort out, clean	2
正式	zhèngshì	*adj.*	formal	1
证书	zhèngshū	*n.*	certificate	9
之前	zhīqián	*n.*	time before	5
支持	zhīchí	*v.*	support	4
支配	zhīpèi	*v.*	arrange, allocate	10
只	zhī	*measure word*	(for certain animals)	5
值班	zhíbān	*v.*	be on duty	4
职位	zhíwèi	*n.*	position	1
纸版	zhǐbǎn	*n.*	hard copy	9

WORD	PINYIN	PART OF SPEECH	MEANING	UNIT
至于	zhìyú	*prep.*	as for	3
制订	zhìdìng	*v.*	make	3
质量	zhìliàng	*n.*	quality	9
制作	zhìzuò	*v.*	manufacture, make	5
致辞	zhìcí	*v.*	make a speech	4
中甸	Zhōngdiàn	*n.*	Zhongdian	8
忠实	zhōngshí	*adj.*	loyal	11
主持	zhǔchí	*v.*	host	6
主任	zhǔrèn	*n.*	director	4
主题	zhǔtí	*n.*	theme, topic	4
助理	zhùlǐ	*n.*	assistant	4
住宿	zhùsù	*v.*	get accommodation	1
祝愿	zhùyuàn	*v.*	wish	6
专门	zhuānmén	*adv.*	specially	1
专心	zhuānxīn	*adj.*	focused	10
专业	zhuānyè	*n.*	major	1
转	zhuǎn	*v.*	transfer	3
转眼	zhuǎnyǎn	*v.*	in a flash	12
状态	zhuàngtài	*n.*	status	10
准确	zhǔnquè	*adj.*	accurate, precise	6
兹定于	zī dìng yú		scheduled for	5
仔细	zǐxì	*adj.*	careful	2
紫外线	zǐwàixiàn	*n.*	UV rays	9
自费	zìfèi	*v.*	pay one's own expenses	3
自己来	zìjǐ lái		do by oneself	7
自习	zìxí	*v.*	self-study	4
自由	zìyóu	*adj.*	free	3
总结	zǒngjié	*v./n.*	summarize; summary	5
总之	zǒngzhī	*conj.*	in sum	2
走遍	zǒubiàn	*v.*	travel all over	12

WORD	PINYIN	PART OF SPEECH	MEANING	UNIT
足迹	zújì	*n.*	footprint	11
组织	zǔzhī	*v.*	organize	2
最爱	zuì' ài	*adv.*	favourite	8
最晚	zuìwǎn	*adv.*	the latest	5

WORD	PINYIN	PART OF SPEECH	MEANING	UNIT
遵守	zūnshǒu	*v.*	abide by, observe (the rules)	4
作品	zuòpǐn	*n.*	works	9
作为	zuòwéi	*prep.*	as	2
作息	zuòxī	*v.*	work and rest	4

Macmillan Education
4 Crinan Street
London N1 9XW
A division of Macmillan Publishers Limited
Companies and representatives throughout the world

ISBN 9780230406438

Published by arrangement with Macmillan Publishers (China) Limited

Publishers: Charlotte Liu, Cai Jianfeng
Project management: Mary-Jane Newton, Miao Qiang
Authors: Qi Shaoyan, Tan Qiuyu
Academic advisors: Simon Greenall, Huang Dian
Editors: Wang Jianbo, Li Caixia, Meng Jiawen, Eric Leher

Audio materials produced by DoubleDouble Creative & Production and Beijing Foreign Language Audiovisual Press

The author and publishers would like to thank the following for permission to reproduce their artwork/photographic material:

1TU: pp12(tr), 15, 43(ld), 44(tl, ml), 51, 56(br), 74-75(background), 94(bl), 97(bl), 100(b), 107(bl), 108(tl, br), p113(b: Dali photographs), 117(ra-rd), 123(br), 124(t), 125(bl), 126(bl: diving), 131, 141(tr), 150(rb), 170(br), 172(bl), 178(bl), 173&179 (r: travel items); Corbis: pp65 (rc, rd), 150(ra); DigitalStock/Corbis: p126(bl: town); Digital Vision: p11(br); ImageSource: pp126(bl: apartment), 150(b); Panorama Media: pp12(tl, ml, bl), 21(bl), 43(la, lb, lc), 44(bl), 73(t), 96(ml), 108(tr, bl), 128(ml), 135(bl), 152(b), 155, 164(ml); PhotoDisc: pp174-175(background); PhotoDisc/Getty Images: pp19(bl), 65(ra), 80(ml), 83(br), 95(bl), 126(bl: skiing), 183(r); Thinkstock/Design Pics: p119; Thinkstock/iStock: pp22-23(background), 27, 46-47(background), 48(b), 58-59 (background), 67, 79, 86-87 (background), 91, 98-99 (background), 103, 110-111(background), 126-127(background), 138-139(background), 143, 150-151(background), 162-163(background), 180-181(background); Thinkstock/Top Photo Group: p231(b); Thinkstock/View Stock: pp34-35(background), 39, 155; He Yongjun: pp65(rb), 177(t); Tommy Pow: p182(b); Wang Jianbo: pp55(bl), 66(br), 148(l), 176(tl), 182(bl); Wang Yi: p176(background)

Cover photographs by Panorama Media (m); 1TU (tl), (tr), (br); Fotolia (bl)

We would like to thank the following reviewers and teachers for their valuable and insightful comments:
Huang Dian (Senior Lecturer in Chinese at the University of Westminster and Chair of the British Chinese Language Teaching Society) and her pilot class, Qi Yanrong (Instructor in Department of Modern Languages, Literatures & Linguistics, University of Oklahoma), Wang Jianling

Printed and bound in China
2019 2018 2017 2016 2015 2014
10 9 8 7 6 5 4 3 2 1